Latin S
and idiom

A Composition Course

R. Colebourn, M.A.

Bristol Classical Press

General Editor: John H. Betts

First published in 1948 by Methuen & Co.

Reprinted (with permission)
1987, 1991, 1992, 1994, 1995, 1997, 1999, 2000, 2001 by
Bristol Classical Press
an imprint of
Gerald Duckworth & Co. Ltd
61 Frith Street
London W1D 3JL
e-mail: inquiries@duckworth-publishers.co.uk
Website: www.ducknet.co.uk

All rights reserved. No part of this publication
may be reproduced, stored in a retrieval system, or
transmitted, in any form or by any means, electronic,
mechanical, photocopying, recording or otherwise,
without the prior permission of the publisher.

A catalogue record for this book is available
from the British Library

ISBN 0-86292-265-8

Printed in Great Britain by
Booksprint

CONTENTS

	PAGE
PREFACE	v
INTRODUCTORY CHAPTER	1
1. QUESTIONS (I)	6
2. USE OF INFINITIVES	9
3. PARTICIPLES (I)	11
4. PARTICIPLES (II): ABLATIVE ABSOLUTE	14
5. PARTICIPLES (III): FURTHER POINTS	17
6. GENITIVE CASE USES (I). REVISION EXERCISES	20
7. REPORTED STATEMENTS (I)	22
8. COMMANDS	26
NOTE ON THE SEQUENCE OF TENSES	29
9. REPORTED COMMANDS	31
10. ADVERB CLAUSES OF PURPOSE	34
11. ADVERB CLAUSES OF RESULT	37
12. REVISION EXERCISES	40
13. NEGATIVES	42
14. REPORTED STATEMENTS (II)	45
15. TIME EXPRESSIONS	48
16. REPORTED QUESTIONS	51
17. TRANSLATION OF ABSTRACT NOUNS	55
18. ABLATIVE CASE USES (I). REVISION EXERCISES	58
19. PLACE EXPRESSIONS	61
20. QUESTIONS (II): 'NUM QUIS', 'UTRUM . . . AN'	64
21. FINAL CLAUSES AND COMMANDS: FURTHER POINTS	67
22. REPORTED SPEECH CLAUSES: FURTHER POINTS	70
23. FEAR CLAUSES	73
24. REVISION EXERCISES	76
25. DATIVE CASE WITH VERBS	78
26. PASSIVE OF INTRANSITIVE VERBS	81
27. FINAL RELATIVE CLAUSES	84
28. CONSECUTIVE RELATIVE CLAUSES	87
29. PREDICATIVE DATIVE	90
30. DATIVE CASE USES. REVISION EXERCISES	93
31. OBLIGATION: THE GERUNDIVE	96
32. IDIOMS OF PRICE AND VALUE	100
33. THE GERUND	103
34. GERUND AND GERUNDIVE	106

		PAGE
35.	TRANSLATION OF 'TO' WITH INFINITIVE	109
36.	REVISION EXERCISES	112
37.	USE OF RELATIVE WORDS	114
38.	IDIOMS OF THE COMPARATIVE AND SUPERLATIVE	117
39.	INDEPENDENT SUBJUNCTIVES	120
40.	IMPERSONAL VERBS	123
41.	TRANSLATING 'OF' IDIOMS	127
42.	GENITIVE CASE USES (II). REVISION EXERCISES	130
	CONDITIONS: A GENERAL SURVEY	133
43.	INDICATIVE CONDITIONS	134
44.	SUBJUNCTIVE CONDITIONS	137
45.	ADVERB CLAUSES OF TIME	141
46.	THE CONJUNCTION 'CUM'	144
47.	THE CONJUNCTION 'DUM'	148
48.	REVISION EXERCISES	151
49.	IDIOMS WITH 'QUIN'	153
50.	'WITHOUT', 'INSTEAD OF', 'SO FAR FROM'	156
51.	IDIOMS OF PREVENTION: 'QUOMINUS' AND 'QUIN'	159
52.	'SOME', 'ANY', 'EACH', &c.	162
53.	'WHOEVER', 'WHENEVER', 'WHEREVER'	166
54.	ABLATIVE CASE USES (II). REVISION EXERCISES	169
55.	CAUSAL CLAUSES	172
56.	CONCESSIVE CLAUSES	176
57.	CONDITIONS: FURTHER POINTS	179
58.	ORATIO OBLIQUA (I)	182
59.	ORATIO OBLIQUA (II): SUBORDINATE CLAUSES	186
60.	GENERAL REVISION EXERCISES	190

APPENDICES:
THE ROMAN CALENDAR	197
ROMAN MONEY	198
NARRATIVE PROSE	199
PROSE COMPOSITION PASSAGES	204
NOTES TO PROSE PASSAGES	231
VOCABULARY	239
INDEX AND SUMMARY OF CASE USES	279
INDEX AND SUMMARY OF CLAUSES	280
INDEX OF LATIN WORDS	281

PREFACE

A note on the *plan of the book* follows the list of contents. It will be seen that the course sets out to be flexible enough to provide for a variety of needs and aims. It covers broadly the same ground as many other books of 'Latin Prose Composition', and its individuality depends mainly on: (1) manner of presenting the material, (2) order of topics, and (3) standard of exercises and range of vocabulary.

PRESENTATION. A bald outline treatment, a mere series of 'rules and exercises', has been avoided, as both inadequate and educationally unsound. It is the duty of the teacher and the text-book to unfold the logical, rational basis of the language. On the other hand, the pupil must not be drowned in a sea of words or a flood of detail. To prevent 'woolliness' the chapters on the chief constructions end with brief *summaries* in note form; when such formulae *follow* a reasoned survey, their usefulness outweighs their dangers. To many chapters are appended groups of quotations, not so much for an inductive approach as to show the construction 'in action' and to illustrate its idiomatic use.

ORDER. A *course*, unlike a work of reference, cannot adopt a purely logical order. Every teacher has his preferences, and his good reasons for them; but the guiding principle must be: what does the pupil need first for his *reading*? (Subject to this principle, the text-book should allow a measure of latitude to the teacher using it.) When introducing the basic constructions, this course concentrates attention on the essential pattern; details and refinements are either reserved for a later chapter, or marked with an asterisk. The asterisked paragraphs may be omitted, or deferred, if wished: the A exercises make no reference to them.

EXERCISES. Here, too, flexibility is essential. The rank and file of pupils, especially when time is short, are fully occupied in mastering idiom and construction, without the distraction of a wide vocabulary; and the sentences set in examinations recognize this fact. For these, the A exercises provide a minimum course, with a rigidly restricted but carefully selected, repetitive, vocabulary. For those of greater ambition or aptitude, the A exercises may be useful for rapid (or oral) work, but the B exercises afford a wider range of idiom and vocabulary, and more complex and varied sentences.

Revision exercises (an essential feature of a practical course) occur at frequent intervals; they also are of A and B standard.

PROSE COMPOSITION. Sixty passages, forming an easier and a harder series (each series carefully graduated in difficulty and vocabulary), are grouped together at the end of the book; but the points after which they may be taken are clearly set out on page x. These passages are preceded by advice on prose-writing, and *alternate* passages are fully annotated with aids and references (pages 231–238). Several passages have been taken, by permission of the University of London, from their General School Examination papers; a few others are based on extracts in J. M. Cobban's reader *Pax et Imperium*.

I gratefully acknowledge help and criticism from several sources, most of all from R. H. Barrow, Esq., H.M.I., and J. M. Cobban, Esq., Headmaster of Abingdon School. Their comment, criticism and advice, both general and detailed, have substantially improved the book. In the task of word-selection Professor Lodge's list ('A Vocabulary of High School Latin') has once again been a most valuable guide and check.

R. C.

PLAN OF THE BOOK

TEXT

The text is arranged in *five* sections, each of *twelve* chapters. In each section, the *sixth* and *twelfth* chapters provide revision. The *sixth* contains little new work (a few points of case usage only) and provides intermediate revision; the *twelfth* contains no new work but consists simply of revision sentences.

The first section (chapters 1–12) is roughly parallel with the latter part of *Mentor* and may be regarded as alternative to it (though more detailed in its treatment of some points). But this course is *not in any way tied* to *Mentor* or *Civis Romanus*; it may equally well follow any beginners' books which cover the elements up to a suitable point.

Continuous Oratio Obliqua is dealt with last of all, in chapters 58 and 59; but may be taken much earlier if preferred.

Throughout the text, points of refinement and details not usually required in a minimum course are placed in asterisked paragraphs, or (if only brief) in footnotes. These may be omitted or deferred without difficulty, as they are not involved in the A exercises. (A few points thus treated at an early stage are, however, allowed to arise in considerably later A exercises.)

EXERCISES

Sentences in A exercises are direct, straightforward, and confined to the point in hand, and based on a restricted vocabulary adapted to the requirements of 'Ordinary Level' sentences. They form a self-contained minimum course, and, within limits, the order in which the chapters and the A exercises are taken may be varied at will. The sentences in B exercises are more varied in structure, content and vocabulary, and contain a larger element of revision of earlier work. The A and B revision exercises are similarly differentiated.

PROSE COMPOSITION

The sixty passages are graded in difficulty and length; and they are arranged in two series. The easier series (nos. 1–30) is more straightforward in idiom and limited in vocabulary, though its later pieces afford some scope for adapting the English. The harder series (nos. 31–60) involves a wider range of idiom and vocabulary, and more difficult 'turning'.

The prose passages are not designed as exercises on specific chapters, but they are related to the syntax course thus:

	EASIER SERIES		HARDER SERIES				
Nos.	1–3	and	31, 32	may	follow	chapter	30
,,	4–6	,,	33, 34	,,	,,	,,	36
,,	7–9	,,	35, 36	,,	,,	,,	42
,,	10–12	,,	37, 38	,,	,,	,,	48
,,	13–15	,,	39, 40	,,	,,	,,	54
,,	16–30	,,	41–60	,,	,,	,,	60

The *odd-numbered* passages in both series are provided with notes and references, which will be found on pages 231–238. (Help given in the notes is not usually repeated in the vocabulary.) The notes have been placed apart from the passages so that they may be used in whatever way may be desired.

INTRODUCTORY CHAPTER

A. SUBORDINATE CLAUSES

1. Much of this book is concerned with various kinds of subordinate clauses (or dependent clauses) and the ways of expressing them in Latin. It will be a great help to understand this brief account of subordinate clauses (§§ 2–5): it applies, of course, not to Latin only, but also to English, and to most other languages studied in schools.

2. Every subordinate clause is either a noun clause, an adjective clause, or an adverb clause. That is to say, it is doing the work of a noun, an adjective, or an adverb in the sentence of which it forms part.

3. (*a*) NOUN CLAUSES

The majority of noun clauses are clauses of *reported speech*. So far as grammar is concerned, there are four different kinds of speech: statements, commands, questions and exclamations. Therefore (since anything we say may be reported) there are four kinds of reported speech.

(1) REPORTED STATEMENT:
   'I am coming'   'Venio'
   He says *that he is coming*   Dicit **se venire**

(2) REPORTED COMMAND:
   'Come'   'Vĕni'
   I demand *that he should come* Postulo **ut veniat**

(3) REPORTED QUESTION:
   'Are you coming?'   'Venisne?'
   I ask *if he is coming*   Rogo **num veniat**

(4) REPORTED EXCLAMATION:
   'How rich you are!'   'Quam dives es!'
   I realized *how rich he was* Perspexi **quam dives esset**

4. (b) ADJECTIVE CLAUSES

These are introduced by relative words, and are generally called *relative clauses*. These should be familiar already; but it should be remembered that, besides the relative pronouns, there are also relative adverbs and adjectives. Such words as *ubi, unde, qualis, quantus,* are more frequently used to form relative clauses in Latin than are their equivalents in English.[1] (See *ch.* 37.)

5. (c) ADVERB CLAUSES

The most important kinds of adverb clause are:

(1) of TIME: I went away *before he arrived*
              When she got there the cupboard was bare
(2) of PLACE: I will meet you *where the bus stops*
(3) of REASON: *Because you are young,* I will forgive you
(4) of PURPOSE: He hid *so that we should not see him*
(5) of RESULT: He hid so well *that we did not see him*
(6) of CONDITION: *If he had waited* he would have been late
(7) of CONCESSION: *Although I waited an hour,* no one came
(8) of MANNER: He behaved *as he had been told to*
(9) of COMPARISON: He behaved better *than I had expected*

In some kinds of subordinate clause (notably relative clauses, and some clauses of reason and condition) the Latin expression corresponds so exactly to the English that there is no need to explain it. The rest will be dealt with in the course of this book. This introductory survey gives a 'bird's-eye view' of the ground to be covered.

---

[1] In Latin, relative words are often used to introduce clauses which are not subordinate at all, but quite independent: they are so used even after a full stop. In English this use is much rarer (never after a full stop). But we freely use 'continuing' relative clauses, which are not really subordinate: contrast *I sent for the doctor, who came at once* with *I sent for the doctor who came before.*

B. THE SUBJUNCTIVE MOOD

6. Many of the expressions explained in this book involve the subjunctive mood. To those who understand something of the principles underlying its use, Latin syntax will seem far less arbitrary and mysterious.

The name *subjunctive* ('subjoined' or 'subordinate') is misleading. On the one hand, many subordinate clauses do not require it; while on the other hand a subjunctive verb is often *non-dependent*—*i.e.* not in a subordinate clause. The distinction between subjunctive and indicative in Latin was a quite different one. In general, the indicative was used for *facts*, the subjunctive for *notions* or *ideas*—whether in the mind of the speaker (*e.g.* wishes, commands) or in some one else's mind (*e.g.* reported questions and commands, purposes, 'quoted reasons').

7. The subjunctive forms, moreover, were used in simple sentences long before they were extended to subordinate clauses —in fact, before subordinate clauses were in use at all. For the idea of dependence, or subordination, developed gradually. The 'conjunctions' which we find introducing various dependent clauses were in origin either adverbs, *e.g. Latin* nē, ut (*how*), si (*so*), num and dum (*now*), *English* before, than; or pronouns, *e.g. Latin* cum, quam, quod, *English* that, whether; or even verbs, *e.g.* licet (*granted*).[1]

The notions or ideas which were originally conveyed by the subjunctive mood may be divided into four types:

(1) wishes (OPTATIVE subjunc.): *e.g.*
    If only he would come! Utinam veniat!
(2) commands and exhortations (JUSSIVE subjunc.): *e.g.*
    Let him not enter Ne ingrediatur
    Let us depart   Discedamus[2]

---

[1] *Than* is the same word as *then*; *whether* is *which of two* (*cf.* utrum).
[2] The same notion in question form is usually called *deliberative*. *What are we to do? Are we to depart?* Quid faciamus? Discedamus?

(3) possibilities (POTENTIAL subjunc.): *e.g.*
> *What would happen then?* Quid tum fiat?
> *Some one may say* . . . Dicat aliquis . . .

(4) thoughts quoted from some one else (OBLIQUE and SUB-OBLIQUE subjunc.). Non-dependent subjunctives of this class were used, but they are rare; they do not appear in this book.

8. It is easy to see how some types of dependent subjunctive developed out of the non-dependent uses, how two sentences, that is, came to be regarded as a single whole:

> Te rogo. Quid faciam? *I ask you: what am I to do?*
> Te rogo quid faciam *I ask you what I am to do*

In the technical terms of grammar, we can see how *parataxis* ('arranging side by side') gave place to *hypotaxis* ('arranging one under the other'). Further fairly self-obvious instances are:

(i) the growth of fear-clauses from wishes:

> Timeo: ne veniat! *I am afraid: may he not come!*
> Timeo ne veniat *I am afraid lest he may come*

(ii) the connexion of subjunctive conditions (§ 430) with wishes accompanying subjunctives of possibility:

O si adesset! Beatus essem[1] *If only he were here! I should be happy*
Si adesset, beatus essem *If he were here I should be happy*

In some other types of clause, however, *e.g.* clauses of result (*ch.* 11) and cum clauses (*ch.* 46), it is less easy to see why the subjunctive came to be used. It seems as if subordinate clauses of the other types grew up first, and it then began to be felt that not only those particular 'notions', but 'notions' or ideas in general, were best expressed by the subjunctive mood, which neatly distinguished them from the speaker's direct assertions of fact.

[1] *O si* (like *utinam*) introduced wishes, but was not used in classical prose.

9. Thus, as time went on, the subjunctive came to be used more widely; and in particular it was found very useful for distinguishing quoted thoughts, statements, &c., from those of the writer or speaker himself. We can trace this widening process going on in Latin literature: we can see how even an interval of a few years—such as divided Livy from Cicero and Caesar—brought a new way of looking at some expressions.

But there are many questions about the use and meaning of the subjunctive which cannot be answered, owing to our lack of information about the earlier stages of the Latin language. In any case this book would not be the place for a full account; and these paragraphs are intended only to lay the foundations for an intelligent approach to Latin syntax. In particular, it is impossible to discuss here the *changes* of idiom—the historical aspect. The usages explained in the following chapters are those of Cicero and Caesar, even though some of the quotations cited actually come from later writers, notably Livy and Pliny.

1

QUESTIONS (I)

11. There are two kinds of questions.

Some begin with an interrogative word, such as *who*, *where*, *why*. This word (in Latin as in English) is put first.[1]

The chief interrogative words are:

quis *who*	quotiens *how often*
quid *what*	quando *when*[2]
qui, quae, quod *what* (adj.)	cur *why*
uter *which of the two*	ubi *where*
qualis *of what sort*	quo *where to*
quantus *how big*	unde *where from*
quot (indecl.) *how many*	quomodo *how* (*in what way*)

Questions of this type may be called **qu-** questions.

12. Those of the second type have no such word in them. These are the questions which are answered by *Yes* or *No*. Let us call them 'fact questions', because they offer us a fact to agree or disagree with. They need some sign to distinguish them from plain statements of fact. In English, and French, inversion provides this; in Latin **-ně** is added to the first word. If one word in the question is emphatic, it comes first and carries the *-ně*. If no other word is especially emphatic, the *verb* comes first and carries the *-ně*.

> Is your brother coming? Venitne frater tuus?
> Is your *brother* coming? Fraterne tuus venit?[3]

---

[1] Except for a preposition governing it. But: *Qua in urbe . . .?* (adj.—prep.—noun). Remember also: *quocum, quacum, quibuscum.*

[2] *N.B.* 'When' in a *question* (direct or reported) is **quando**. 'When' as a time conjunction (in *adverb clauses*) is *never* **quando**.

[3] This corresponds to Engl. *Is it your brother that is coming?* and French *C'est ton frère qui vient?* There are no such expressions in Latin, where emphasis is expressed by word-order.

13. If there is a *non* in the question, put it first:

Isn't your sister beautiful? **Nonne** pulchra est tua soror?

14. A question such as this is not *really* a question, a search for information. It is a *leading question*; it invites the answer *Yes*,[1] and has the force of a positive statement, such as 'Your sister is beautiful, isn't she!' The Latin for this statement will be the question: 'Nonne pulchra est soror tua?'

15. Similarly a question may have the force of a negative statement, and invite the answer *No*. It will then start in Latin with **num** (*surely not*):

Surely your father isn't ill?
Your father isn't ill, is he? } **Num** pater tuus aeger est?

16. SUMMARY—QUESTIONS.[2]

There are two kinds of questions: **qu-** *questions* and *fact questions*. *No question can be both at once:* it is wrong to put **-ně** *and* an interrogative word in the same sentence.

Fact questions in turn are of three kinds:

(i) **-ně** added to the first word marks a genuine question;
(ii) **nōnně** invites the answer *Yes*;
(iii) **num** invites the answer *No*.

17. Study these further examples of fact questions:

1. (*a*) Placetne tibi hic liber? (*b*) Num tibi placet hic liber?
2. (*a*) Cupisne abire? (*b*) Num cupis abire?
3. (*a*) Tune idem putas? (*b*) Nonne tu idem putas?
4. Nonne urbs nostra bene munita est?
5. Hodiene sunt ludi?
6. Nonne haec saepe iam audivistis?
7. Unāne legione hanc urbem oppugnabis?
8. Num barbarorum Romulus rex fuit?

---

[1] This may not be the answer received, or even the one expected.
[2] Alternative questions are dealt with in §§ 202, 203; deliberative questions in § 393.

Exercise 1A

1. Where are you?
2. Where are you going?
3. Are you accusing me?
4. Are you really accusing me?
5. Has your friend come?
6. Your friend has come quickly, hasn't he?
7. You aren't angry, are you, mother?
8. Have *you* learnt these words?
9. Why have you not learnt all the words?
10. How many words do you already know?
11. Where was the money found?
12. Where have the others fled to?
13. Surely the ambassadors have not departed?
14. How many times have you lost the book?
15. Which of the two consuls[1] has died?
16. What sort of books have you bought?
17. Do you not consider our city beautiful?
18. Was it your father whom I saw today?
19. They aren't sending me away, are they?
20. When did you receive this letter?

Exercise 1B

1. In what village do these peasants live?
2. Was it not in this village that you were born?
3. Did that boy really say such things to his sister?
4. Where has he gone, and why did he not stay with us?
5. To which of the two brothers[1] did you give the reward?
6. How many soldiers were wounded in the battle yesterday?
7. Have you thanked all those from whom you received gifts?
8. How did the thieves open the window?
9. Have I not been accused without reason by my enemies?
10. Will the gods allow such (*tam*) cruel men to live?

---

[1] Do not use the genitive: *which of the two consuls:* uter consul. (But use the gen. of a pronoun, *e.g. which of us two:* uter nostrum. The reason for the difference should be obvious.) This applies to *uter, uterque, neuter, quis,* and *quisque.*

2

USE OF INFINITIVES

21. The infinitive of a verb is that form of it which plays the part of a noun in its sentence. In a Latin sentence an infinitive may act as subject, object or complement.

22. These verbs, with an infin. as object, are common[1]:

possum *I can*
vŏlo *I wish, I am willing*
nōlo *I am unwilling*
mālo *I prefer*[2]
cōnor (1) *I try*
timeo (2) *I am afraid*
statuo (3) *I decide, resolve*
constituo *I decide, resolve*
audeo, -ēre, ausus sum *I dare*

soleo, -ēre, solitus sùm *I am accustomed*
cupio, -ĕre, cupīvi, cupitum *I desire*
disco, -ĕre, didici *I learn*
incipio, -ĕre *I begin*
coepi[3] *I began*
dēsino, -ĕre, dēstiti[4] *I cease*
scio (4) *I know how*

23. These verbs take a person object *and* an infin. object:

iubeo, -ēre, iussi, iussum *I order*
veto, -āre, vetui, vetitum *I forbid, I order . . . not*[5]
sino, -ĕre *I allow* (*give permission*)
patior, pati, passus sum *I allow* (*do not prevent*)
prōhibeo (2) *I prevent* (*N.B. Engl.* I prevent you *from* going)
cōgo, -ĕre, coēgi, coactum *I compel*
doceo, -ēre, docui, doctum *I teach*

e.g. Te ire iubeo   Mater nos legere docuit

---

[1] Another name for an object infin. is *prolative infin.*

[2] Malo ire quam manere *I prefer going to staying; I'd rather go than stay.*

[3] The perfect stem of *incipio* is not to be used: use *coepi* instead. *N.B.* **Coepi** does not mean *I begin*, but *I began* (or *I have begun*). The passive voice of *coepi* (*i.e.* **coeptus sum**) is used with passive infinitives: *e.g. The matter began to be discussed* Res agi coepta est.

[4] *Dēstiti* (from *dēsisto*) is the usual Latin for *I ceased.*

[5] If the order is negative, *iubeo* may not be used.

24. An infinitive is used as the subject of various verbs and expressions, notably these:

>   (mihi) placet   *it pleases me, so I resolve*
>   (me) iuvat   *it pleases me*
>   (mihi) mos est   *it is my custom*
>   (mihi) necesse est[1]   *it is necessary for me; I must*

Caesar decided to pitch camp   Caesari placuit castra ponere

25. Remember that the infinitive is a *neuter* noun, and any adjectives qualifying it must be in the neuter:

> Diutius manēre **periculosum** erit
> **Dulce et decorum** est pro patria mori

26. An infinitive is used with: paratus sum *I am ready*; in animo habeo *I intend*.

Exercise 2

1. It does not please me to wait here longer.
2. You ought not to allow the faithful dog to die.
3. It is very difficult to defeat the Romans' battle-line.
4. Most men would rather watch the games than work.
5. Agricola ordered his army to advance into Caledonia.
6. The soldiers began to complain because of the difficulties of the march.
7. However, they were compelled to march very swiftly.
8. No-one dared any longer to resist.
9. We have been ordered not to return there before night.
10. Who can teach us to read well? We have often tried to learn how[2] to do that.
11. The natives, who had been in the habit of placing their towns on hills, are beginning to live in the plains.
12. The fear of unknown danger prevented us from entering the wood.

---

[1] *Necesse* is an indeclinable adjective used only to qualify infinitives. *A necessary delay:* mora necessaria.

[2] In *learn how to, teach how to, know how to, how* is not translated.

3

PARTICIPLES (I)

31. A participle is that form of a verb which plays the part of an adjective (*broken* glass, a *rolling* stone). The ordinary Latin verb has three: the *present participle*, the *perfect participle passive*, and the *future participle* (*e.g.* amans, amātus, amātūrus).

32. The PERFECT PARTICIPLE PASSIVE is the most used; it can be used like the English past participle, *e.g.*

>The prisoners, *set free* by the enemy, returned home
>Captivi, ab hostibus **liberati**, domum regressi sunt
>
>The cavalry pursued the *defeated* Gauls to the camp
>Equites Gallos **superatos** ad castra prosecuti sunt

33. The perfect participle of a *deponent verb* is active in meaning. This fact makes deponent verbs very useful.

>The cavalry, *having pursued* the Gauls, took their camp
>Equites, Gallos **secuti**, castra eorum ceperunt

But *no verbs except deponents* have a perfect participle with active meaning: *having arrived* is NOT perventus.

34. The PRESENT PARTICIPLE has the same meaning in Latin as in English, but is used with greater care. Compare:

>(i) *Crossing the river, the boy fell from the bridge*
>   Flumen **transiens**, puer de ponte decidit
>(ii) *Crossing the river, the boy entered the city*
>   Flumen **transgressus**, puer urbem intravit

Where one action *follows* the other, as in (ii), the present participle may not be used in Latin; it is used only when the two actions named are *simultaneous*.[1]

---

[1] In English, to show that the actions are simultaneous, 'while' is often used: *e.g. While crossing* the river, the boy fell in.

—vrvs

*35. The FUTURE PARTICIPLE has active meaning (*e.g.* scripturus *about to write, going to write*). It is most commonly used as a complement to the verb *esse*, to express *likely to, intending to*.

>Hostes bellum illaturi erant
>*The enemy were likely to make war*

Facite quod vobis libet: daturus non sum amplius
Do whatever you like: I don't intend to give any more

36. Examples to be translated into English, first without, then with, the words in italics:

1. Hostes, *a Romanis superati*, fugerunt.
2. Praedones (pirates) *a Pompeio capti* punientur.
3. Pompeius, *in Asiam missus*, multas victorias reportavit.
4. Pompeius praedones *captos* punivit.
5. Cicero epistolam *a filio suo missam* lēgit.
6. Cicero epistolam *lectam* deposuit.
7. Equites Romani, *Gallos secuti*, magnum numerum occiderunt.
8. Pompeius, *cum multis navibus profectus*, praedones brevi oppressit (crushed).
9. Puerum *in silva latentem* invēnimus.
10. Nauta *in navem conscendens* in mare incidit.
11. Magister mihi *scribenti* errorem monstravit.
12.[1] Nonne hostes castra oppugnaturi sunt?

[1] On § 35.

Exercise 3A

1. We saw the enemy's[1] forces drawn up near the shore.
2. Why are you afraid of the falling stones?
3. Having spoken these words, they began to weep.
4. The prisoners, set free by the king, gave thanks to him.
5. The ambassadors found Cincinnatus working in the fields.
6. Advancing to the bank of the river, they halted near the bridge.
7. Roscius was murdered while returning from a dinner-party.
8. The natives, defeated in[2] this battle, began to despair.
9. They were all killed fighting bravely for their country.
10. Following the guide, we came to an unknown town.

Exercise 3B

1. The sailors, having been ordered to repair the ship, finished the task before night.
2. Setting out for Italy, Caesar left a large army in Gaul.
3. Soon, warned about the Gauls' plans, he decided to return thither.
4. We saw a large number of gladiators carrying shields and swords.
5. Pursuing the enemy[1] across the plain, our men captured their camp.
6. Pursuing the enemy across the plain, our men were hindered by the swamp.
7. Born in Spain, I came from there as a boy[3] to Britain.[4]
8. We are likely to die unless you send[5] food to us at once.
9. While coming down from[6] the mountain, the shepherds heard our shouts.
10. The ambassadors sent by the Thebans have been cruelly put to death.

[1] Always plu. in Latin.
[2] Abl. of instrument.
[3] Just *puer*: the *as* does not appear in the Latin expression.
[4] With names of countries, use *in*, not *ad* (and *ex*, not *ab*).
[5] Tense?
[6] down from: *de* + abl.

4
PARTICIPLES (II): ABLATIVE ABSOLUTE

41. The train, *being late*, was travelling at high speed
The train being late, I missed my appointment

In both these sentences, *being late* qualifies *the train*. In the first, *train* is subject; but in the second the subject is *I*; and *train* stands outside the main framework of the sentence. The phrase *the train being late* could be detached, and still a complete structure would be left. A phrase, made up of a <u>noun</u> and a <u>*participle*</u>, which <u>can</u> be thus <u>detached</u> is called an **absolute phrase** (*absolute* meaning *unattached*).

> *The game finished*, we returned to school
> *The rain having stopped*, they resumed their journey
> *Work being impossible*, we were all sent home

42. Absolute phrases are much commoner in Latin than in English. The noun and participle are in the ablative case, and the phrase is called an **Ablative Absolute**.[1]

Pecunia accepta, Sibylla libros tradidit
(*The money received*, the Sibyl handed over the books)
Having received the money, the Sibyl handed over the books

43. Observe the *natural* English in this example. Having no perfect participle active (except of deponents), Latin uses absolute phrases a great deal; English avoids them, and has a variety of expressions which can be used instead: *e.g.*

Having captured the camp,
After capturing the camp, } the soldiers carried off the loot
When they had captured the camp,
Milites **castris captis** praedam abstulerunt

---

[1] Ablative, because it may denote *time when*, *cause*, or *attendant circumstances*. Compare with the examples above the equivalent clauses *When the game was finished*, *Since the rain had stopped*, *As work was impossible*.

> *On learning of these events,* Caesar started for Gaul
> **His rebus cognitis,** Caesar in Galliam profectus est
>
> *When the envoys had departed,* }
> *After the departure of the envoys,* } the plan was changed
> **Legatis (iam) profectis,** consilium mutatum est

44. The ablative absolute is a 'last resort' in translating. If the noun which the participle qualifies stands in the main framework of the sentence, *or is referred to there,* it would be *quite wrong* to use an abl. abs.:

> *The soldiers, having captured the camp, looted it*
> *The soldiers looted the captured camp*
> Milites **castra capta** diripuerunt

45. Quotations to study: translate them first literally, then suggest the most natural English for them:

Caesar,[1] equitibus praemissis, subsequebatur omnibus copiis.

(*News of the storm reaches Caesar*) His rebus auditis, Caesar[1] ipse ad naves revertitur (*returns*).

Brevi spatio (*breathing-space*) interiecto, hostes ex omnibus partibus impetum fecerunt.

Profecto avunculo (*uncle*), ipse reliquum tempus studiis impendi (*I spent*).

Haec dicente consule, cives circumfunduntur (*flock around*).

Tum Caesar omnibus portis eruptione (*sortie*) facta, equitatuque emisso, celeriter hostes in fugam dat.

Hoc proelio trans Rhenum nuntiato, Suebi (qui ad ripas Rheni venerant) domum reverti coeperunt.

Concursu (*a running together*) ad clamorem facto, Etrusci milites Mucium comprehendunt.

---

[1] Observe the different position of the subject in these sentences. Both are correct; but the order *subject—participle phrase—predicate* is used to emphasize that the doer of the two actions referred to is the same.

Exercise 4A [1]

1. The work having been finished, we left the city.
2. Having prepared a large fleet, Octavianus joined battle with Antonius.
3. Having prepared a large fleet, Octavian led it against Antony.
4. After defeating the Gauls, Caesar demanded many hostages.
5. Learning these facts, the queen resolved to die.
6. Having lost the money, the boy was afraid to return to his mother.
7. Having found the money, the boy brought it to his father.
8. As my spear was broken, I was compelled to fight with my sword.
9. After they had lost many ships, the enemy surrendered.
10. When we heard your words, we wished to follow you.

Exercise 4B

1. When these terms were accepted, the defeated army immediately handed over its arms.
2. Laying aside our fear, we entered the thick wood.
3. As very many ships had been wrecked, not all the soldiers could be taken across at the same time.
4. Advancing to the nearest hill, they pitched camp.
5. Several of our men, falling from the bridge, were carried away by the force of the river.
6. When the bridge was broken down, very many fell into the water and perished.
7. After besieging Troy for a long time, the Greeks adopted a new plan.
8. After besieging Troy for a long time, the Greeks took it.
9. Launching their ships, they withdrew to a neighbouring island.
10. When the Greeks had departed, the Trojans dragged the wooden horse into the city.

[1] Deponent verbs are excluded from Exercise 4A.

5

PARTICIPLES (III): FURTHER POINTS

51. Sometimes, where English uses a participle, Latin cannot do so. When using an intransitive verb, *e.g. venio, resisto*, we cannot express either *having done it* or *having been done*. Sometimes there may be a deponent verb with similar meaning; but if not, a clause must be used instead.[1]

The citizens, *having resisted bravely all day*, were exhausted
Cives, **cum totum diem fortiter restitissent**, defessi erant

Such clauses would usually start, in a narrative, with:

 ubi, postquam *when*[2] (with perfect indic.)
 quod *because*
 cum *when* or *because* (with imperf. or pluperf. subjunc.)

Take special care in translating *having come, having arrived*.

52. Just as the perfect participle may be used for various English expressions (§ 43), so may the present participle:

While reading the book I fell asleep **Librum legens** obdormivi
We pursued the Gauls *as they fled* Gallos **fugientes** secuti sumus
In the reign of Darius (while D. reigned) **Dario regnante**

53. Where in English we use two verbs, joined by *and*, Latin often uses one participle and one finite verb.

> They *collected money and* built a school
> **Pecunia collata** ludum aedificaverunt
>
> Caesar *set forth next year and* captured the pirates
> Caesar **proximo anno profectus** piratas cepit

---

[1] Two other restrictions must be observed:
(a) If a perfect participle of a deponent verb is used in abl. abs., it may not govern an object. It would be *wrong* to say: Equitibus Gallos secutis, castra capta sunt.
(b) The future participle is not to be used in abl. abs.
[2] Never *quando. Quando* is '*when*' *in a question* only.

54. The verb **sum** has no present participle; therefore:
    Tarquin is king   Tarquinius est rex
    Tarquin being king ... Tarquinio rege ...

Similarly: *in Cicero's consulship*   Cicerone consule[1]
           under Camillus' leadership duce Camillo

More such expressions are given in § 177.

But two compounds of **sum** have a present participle: absens *absent* or *in one's absence*; praesens *present* or *in one's presence*.

> *In the absence of the king* I can do nothing
> **Rege absente** nihil agere possum

55. Notice carefully when, and *when not*, to use the pronoun *is* with a participle. [already mentioned]

We pursued *them as they fled*   Eos fugientes secuti sumus
We pursued *those fleeing*   } Fugientes secuti sumus
We pursued *those who fled*   }

Is is used to refer (just as it would if no participle were added) to someone definite already mentioned. *Those fleeing = the fleeing (men)* = fugientes.[2]

56. Quotations to study:

Sabinus, suos hortatus, cupientibus signum dat.

Propter muri altitudinem, paucis defendentibus expugnare (*capture*) urbem non potuit.

Hi, novissimos adorti, magnam multitudinem eorum fugientium concīderunt (*cut down*).

---

[1] The Romans dated their years by giving the names of the two consuls (without any conjunction):
    Cn. Pompeio M. Licinio Crasso consulibus   *In 70 B.C.*

[2] But do not use a participle in this way in the nominative:
    Those approaching were cut off from the camp
    Ei qui appropinquabant castris interclusi sunt.

Exercise 5A

1. We left the island of[1] Sicily and crossed the sea.
2. In Tiberius' reign, Sejanus' influence became greater.
3. On arriving at the shore, my companions saw a ship.
4. I have been accused in my absence; but in my presence you dare to say nothing.
5. While running across the field, we fell into a ditch.
6. The shouts of those resisting aroused the guards.
7. Having escaped from the prison, the sailors hid near the harbour.
8. Claudius attacked the Britons and conquered them.
9. Reaching the gates, we drew our swords and entered.
10. Caesar advanced into the territory of the Nervii, and easily defeated them.

Exercise 5B

1. Suetonius returned with two legions and tried to defend London against the natives.
2. Horace, the famous poet, was born in Manlius' consulship.
3. As I was reading your letter, my wife called me into the garden.
4. Never again were the Britons likely to try to recover their freedom.
5. We have now left the province and reached an unknown region.
6. I never intend to question you about this matter.
7. After waiting in vain for a very long time, we returned home without our brother.
8. Having routed the cavalry, our men pursued the rest of the Gauls as they made for their camp.
9. Caesar released all the hostages and sent them back to Gaul.
10. We manned three ships, set out from the harbour, and sailed round the island.

[1] Latin: 'the island Sicily': the two nouns will be in apposition.

6
GENITIVE USES (I). REVISION (1-5)
part of whole

61. A PARTITIVE GENITIVE is one which names *the whole, of which a part is being considered*: *e.g.* multi civium.

Note 1. The gen. of *nos, vos*, when used partitively, is **nostrum, vestrum**; in other uses **nostri, vestri**.

Many of us are here **Multi nostrum adsunt**

Note 2. 'All of them' looks like a partitive expression; but *all* is not a part. The Latin is *ei omnes*.

We saw *all of them* (=*them all*) **Eos omnes vidimus**

62. The following words often have a partitive genitive depending on them. They are used in nom. and acc. only.

INDECLINABLE NEUTER NOUNS	NEUTER ADJECTIVES AND PRONOUNS
satis *enough*	multum *much*
plūs *more*	quantum *how much*
minus *less*	tantum *so much*
nimis *too much*	
parum *too little*	quid *what*

We have hardly *enough food*	Vix satis cibi habemus
How much money is left?	Quantum pecuniae reliquum est?
What news do you bring?	Quid novi affers?

63. A POSSESSIVE GENITIVE, used as a complement, may express *the duty of, the character of, the nature of*.

It is the duty of Roman soldiers to fight bravely
Militum Romanorum est fortiter pugnare

Boys will be boys Puerorum est talia facere

It is not like a wise man to blame fortune
Non sapientis[1] est fortunam reprehendere

[1] *N.B.* This is the Latin for 'it is not wise to . . .'

Exercise 6A

1. It is the nature of dogs to love their masters.
2. The enemy's cavalry attacked our men as they were advancing.
3. The enemy's cavalry attacked our men and killed several.
4. The enemy's cavalry attacked our men and killed them.
5. Surely it is not prudent to do the same again?
6. What news have you heard recently, my son?
7. The majority of the citizens, on hearing this, desired peace.
8. These sailors show less skill than courage!
9. Why are you unwilling to learn to read?
10. Our men routed the Gauls and captured their camp.
11. Our men captured the camp of the Gauls and burnt it.
12. Is the master willing to allow us to play?

Exercise 6B

1. That orator has too much eloquence and[1] too little sense.
2. As the old bridge was broken down, we had begun to swim across the river.
3. Do you know how[2] to cultivate the garden?
4. Ordering the infantry to follow closely, Caesar himself led out the cavalry.
5. Which of these two men[3] prevented you from drinking too much wine?
6. It was characteristic of all Greeks to disagree among themselves.
7. Few of the bystanders tried to catch the thief as he fled.
8. Because they did not allow us to enter, we resolved to depart at once.
9. It is very foolish to give more money to him.
10. Was it not the consul himself who fell from his horse?

---

[1] Contrast, so no conjunction. [2] See *p.* 10, *n.* 2.
[3] No noun is required in Latin.

7

REPORTED STATEMENTS (I)

71. In English, verbs meaning *say*, *know*, *think*, are followed by a noun clause beginning with the conjunction *that*. Such a noun clause is called a **Reported Statement**.[1]

DIRECT STATEMENT	REPORTED STATEMENT
'He is coming'	His wife says *that he is coming*
	I believe *that he is coming*

A few of these verbs (*e.g. declare, believe, suppose*) are sometimes followed, instead, by an *accusative* and an *infinitive*, to convey the same meaning: *e.g.* I believe *him to be coming*.

72. In Latin, *all* reported statements are expressed by the 'accusative and infinitive' method. The subject of the statement is in the acc. (notice above how *he* changes to *him*).

'Magister advenit' Pueri dicunt **magistrum advenire**

73. The tense of the infinitive is the same as that of the verb in the original (or direct) statement. It is not affected by the tense of the verb of saying (*&c.*) on which it depends.

'Britain is an island'	'Britannia **est** insula'
We know *that Britain is an island*	Scimus **Britanniam esse insulam**[2]
The Romans thought *that Britain was an island*	Romani putabant **Britanniam esse insulam**
'Marcus will come'	'Marcus **veniet**'
I hope *that Marcus will come*	Spero **Marcum venturum**[2] **esse**
They replied *that Marcus would come*	Responderunt **Marcum venturum esse**

[1] Or *Indirect Statement*. In this book the term *Reported* is used.

[2] Observe that the complement, which has to be in the same case as the subject, becomes acc. too. This applies to participles in the compound tenses of verbs, since they are really complements.

74. In an acc. and inf., the pronoun subject *must not* be left out.

'Veniet'   Credo **eum** venturum esse

If the English word *he, she, they* (or *him, her, them*) in the *that*-clause refers to the speaker (or thinker), use **se**; if it refers to someone else, use the proper part of **is**. In the same way, *his, her,* or *their* will be **suus** only if it refers to the speaker, *i.e.* if it represents *my* or *our*. Otherwise use **eius, eorum**. Think of the original words that are being reported.[1]

'I shall return to my own country'	'In patriam meam redibo'
He says he will return to his own country	Dicit se in patriam suam rediturum esse
'He has worked well'	'Bene laboravit'
We know that he has worked well	Scimus eum bene laboravisse

75. SUMMARY—REPORTED STATEMENTS

English (usually)—*that*-clause.

Latin—acc. and inf.: no conjunction.

> VERB: *Mood:* Infinitive.
> *Tense:* the same as in the direct speech.

The acc. subject must always be expressed.

Se and *suus* in reported speech refer to the speaker.

76. Some common verbs introducing reported statements:

(tibi) dīco (3) *I say*[2]	audio *I hear*
(tibi) affirmo (1) *I declare*	puto (1) *I think*
(tibi) respondeo, -ēre, respondi, responsum *I answer*	crēdo, -ěre, credidi, creditum *I believe*
(te) certiorem facio *I inform* (lit. *I make (you) surer*)	scio (4) *I know*
	cognosco, -ěre, cognōvi, cognitum *I find out*
(tibi) nuntio (1) *I report*	
(te) doceo *I teach, tell*	spēro (1) *I hope*
scrībo (3) *I write*	nego (1) *I deny*

[1] This rule does not prevent *se* and *suus* from being used in the ordinary way, to refer to the subject of the reported statement, as long as no ambiguity results:

'Hostes se receperunt' Equites nuntiant hostes se recepisse

[2] *Inquam, inquit* are used only with the actual words (direct speech).

Exercise 7A

PART 1—DIRECT AND REPORTED STATEMENTS

1. The enemy are winning. 2. He says that the enemy are winning. 3. We heard that the enemy were winning.
4. My friend will send a letter. 5. I know that my friend will send a letter. 6. I thought my friend would send a letter.
7. Large rewards will be given. 8. I have been informed that large rewards will be given. 9. The general answered that rewards would be given to the brave.
10. He has been elected consul. 11. Have you heard that he has been elected consul? 12. You informed us that he had been elected consul again.
13. The new school will be larger. 14. We hope the new school will be larger. 15. We found out that the new school would be larger.

PART 2—USE OF se, suus

1. The merchant told us that he had come from Italy.
2. We replied that he had come to a very beautiful region.
3. The old man thought that his son was calling him.
4. I do not believe that all his slaves will be set free.
5. I hope I shall build a new house here.
6. We do not think he is speaking the truth.
7. My wife has written that she and the children are well.
8. The consul declared that he would beat the enemy before the winter.
9. The senators replied that he could not do this.
10. Our friends informed us that they would follow us after dinner.

Exercise 7B

1. We read that in Nero's reign the city of Rome was destroyed by fire.
2. Many used to believe that Nero had himself set fire to that city.

3. When were you informed that your companions were safe?
4. You did not say that you wished to stay here with me.
5. The natives believe that these trees are sacred to the gods.
6. Who does not know that Fortune always helps the brave?
7. The messenger replied that several tribes had taken up arms.
8. I shall not try to deny that I have often neglected my duties.
9. The master said that he had written the boys' names in a book.
10. Apollo had told the Athenians that they would be saved by wooden walls.

Exercise 7C

1. We were told yesterday that our grandfather was ill; to-day we hear that he has died.
2. Although we knew that you had been ill, we thought you would try to come.
3. Caesar was informed by his patrols that the column had halted in the valley.
4. The soldiers openly said that an excellent chance of victory was being missed.
5. Surely the witnesses do not deny that they heard your voice?
6. Glaucus hoped that by a spell Scylla would be compelled to love him.
7. I hope you will write to me often and send many gifts.
8. Our ancestors thought that the poor ought to hold the nobles in honour.
9. My companions declared that we should arrive before night at the robbers' cave.
10. The old men replied that old age seemed more pleasant to them than youth.

8

COMMANDS

81. Commands in the *2nd person* are expressed thus:
(a) if positive, by the imperative;
(b) if negative, by **nōlī, nōlīte** with the infin.

N.B. Non, nemo, numquam, nihil may not be used in commands.

Send no one (Do not send anyone) Noli quemquam mittere

82. Commands in the *1st and 3rd persons* are expressed by the subjunctive mood (present tense). This subjunctive is called 'jussive'. The negative word is not *non* but **nē**.

> *Let us not stay here* Ne hic maneamus

And not is **nēve** (not *neque*). *Neither ... nor* is **nēve ... nēve**.

> *Let the soldiers neither blame nor despise their general*
> Milites neve culpent neve contemnant ducem

83. Sometimes the word *let* really does mean *permit*:

> *Let me go with you* Sine me tecum ire

*84. Note these idiomatic forms of command:

Mind you come[1]*:* fac venias; fac ut venias; curā ut venias.
Mind you don't come: cave ne venias.

*85. Second person negative commands are sometimes expressed by **ne** and the perfect subjunctive:

> *Do not cross that river* Ne transieris illud flumen

But this expression is not much used in literary prose; it is mainly colloquial, and should be avoided.

There is, however, one exception. If there are two commands

---

[1] Or *see that you come, take care to come, be sure to come*.

in a sentence, and the second of them is negative, then (since *et noli . . .* is impossible) we must say:

Do not (either) praise or imitate such a man
Talem virum ne(ve) laudaveris neve imitatus sis

Come with me and do not wait for them
Veni mecum neque eos exspectaveris

If both commands are negative, they are connected by *nēve*; if only the second is negative, *neque* is used.

*86. The future imperative (*amātō, amātōte*) may be disregarded at present. Its use is explained in § 437.[1]

NOTE ON *ask for, look for, wait for*

87. There are some common verbs in English which are intransitive, but are translated by transitive verbs in Latin. Amongst others, note especially:

I *wait for* you   te exspecto (*cf.* I await you)
I *look for* you   te peto; te quaero (*cf.* I seek you)
I *ask for* money   pecuniam rogo[2]

It would be *quite wrong* to put these *objects* in the dative.

---

[1] But the only imperative of *memini* (I remember) is *memento(te)*; and of *scio* (I know), *scito(te)* 'let me inform you . . .'

[2] It is sometimes said that *rogo* may have two objects, the *person* asked and the *thing* asked for (*e.g.* te pecuniam rogo). This is not quite true: briefly summarized, the facts are these:

(*a*) *Rogo* (=ask) has a *person* as object; in addition it may have as a second object any of the following:
  (i) a clause (so in Engl.: I ask you *what you mean*);
  (ii) a neuter pronoun: *e.g. I asked you that:* illud te rogavi.
  (iii) the noun *sententiam:*
    The consul asked me my opinion Consul me sententiam rogavit
(So too in the passive: Sententiam rogatus sum.)

(*b*) *Rogo* (=ask for) has a *thing* as object: **pecuniam** rogo; if the person asked is to be expressed, *ab*+abl. must be used:
  I asked him for money (say *I asked-for money from him*)
  Pecuniam **ab** eo rogavi (*or* Pecuniam **ab** (**ex**) **eo** petivi).

Exercise 8A

1. Do not fear the bull: let us wait for our friends.
2. Let us not stay here any longer.
3. Give me the money which you have found.
4. Let all brave citizens defend the state.
5. Father, let me go to the games to-day, although it is raining.
6. Let us start at once and travel very fast.
7. He is not to work in the fields.
8. Do not drink water: let us ask for the best wine.
9. Do not buy that house; live near the sea.
10. Send me more money, for I cannot buy bread.

Exercise 8B

1. Let us destroy the temples of the old gods.
2. Everyone is to wait here for the arrival of the guides.
3. Let us not fear or despair, although we are in serious danger.
4. Mind you cease playing in the wood before night.
5. Remember always that you are a Roman citizen.
6. See that you do not spend too much money.
7. Let me assure you that your friends miss you.
8. Follow us and do not speak.
9. Take care to post guards at[1] all the gates.
10. Let us board your ship; we are willing to give a very large sum[2] of money.
11. Do not write to me or ask me for help.
12. Neither the cavalry nor the infantry are to pursue the fugitives across the swamp.

[1] ad. [2] *a large sum of money:* magna pecunia.

THE SEQUENCE OF TENSES

90. The tense of a subordinate verb tends to be influenced by the tense of the verb in the main clause on which it depends. The main verb 'sets the pace' for the whole sentence. This is true in most languages of the European family.[1]

He says that he {has come / is coming / will come} *but* He said that he {had come / was coming / would come}

There are two groups of tenses. Those referring to present or future time are called the **primary** tenses; those referring to past time the **secondary** or **historic** (*i.e.* story-telling, narrative) tenses. In Latin it works out thus:

PRIMARY TENSES	HISTORIC TENSES
Present	Imperfect
Future	Future-in-the-Past[2]
Perfect (*in subord. clauses*)	Pluperfect
—	Perfect (*in main clauses*)
Future Perfect	—

The imperative mood is primary.

The only difficulty is over the Latin perfect. In those *subordinate* clauses where strict sequence applies, it stands in the primary group, with the pluperfect corresponding to it in the historic group. But a perfect in a *main* clause is historic. The perfect tense had become the ordinary narrative tense in Latin,[3] and even where we should translate it by the English present-perfect *I have done*, it was to the Romans a *past* tense, denoting an action already finished.

Whichever of the two groups the main verb belongs to, the subordinate verbs will tend to be chosen from the same group; primary will follow primary, historic will follow historic.

---

[1] Greek is the exception.
[2] *i.e.* Engl. *he would do*, Latin (in subjunc.) *facturus esset* (§ 162).
[3] The same thing has happened over again in French: in *spoken* French the ordinary narrative tense is the compound past, *j'ai parlé*.

This tendency to 'follow suit' is much stronger in some kinds of subordinate clause than in others. The first rule of languages is *to express what you have to say*, and rules of grammar are to help, not impede, this expression. Now, some subordinate clauses are concerned with *facts* (this is notably true of relative clauses and adverb clauses of result). These readily disregard sequence rules in order to state their facts precisely. But in clauses dealing with *ideas* or *thoughts* (above all in reported speech clauses), the force of the sequence-tendency is very great.[1]

EXAMPLES

(*a*) SEQUENCE DISREGARDED:

Relative clause: I lent him a book which explains chess
　　　　　　　　The prisoner who escaped will be caught

Result clause: He is so old that he could not travel with us
　　　　　　　I worked so hard yesterday that I am still tired

(*b*) SEQUENCE STRICTLY OBSERVED:

Reported speech: 'Where are you going?'
　　　　　　　　Ask him where he is going
　　　　　　　　I asked him where he was going

Purpose clause: I am saving up so that I can buy a present
　　　　　　　　I was saving up so that I could buy a present

---

[1] *N.B.* The principle of sequence concerns finite verbs only, and never affects infinitives (*cf.* § 73).

The impression is often given that, where sequence operates, the subordinate verb must be in the subjunctive. This is not so: in Latin, of course, subordinate clauses expressing ideas or thoughts do normally have their verbs in the subjunctive; but there is no *necessary* connection between this mood and the sequence of tenses. For example, subjunctive verbs in result clauses (*ch.* 11) are little affected by the sequence principle.

9

REPORTED COMMANDS

91. REPORTED COMMANDS[1] in English are expressed by an infinitive, or (less often) by a noun clause:

DIRECT COMMAND	REPORTED COMMAND
'Pay the money'	We ordered (begged, asked, told) him *to pay the money*
'Let him be set free'	We ordered (advised, urged) *that he should be set free*

92. In Latin, **iubeo** and **veto** have an infin. (*never a clause*) depending on them. Remember: *te ire iubeo; te ire veto*.

Iubeo is never followed by a negative. *To order not to* must be translated by **vetare** (*to forbid*).

The general ordered the cavalry not to attack at once
Dux equites statim impetum facere vetuit

93. All other verbs of commanding have a clause, *never an infin.*, depending on them. This clause is introduced by **ut** (=*that*) in a positive command, but by **nē** (=*that . . . not*) in a negative command. The verb is in the subjunctive mood, present tense in primary sequence, imperfect tense in historic sequence—*i.e.* after a past main verb.

He urges us *not to yield*   Nos hortatur **ne cedamus**

He begged his friends *to stay* Amicos oravit **ut manerent**[2]

He proposed *that a new city should be founded*
Monuit **ut nova urbs conderetur**

---

[1] *N.B.* The technical term *command* includes requests, advice, &c. For purposes of grammar, *he begged me to go, he persuaded me to go, he besought me to go* are commands no less than *he ordered me to go*.

[2] Not 'oravit ut amici manerent': it is a common mistake to transfer the person-word to the subordinate clause. If it is with the main verb in English, it is so in Latin too.

94. Se and **suus** refer, just as in reported statements, to the speaker. Think of the actual words of the order.

My uncle asked me *to go with him* ('Go with **me**')
Avunculus me rogavit **ut secum irem**

95. SUMMARY—REPORTED COMMANDS

English—infinitive (sometimes *that*-clause).
Latin—CONJUNCTION: **ut** for positive command,
   ne for negative command.
   VERB: *Mood:* Subjunctive.
      Tense: in primary sequence, present,
          in historic sequence, imperfect.

But: *te ire iubeo, te ire veto.*

96. List of common verbs introducing reported commands:

(te) rogo (1) *I ask*	(tibi) persuādeo, -ēre, -suāsi, -suāsum *I persuade*
(te) ōro (1) *I beg, entreat*	
(te) moneo, admoneo *I advise, warn*	(tibi) impero (1) *I command, order*
(te) hortor, cohortor (1) *I encourage, urge*	(tibi) praecipio (3) *I instruct*
	(abs te) peto, petere, petīvi, petītum *I ask, beg*

Beware of the English verb *tell*. I tell you *to* means *I order you to*, and *dico* must not be used. For ordering, *impero* is rather a formal word; the ordinary word is *iubeo*.

97. Quotations to study:

Servo magnis praemiis persuadet ut litteras ad Caesarem deferat (*deliver*).

Milites cohortatus est ut pristinae (*traditional*) virtutis memoriam retinerent.

Cives manūs ad curiam (*senate-house*) tendebant, orantes ut sibi liberos et fratres redderent.

(*A murdered friend's ghost appears*) Idem ille rogare visus est ut mortem suam ulcisceretur (*avenge*).

Caesar imperat Cassivellauno ne Mandubracio neu[1] Trinobantibus noceat (*do harm to*).

---

[1] Wherever *not* is ne, *nor* or *and not* is neve, neu (*cf.* § 82.)

Exercise 9A

1. My uncle ordered the sailors to prepare the ship.
2. He asked me to cross the sea with him.
3. The others were urging the old man to go back.
4. They begged him not to despise the danger.
5. But he ordered the sailors not to change the course.
6. I entreat you not to speak in such a loud voice.
7. Nobody will persuade me to do the same again.
8. My mother urged me to start and to leave her behind.
9. We were warned not to try to escape by sea.
10. We advise you not to wait for your wife.

Exercise 9B

1. Varro had ordered Minucius not to challenge the enemy to battle while[1] he was away.
2. Jurymen, I advise you to acquit the defendant because of his youth.
3. The old man persuaded us to seek safety by flight.
4. My brothers ask me to tell you that they are not willing to sell the farm.
5. I urged them to confess that they had taken up arms against us.
6. The general ordered three cohorts to advance and seize the nearest hill.
7. The natives begged Caesar to let them[2] go back to their kinsfolk.[3]
8. The boys had been warned not to swim in that part of the lake.
9. My father told me not to go near the river: ought I not to obey him?
10. Do not try to persuade me to give up hope of victory.

[1] Abl. abs.
[2] Say: begged Caesar that they might ... The word *let* is here only an English device to make possible the use of an infin.; it should not be translated.
[3] *sui*.

10

ADVERB CLAUSES OF PURPOSE

101. The purpose of an action may be expressed in a *phrase* or a *clause*: I've been to London *to see the queen*; I stood up *so as to see better*; I wrote to him *so that he should not worry*. Purpose *phrases* are less common in Latin than in English; they will be explained later. An English purpose phrase will often have to be turned into a Latin purpose clause.[1]

102. Adverb clauses of purpose are often called **final clauses**.[2] In Latin, they are introduced by **ut** (*so that*), or (if they are negative) by **nē** (*lest* or *so that . . . not*). (*Ut* cannot introduce a negative purpose.) The verb is subjunctive, and present tense in primary sequence, imperfect in historic sequence (§ 90).

Fight *so that you may be free* Pugnate **ut liberi sitis**

I've been to London *to see the queen* (*so that I might see the queen*) Londinium ivi **ut reginam viderem**

The soldiers fought bravely *so as not to be beaten*
Milites fortiter pugnaverunt **ne vincerentur**

103. An infinitive *never* expresses purpose in Latin.

104. Sometimes the purpose clause precedes the main clause: it is a matter of emphasis: compare *I stayed in bed so that I should get better* with *So that I should get better I stayed in bed*. The order will be the same in Latin as in English, for the same reason. Do not interchange the clauses.

105. A purpose is a *thought* or *idea* in someone's mind: therefore in final clauses, **se** and **suus** refer to the thinker, just as in reported speech clauses (§§ 74, 94).

---
[1] In turning phrases into clauses, mistakes are often made over the number and person of the verb. Think it out in English first: *e.g.* I've been to London so that *I* could see the queen.
[2] Because they state the *end* to which the action is directed.

He gave the jurors bribes *so that they would acquit him*
Iudicibus praemia dedit **ut se absolverent**

106. SUMMARY—FINAL CLAUSES

CONJUNCTION: **ut** (*so that*) for positive purpose;
nē (*lest, so that ... not*) for negative purpose.
VERB: *Mood:* Subjunctive.
Tense: in primary sequence, present;
in historic sequence, imperfect.

107. Quotations to study:

Magister pueros extra urbem ducere solitus erat ut corpus exercerent.

Caesar ex provincia egressus erat uti se a contumeliis (*insults*) inimicorum defenderet.

Unus ex eis, ut iusiurandum (*oath*) solveret, in castra rediit.

Haec ad te scripsi pluribus (*at greater length*) ut videres te quoque debere illam monere.[1]

Exercise 10A

PART I

(i) Change the purpose phrase into a clause; (ii) state the tense and conjunction required in Latin; (iii) translate:

1. We come to school to learn.
2. Mucius went to the camp to kill the king.
3. He hid himself so as not to be seen.
4. The Gauls are advancing in order to capture Rome.
5. The enemy advanced to attack the city.
6. I have come to pay the money.
7. So as not to be caught, avoid the roads.
8. We shall run away so as not to be punished.

---

[1] In a sentence such as this, we should translate *scripsi* by *I have written*; but to the Romans a perfect, in a main statement, was a past tense; and so the subordinate verb is imperfect (*scires*). (Exceptions occur; but you should follow the normal rule, that *a perfect main verb is historic*.)

PART 2

1. I am writing this letter to warn you of the danger.
2. Brutus decided to kill Caesar so that the state might be free.
3. So that she would not lose the gold, the woman hid it[1] under the earth.
4. The orator was standing on the table so that all might see him easily.
5. Horatius swam across the river so as not to be captured by the Etruscans.
6. My wife will go to the market to buy food and wine.
7. Lest the prisoners should escape, close all the gates at once.
8. They kept silent, so that we should think them wise.

Exercise 10B

1. To attack the inhabitants of that region, Caesar was forced to send for his fleet.
2. Let us send out patrols, so as not to be taken off our guard by the enemy.
3. Twenty thousand citizens had assembled to watch the games.
4. Let us go out on to the shore to look for (some) fish.
5. As a young man he had come to Italy to get rich.
6. To avenge the death of Patroclus, Achilles determined to kill Hector.
7. Hide[2] behind this tree so that your sister won't find you.
8. To defend themselves against the attacks of the natives, they surrounded the city with very high walls.
9. Verres has sent us to this temple to carry away the famous statue of Hercules.
10. So that Hippomenes should not defeat her, Atalanta threw down a golden apple.

---

[1] Omit: it is usually safe to leave out an unstressed *it* in Latin, when it refers to something already mentioned.

[2] The Latin verb is transitive.

11

ADVERB CLAUSES OF RESULT

111. I was so tired *that I fell asleep*
It gave me such a shock *that I have not recovered*
So difficult is the task *that few will succeed*

Adverb clauses of result (or *consequence*) are commonly called **consecutive clauses.** Their main clause contains the 'signpost' word *so* or *such*—a helpful identification-mark.

112. The conjunction in English is always *that*, in Latin always **ut**. The verb is in the subjunctive, and the same tense is used as would have been used in a simple sentence.[1]

I was so tired *that I slept for a long time*
(Diu dormivi) Tam defessus eram **ut diu dormiverim**

For a *future* subjunctive, the future participle + *sim* is used.

We are so tired *that we shall not work to-morrow*
Tam defessi sumus **ut cras laboraturi non simus**

113. The demonstrative words used as 'signposts' are:

talis *such (in kind)*	tam (with adj. or adv.) *so ...*
tantus *so great; such (in amount)*	adeo (used with verbs) *so much, to such an extent*
tot *so many*	ita *so* (=*in such a way*)

These words are emphatic: always put them *first*. This is done sometimes in English (*e.g.* So difficult is the task ...) but in Latin it is the normal rule.[2]

They were so terrified by the war cry that they fled
Adeo clamore perturbati sunt ut fugerint

---

[1] Result clauses express *events*, not ideas or thoughts. They are, therefore, little affected by the strict sequence rules (§ 90).
[2] Occasionally there is no signpost demonstrative: *e.g.*
    We had been travelling a long time; so that we were tired
    Diu iter feceramus, ut defessi essemus.

114. Carefully distinguish negative consecutive clauses from negative final clauses; the English may be rather similar.

They ran fast so that we could not catch them
Celeriter cucurrerunt ne se caperemus — thought ∴ se

They ran so fast that we could not catch them
Tam celeriter cucurrerunt ut eos capere non possemus

These examples illustrate another difference between final and consecutive clauses. A purpose is a kind of thought; so *se* is used to refer to the thinker. A result, on the other hand, is event, not thought; so *them* becomes eos, not se.

115. SUMMARY—CONSECUTIVE CLAUSES

    CONJUNCTION: **ut** *always.*

    VERB: *Mood:* Subjunctive.
          Tense: as if in a simple sentence.

Demonstrative (Engl. *so* or *such*) first in main clause.

116. Quotations to study:

Nullus liber est tam malus[1] ut non aliqua parte (*in some part*) prosit.

Eiusmodi (=tales) tempestates sunt consecutae uti opus necessario intermitteretur.[2]

(*Postumius spurs on his troops*) Tantum iniecit ardoris ut non ultra (*any more*) sustinuerint impetum Aequi.

(*Cicero appeals to Antony's patriotism*) Maiores tuos respice, atque ita rem publicam gere ut natum esse te cives tui (*your fellow citizens*) gaudeant.

Verres per triennium (*3 years*) Siciliam ita vexavit ... ut ea restitui nullo modo possit.

---

[1] *Tam malus* has been displaced from the beginning by the even more emphatic *nullus*.

[2] Notice the imperf. tense. You will observe in reading that Caesar, unlike other writers, lets the strict sequence rule limit his choice of tense in consecutive clauses. In the example in § 113 Caesar would have written *fugerent*.

Exercise 11A

1. We have run so quickly that we are tired.
2. The storm was so great that we did not come.
3. I had bought so many books that I could not carry them.
4. They are so stupid that they have learnt nothing.
5. So wide was the river that we could not build a bridge.
6. Such[1] was the courage of the soldiers that they withstood all the attacks.
7. You have behaved in such a way that we shall never praise you.
8. He asked such[1] a high price that I did not buy the house.
9. Our men fight so keenly that they will easily defeat the Gauls.
10. The wall is so high that we cannot see the flowers.

Exercise 11B

1. I have heard so many speeches lately that I do not wish to be present in the senate to-day.
2. You sing so badly that nobody wishes to hear you.
3. The king was so cruel that he was driven out of his kingdom by the angry citizens.
4. Beyond this valley the road becomes so narrow that it is difficult to advance farther.
5. Such was the enthusiasm of the soldiers that the general ventured to join battle at once.
6. The theatre is so huge that all the inhabitants can watch the play at once.
7. So completely did the guide deceive us that we did not foresee the ambush.
8. The illness is so serious that he will die to-morrow.
9. The determination of the Christians is such that they are unwilling to pray to our gods.
10. You have cut down so many trees that there is no longer any shade in the garden.

[1] Not *talis*.

12

REVISION EXERCISES

Exercise 12A

1. He spoke in a loud voice so that all might hear him.
2. He spoke in such a loud voice that all of us could hear him.
3. Order the sailors to embark at once.
4. Let us go out into the woods to pick fresh flowers.
5. The old man called his sons together and told them that he wished to sell the farm.
6. Tell those boys not to throw stones into this garden.
7. They asked their mother to give them more money.
8. To learn to write well, read the best books.
9. Their joy was so great that they drank too much wine.
10. So as to reach the village before night, travel more quickly.
11. The cavalry were ordered to pursue those fleeing.
12. The leaves were so thick that we could not see the birds.
13. Surely you do not believe that I shall try to escape through the window?
14. The guards are so careless that I shall try to escape through the door.
15. We have been told not to stand under that tree.
16. Caesar had already ascertained that ambassadors would be sent by several tribes.
17. These merchants have sold so much plunder that they are very rich.
18. If they are guilty, let them be punished severely.
19. When informed that the cruel king was dead, they said they were glad.
20. Let us neither fight nor work on behalf of the patricians.

Exercise 12B

1. Do not think that the gardens which we have seen are more beautiful than mine.
2. The dictator had ordered the master of the horse[1] not to join battle in his absence.
3. We had so often been deceived by false rumours that we did not fear the real danger.
4. The archers had been ordered to lie hidden in ambush near the ford.
5. I am sure that, when a larger ransom has been paid (*use participle*), we shall be released at once.
6. When we saw the bones, we were so terrified that we fled from the cave.
7. I do not think it is necessary to ask the same (question) again.
8. So that his opponents should not put him to death, Marius hid[2] in a swamp near the coast.
9. These hostages wish to beg us to send them back to their kinsfolk.
10. Be sure to advise your brother to help us in our difficulty.[3]
11. To pay the money, I was forced to sell the farm which had been left to me by my father.
12. Deliver this letter to Cicero and do not wait for an answer.
13. The slave did not dare to deny that he had himself prepared the poison.
14. I believe you have hidden the books on purpose: mind that you do not waste time thus to-morrow.
15. So as to govern the new province well, let us learn the language of the natives.

[1] Magister Equitum: (the Dictator's second-in-command).
[2] Transitive in Latin.
[3] Pres. part. of *laboro*.

13

NEGATIVES

131. Common negative words are:

nēmo[1] *nobody*
nullus *no* (adjective)
nihil *nothing* (indecl.)
neuter *neither one*

neque ... neque[2] *neither ... nor*
numquam *never*
nusquam *nowhere*
ne ... quidem[3] *not even*

132. 'Any' after a negative word is *quisquam, quidquam* (pronoun) or *ullus* (adj.). But this does not apply where the negative is plain *non*. 'Not any' is *nemo, nihil, nullus*.[4]

Et cannot be used before negatives: *and ... not* is **neque**. So:

and nobody	becomes	*nor anybody*	nec quisquam
and nothing	,,	*nor anything*	nec quidquam
and no ...	,,	*nor any*	neque ullus
and never	,,	*nor ever*	neque umquam

And so on; but remember that the English for *neque* in such expressions is *and ... not* (sometimes *but ... not*).

We waited all day *and did not see anybody*
Totum diem exspectavimus **neque quemquam vidimus**

---

[1] Always singular (as in English); for declension, refer to grammar.

[2] Caesar uses *nec* only before consonants, *neque* anywhere. So with *ac* and *atque*.

[3] Only one word can stand between the parts: *not even I* ne ego quidem, but *not even a Roman citizen* ne civis quidem Romanus. Do not confuse the adverb *nē* in this expression with the conjunction *nĕ*. It sometimes causes difficulty if the *not even* happens to occur in a consecutive clause:

He was so angry that *not even the innocent* dared to speak
Tam iratus erat ut ne innocentes quidem loqui ausi sint.

[4] 'Hardly any' is *nemo ferē, nihil ferē, &c*. (Do not use *vix*.)

*133. A double negative, with **non** coming *second*, makes an emphatic affirmative.

Nihil non feci *There was nothing I didn't do: I did everything*

Do not confuse this with a double negative in which **non** stands *first*, such as:

> non nulli *by no means none—a good many, quite a number*
> non nihil *by no means nothing—a good deal*

*134. Haud (*not*) negatives a single word only (generally an adverb), never a whole sentence.[1]

> haud procul *not far off*   haud dubiē *undoubtedly*

135.   *He neither saw nor heard them*
     Neque vidit eos neque audivit

   Nobody either saw or heard them
   Nemo eos aut vidit aut audivit

After a negative, *either . . . or* is **aut . . . aut**.[2]

136. *Neither Apollo nor Minerva encouraged the Trojans*
     Neque Apollo neque Minerva Troianos hortata est

With *neither . . . nor* (just as with *either . . . or*) the two subjects are not 'added up' to make the verb plural: the verb agrees with the nearer subject—*i.e.* normally the last one.[3]

---

[1] Do not use *haud* with verbs (except *scio*: § 205).

[2] Distinguish between (*a*) the emphatic *either . . . or* ('one or the other, but not both'): *aut . . . aut*, and (*b*) the unemphatic *either . . . or* ('one or the other, it doesn't matter which'): *vel . . . vel*.
    (*a*) Aut vincere aut mori constituimus
    (*b*) Hoc vel hodie vel cras facere volo
The enclitic *-ve* has the same force as *vel*, but is not used in pairs.

[3] The same rule (agreement with the nearest subject) holds for subjects joined by *and*, if all or any of the subjects are *things*. If all the subjects are *persons*, it is correct to 'add them up' (just as in English or French). (But Latin writers, especially Caesar, often follow the 'nearest subject' rule even then.)

Exercise 13A

1. We did not leave anyone there.
2. We have neither given nor sold any bread to them.
3. I watched for a long time, but did not see anything.
4. They departed secretly, and never came back.
5. Not even the bravest soldiers dared to climb the rampart.
6. We have neither seen nor heard the enemy's patrols.
7. I have allowed no-one either to enter or to leave.
8. When the sad news was brought, neither the king nor the queen spoke.
9. Why did you not invite even your own sister's sons?
10. Neither of the consuls[1] will come to the senate to-day.

Exercise 13B

1. Although I searched in the valley, I did not find any flowers anywhere.
2. None of us is willing either to eat your bread or to drink the wine which you have brought.
3. They had travelled so often through those regions that they did not fear even the fierce lions.
4. He left no stone unturned[2] to recover the lost silver.
5. He has quite frequently told me that he knows[3] you.
6. A battle was fought *and* the Romans came off undoubtedly victorious.
7. You will easily be able to cross the river either by means of a bridge or by a ford.
8. Hardly anywhere have the chieftains now either power or influence.
9. I have been told that neither of these men[4] wishes to undertake the work.
10. Coriolanus was so angry that neither his mother nor his wife could influence him.

[1] Say '*neither consul*': it would be wrong to use the genitive in Latin.
[2] 'He did-not-do nothing.'
[3] Refer to vocabulary.
[4] Pronouns are an exception to the rule in note 1 : one could not say 'neither this-man': a gen. *must* be used: see *p*. 8, n. 1.

14

REPORTED STATEMENTS (II)

141. Dico never introduces a *negative* reported statement. *To say that . . . not* becomes *to deny*: negare.

He says that he will not come Negat se venturum esse

So with the expressions given in § 132: *e.g.*

He said that he had seen no-one Negavit se quemquam vidisse

This restriction does *not* apply to any verb except *dico*:

He replied that he had seen no-one Respondit se neminem vidisse

142. Further verbs introducing reported statements:

(*a: cf.* § 143)
spēro (1) *I hope*
(tibi) polliceor (2) *I promise*
(tibi) promitto, -ĕre, -mīsi, -missum *I promise*[1]
(tibi) minor (1) *I threaten*[2]
iūro (1) *I swear*

intellego, -ĕre, -lexi, -lectum *I realize*
exīstimo (1) *I think*
arbitror (1) *I think*[3]
memini, meminisse *I remember*[4]
ferunt *men say*[5]

(*b*)
doceo, -ēre, docui, doctum *I teach, I tell*
disco, -ĕre, didici *I learn*
pro certo habeo *I am sure*

(*c: cf.* § 144)
necesse est *it is inevitable*
manifestum est *it is clear*
appāret *it is evident*
(inter omnes) constat *it is common knowledge*

---

[1] *Polliceor* is much the commoner word; you *need not* use *promitto*.

[2] Also used with a 'thing-object': tibi mortem minor *I threaten you with death*. Note the difference from English.

[3] *Thinking* (participle) is best translated by *arbitratus*—not by a present participle. (Some writers—not Caesar—use *rătus*.)

[4] The perfect tense-form has present meaning: *I remembered:* memineram. *Imperative:* memento(te).

[5] Never with a definite subject.

143. In English, the verbs in § 142 (*a*) are often followed by an infinitive: I hope, promise, threaten, swear *to come*; but in Latin, a clause of reported statement must *always* be used. Before attempting to translate, change *He promised to come* into *He promised that he would come* (and so on).

> *They promised to repay the money at once*
> Polliciti sunt se statim pecuniam reddituros (esse)

The infinitive in the reported statement will be *future*: this is obvious as soon as the English is changed into clause form. Reminder: 'Every promise is a promise *that*; every hope is a hope *that*'—and so on.

144. An acc.-inf. may be the *subject* of a verb or expression such as those in § 142 (*c*).

> *It is well known that hardly anyone survived the disaster*
> Satis constat neminem fere cladi superfuisse

145. English uses the impersonal expressions *it is said, it is thought, &c.* Latin avoids using *dicitur, creditur, fertur, nuntiatur, &c.*, impersonally. Before translating, change the English into the personal form: *e.g.*

> *It is said that the Romans were brave soldiers*
> (*The Romans are said to have been brave soldiers*)
> Romani dicuntur milites fortes fuisse

146. Similarly the impersonal *it seems* is avoided in Latin:

> *It seems that we were wrong* Videmur erravisse

But in the compound tenses of these verbs (except *videor*), the impersonal forms are correct:

 It was reported that the envoys were approaching the town
 Nuntiatum est legatos oppido appropinquare
But:

> *It seemed that we were wrong* Visi sumus errare

Exercise 14A

1. The consul said that the enemy would never defeat us.
2. We believed that the enemy would never defeat us.
3. I swear never to deceive you.
4. It is related that Homer was blind.
5. It was generally known that he had been elected by a disgraceful trick.
6. I hope to see you and your wife there.
7. It is inevitable that the guilty should pay the penalty at last.
8. Thinking that the enemy were approaching, the commander drew up his battle-line.
9. It seemed that they had decided not to yield.
10. Promising to bring back a great weight of gold, they started off.

Exercise 14B

1. It is clear that you also hold the same opinion.
2. You will be set free if you promise to give back the plunder.
3. It seems, my son, that you prefer wealth to fame.
4. It is well known that the Germans are more cruel than the Gauls.
5. The guards said that no-one had tried to enter the citadel.
6. It was reported that ten ships had been wrecked by the force of the wind.
7. Supposing that our companions had not yet started, we travelled slowly.
8. It is said that Catiline threatened to overthrow the state.
9. We hope to return safely when the war is finished.
10. Do not promise to hand over hostages to these ambassadors.

15

TIME EXPRESSIONS

151. When a noun is used in a *time phrase*,

(i) TIME WHEN is expressed by the abl. with *no preposition*:

    eo anno *in that year*   bello civili *in the civil war*

(ii) TIME WITHIN WHICH by the abl. with *no preposition*:

    brevi (tempore) *in a short time*   triduo *in 3 days*

(iii) TIME FOR WHICH (extent of time) by the acc. with *no preposition*:

    decem annos manserunt *they stayed for ten years*

N.B. In a *negative* sentence, *e.g. I haven't seen him for two years*, the *for* does not denote extent of time. In Latin it is expressed as *time within which*: Eum **biennio** non vidi.[1]

152. Notice the tense used (in most languages except English) where the action is, or was, still going on:

I have been waiting for three hours Tertiam iam horam exspecto
He had been king for over 4 years Quintum iam annum regnabat

153. PREPOSITIONS are used in some time phrases:

Intra (+acc.), used instead of the abl. of time within which, emphasizes that the action was over in *less than* the period:

    The war was brought to an end *inside six months*
    Intra sex menses bellum confectum est[2]

Per (+acc.) emphasizes duration: *throughout:*

    Per totam noctem clamores audiebantur

Sub (+acc.) *towards*: sub noctem, sub vesperum, sub lucem
De (+abl.) *starting from*, esp. in Caesar: de tertia vigilia

---

[1] So in American: *I haven't seen him in years.*
[2] *sex mensibus* would imply *by the end of six months*. Compare the difference in French between *dans six mois* and *en six mois*.

Ad (+acc.) *until*: ad multam noctem, ad solis occasum
Post hominum memoriam *within human memory*
Ex eo tempore *ever since that time*
Ad tempus *in time, punctually*
In tempore *in the nick of time*

154. AGE can be stated by *natus* + acc. of extent of time:
a boy ten years old puer decem annos natus

155. In phrases with *abhinc*, the order of words is fixed:
ten years ago abhinc annos decem

156. With *ante, post*, use abl. of measure of difference:
ten years earlier (later)[1] decem ante (post) annis

157. *In so-and-so's reign, consulship, &c.* (refer to § 54): *e.g.*
Tarquinio rege; Tarquinio regnante; Caesare consule.

158. List of common adverbs and phrases of time:

herī *yesterday*	prīdiē *the previous day*
hodiē *to-day*	posterō diē ⎱ *the following day*
crās *to-morrow*	postrīdiē ⎰
prīmā lūce *at daybreak*	quotā hōrā *at what hour*[2]
sōlis ortū *at sunrise*	prīmā hōrā *at the first hour*[3]
māne *in the morning*	
merīdiē *at noon*	noctū *at night* (*also* nocte)
multō diē *late in the day*	interdiū *by day*
sōlis occāsū *at sunset*	quotīdiē *every day, daily*
vesperī *in the evening*	quotannīs *every year, annually*

[1] The same meaning may also be expressed by the *prepositions* **ante** and **post** with acc., *e.g.* quintum post annum *or* quinque post annos.
[2] The interrogative adj. *quotus* is answered by an ordinal number, as *quot* is answered by a cardinal. *What is the time?* quota hora est?
[3] Between sunrise and sunset there were twelve hours; the sixth was always called *meridiēs* (m.). The night was divided into twelve hours, or (in military language) into four watches (*vigiliae*).

Exercise 15A

1. Having stayed with us for six days, they left yesterday at sunrise.
2. We set sail at noon and sailed on until sunset.
3. They go to the temple of Jupiter every morning.[1]
4. At the age of 37, he was elected consul.
5. Throughout that night they lay hidden in ambush; at dawn they at last appeared.
6. Tarquinius had been king for four months.
7. Our city was founded two hundred years ago.
8. At what hour do you usually dine?
9. They departed a little (*paullo*) after daybreak, and will try to return in the evening.
10. Towards noon the remainder of the enemy surrendered.
11. The nights, which are short in summer, become longer towards the winter.
12. We have been besieging Troy for ten years.

Exercise 15B

1. He went to Africa with his wife and children twenty years ago.
2. He has not been seen by anyone for the last six months.[2]
3. They promised to return the money in two days' time.[3]
4. I hear you have been ill for the past five days.
5. In the following[4] summer, war broke out between the Romans and the Carthaginians.
6. His father, as it happened, had died four months earlier.
7. By day the robbers hide among the mountains; at night they plunder the neighbouring villages.
8. Each year the sailors used to launch their ships in the spring.
9. Ever since then, the gates are closed daily at sunset.
10. The senators met next day at sunrise, and did not adjourn before the ninth hour of the day.

---

[1] 'daily in the morning'. [2] Translate *the last* by *hic*.
[3] Use *biduum*, *triduum* (not *duo dies*, *tres dies*). [4] *proximus*.

16

REPORTED QUESTIONS

161. '*What are you doing?*' He asked me what I was doing
'Quid facis?' Me rogavit quid facerem

When a **qu-** question (§ 11) becomes reported, the interrogative word serves as the conjunction, just as in English.

'*Are you well?*' He asked me whether I was well
'Valesne?' Me rogavit num valerem

In reported fact questions (§ 12) the conjunction in English is *whether* or *if*; in Latin it is **num**. In reported questions *num* does not imply a negative (as it does in direct questions) but is quite 'neutral'.[1]

162. When a question is reported, its verb becomes subjunctive. Just as in English, it is affected by the 'sequence of tenses' (§ 90). If the main verb is *primary*, the tense of the original question remains unchanged[2]; after a *historic* main verb, an original *present* becomes imperfect, a *past* tense (imperfect or perfect) becomes pluperfect, and a *future* becomes future-in-the-past:

'What are you doing?'	'What did you do?'	'What will you do?'
He asks what I *am doing*,	... what I *did*,	... what I *shall do*
He asked what I *was doing*,	... what I *had done*,	... what I *should do*
'Quid facis?'	'Quid fecisti?'	'Quid facies?'
Rogat quid *faciam*,	... quid *fecerim*,	... quid *facturus sim*
Rogavit quid *facerem*,	... quid *fecissem*,	... quid *facturus essem*

[1] Take great care not to confuse the interrogative *if* and *whether* (introducing a *noun clause*) with the *if* and *whether* of an adverb clause of condition. In Latin, *si* never introduces a question.

[2] There is one (rare) exception, an original imperfect:

'*What were you doing?*' I ask him what he was doing
'Quid faciebas?' Eum rogo quid **fecerit** (*perfect*)

The breach of sequence is allowed in English, but not in Latin.

163. These examples show how a *future subjunctive* is formed. *I shall* (future simple) becomes *I am going to:* fut. part. + sim. *I should* (future-in-past) becomes *I was going to:* fut. part. + essem.

164. The list of interrogative words to be used in **qu-** questions has been given in § 11. But *cur* and *quomodo* are not common in reported questions. Instead of *cur*, use **quare or quam ob rem**; instead of *quomodo*, use **quem ad modum**.

*****165.** In a reported fact question, Roman writers sometimes used *-nĕ* instead of *num*. But in writing, use *num* always.

166. SUMMARY—REPORTED QUESTIONS

CONJUNCTION: (*a*) for **qu-** questions, the interrogative word; (*b*) for **fact** questions: **English** *whether, if;* **Latin** *num.*
VERB: *Mood:* Subjunctive.
    Tense: corresponds to the English (but make sure that sequence is observed[1]).

Se and *suus* refer (as in all reported speech) to the speaker.

167. Reported questions depend on verbs meaning *ask*:
(te) rogo, interrogo; (a te) quaero, -ĕre, quaesīvi, quaesītum.
They can also depend on verbs meaning *say, know, &c.: e.g.*

(tibi) dico[2]	intellego	mīror (1) *I wonder*
(te) certiorem facio	cognosco	oblīviscor, -i, oblītus sum *I*
(te) doceo	scio	*forget*
audio	memini	sentio, -īre, sensi, sensum *I*
video	nescio	*perceive*

Reported questions follow such expressions as:
    incertum est *it is uncertain*; mirum est *it is wonderful*

---

[1] When the verb in the English is *simple past*, great care is needed: think what the direct question would have been.

Tell me what you *saw* ('Quid *vidisti*?') Dic mihi quid **videris**
He asked me what I *knew* ('Quid *scis*?') Me rogavit quid **scirem**
The first is a *primary* sequence, and the original perfect is unchanged; the second is *historic*, and present becomes imperf. as explained in § 162.

[2] Principal parts given in earlier verb-lists are not repeated.

168. The clauses following some of the verbs in § 167 are not, strictly speaking, reported *questions*, but reported *exclamations*. But the construction of these is exactly similar, and it is convenient to use the same name.[1]

169. Quotations to study:

Caesar ex captivis cognoscit quae apud Ciceronem (*in C's camp*) gerantur, quantoque in periculo res sit.

Cum ab his quaereret quae civitates quantaeque in armis essent, et quid in bello possent, sic reperiebat (*learnt*).

Videte quantum inter meam sententiam vestramque intersit.

(*Cicero warns the senate*) Nunc autem homines in speculis (*look-out points*) sunt: observant quem ad modum sese unus quisque nostrum gerat.

Quanta multitudo ad hoc iudicium (*trial*) convenerit, vides.

(*Canius had been tricked into buying some 'good fishing-grounds'*) Cumbam (*boat*) nullam videt: quaerit ex vicino, num feriae (*holiday*) piscatorum essent.[2] Negavit ille ... 'Hic piscari nulli solent; itaque heri mirabar quid accidisset.'

Exercise 16A

1. I do not know why he has done this.
2. The master asked the boy what he had seen.
3. He does not realize how great the danger was.
4. We saw at once how great the danger was.
5. Find out if he is willing to go with us.
6. We forgot how many gifts we had sent him.
7. They heard at last where we had gone to.
8. No-one knows whether the enemy's forces will yield.
9. We perceived how difficult the journey would be.
10. Tell me who you are and why you came.

---

[1] All four types of reported speech, therefore, have now been introduced (*cf.* § 2).

[2] After a historic present (*quaerit*) either sequence may be used. (Compare the first quotation.)

Exercise 16B

1. Caesar asked the prisoners how many tribes had conspired against the Roman people.
2. We often forget how we ought to behave.
3. We did not know when[1] we should arrive at the city gates.
4. Find out from (*ex*) your friends whether they will stay here long.
5. It was uncertain where the enemy had gone in the night.
6. Tell me whether you have seen my dog recently.
7. It is wonderful how quickly a boy's money is spent.
8. Two roads lead[2] into this town; do you know by which one he will enter?
9. I remember where I met him and what he promised to do.
10. The general asked his scouts how many horsemen they had observed beyond the hill.

Exercise 16C

1. The old man does not remember how many years he has lived in the same village.
2. Pliny decided to ask Trajan whether he wished the Christians to be punished.
3. It was uncertain which of the two consuls[3] had won the greater victory.
4. The slaves do not know if their master will free them.
5. It is wonderful how often he sings the same song.
6. When questioned by the king, he told us how long he had been in (*apud*) the army.
7. Try to find out where we are going, and when we shall start.
8. Few of you realize how difficult it will be to surround the enemy secretly.
9. I urged the jurymen to reveal how much money they had received.
10. I asked the guards if they knew what had happened the previous night.

---

[1] See *p*. 6, *n*. 2.   [2] Use *fero* (intrans.).   [3] See *p*. 8, *n*. 1.

17

TRANSLATION OF ABSTRACT NOUNS

171. Often, where English uses an abstract noun, it is best to use a REPORTED QUESTION in Latin: *e.g.*

The scouts ascertained *the position of the camp*
Speculatores cognoverunt **ubi castra posita essent**

At last I understood *the cause of his anger*
Tandem intellexi **quam ob rem iratus esset**

172. Common expressions[1] of this kind are:

the size of (*how large it is*): *use* quantus
the nature of (*what it is like*): *use* qualis
the position of (*where it is*): *use* ubi
the origin of (*where it comes from*): *use* unde
the cause of, the origin of (*why it happened*): *use* quare
the motive of, the purpose of: *use* quo consilio
his intentions, his object: *use* quid facturus sit, quid in animo habeat.[2]

173. This is but one of several ways in which abstract nouns were avoided in Latin: Roman writers preferred, as a rule, to convey their meaning in concrete terms—and in particular to put the meaning into *verbs*, whereas English tends to put the meaning into nouns.

174. A NEUTER PRONOUN OR ADJECTIVE may be used:

He expressed the same opinion Idem dixit (censuit)
They had made many preparations Multa paraverant

175. AN INFINITIVE may express the abstract idea:

I prefer death to defeat Mori malo quam vinci
I am vexed at this procedure Id fieri aegre fero

---
[1] These are only suggestions: the point is not to learn a list of equivalents by heart, but to understand the principle.
[2] For this use of the future participle refer to § 35.

176. A RELATIVE CLAUSE is sometimes useful: *e.g.*

He achieved all his ambitions Quae cupiebat omnia effecit

177. A PARTICIPLE PHRASE may be used: the following are among the most common:

> *on the advice* of his father: patre monente
> *with the help* of his friend: amico adiuvante
> *in the reign* of Darius: Dario regnante; Dario rege[1]
> *under Aeneas' leadership*: Aenea ducente; Aenea duce[1]
> *at the suggestion* of Pompey: auctore Pompeio[1]
> *in the absence* of the master: magistro absente
> *on the departure* of the envoys: legatis egressis
> *in* the king's *lifetime*: rege vivo[1]
> *against* his *will*: eo invito[1]
> *without* our *knowledge*: nobis insciis[1]

178. *N.B.* (i) The phrase is not always an abl. abs.; similar phrases may be used in any part of the sentence:

> *in the year of the city's foundation:* anno urbis conditae
> *after the loss of the ship:* post navem amissam

(ii) In particular, notice the difference between:

He was accused in his absence and	*I was accused in his absence*
Absens accusatus est	**Eo absente** accusatus sum
They freed him against his will and	*They entered against his will*
Eum **invitum** liberaverunt	**Eo invito** ingressi sunt

*179. Do not make an abstract noun or expression the subject of a verb expressing *action*. Livy may say:

> Omnia repente mutaverat imperator mutatus
> *The change of commander had transformed the whole situation*

But you would be much wiser to write, as Caesar would have done: Imperatore mutato, omnia repente mutata erant.

---

[1] For the absence of a participle of *sum*, refer to § 54.

Exercise 17A

PART 1: REPORTED QUESTIONS

1. Tell us the cause of his death.
2. He explained to his friends the nature of the journey.
3. We do not know the size of that field.
4. The position of the enemy's camp was uncertain.
5. Do you not realize my object in asking that?
6. No-one suspected the origin of the rumour.

PART 2: PARTICIPLES AND INFINITIVES

7. On his father's instructions he returned the gold to me.
8. By the help of our slaves we found the money.
9. I desire your speedy release from enslavement.
10. Under Caesar's leadership we have conquered the Gauls.
11. In the absence of the consuls we dare not answer you.
12. After the defeat of Pompey, nobody knew Caesar's intentions.

Exercise 17B

1. Having told many lies, he at once realized the stupidity of his answer.
2. To ascertain the depth of the river, the general sent forward several scouts.
3. Tell me why you wish to change your plan without your companions' knowledge.
4. At the suggestion of the sailors we weighed anchor a little before dawn.
5. Caesar wished to be elected consul in his absence.
6. The death of his friend filled him with great sorrow.
7. Hardly anybody then understood the cause of storms.
8. I have remained with him so long that I do not understand his motive for sending me away against my will.
9. Advice is always more useful than complaint.
10. He carefully ascertained the number and size of the harbours on that coast.

18

ABLATIVE USES (I). REVISION (13–17)

181. The exercises which follow assume acquaintance with these uses of the ablative case:

abl. of the agent (**A patre** monitus sum)
abl. of the instrument (**Gladio** interfectus est)
abl. of manner (**Magna voce** locutus est)
abl. of respect (Caesar **nomine. Sapientia** excellit)[1]
abl. of comparison (**Fratre** sapientior es)
abl. of measure of difference (Fratre **multo** sapientior es)
abl. of time when (**Tertio anno** discessit)
abl. of time within which (**Tribus annis** regressus est)

182. An abl. of the instrument is used with these verbs, which do not govern an object:

ūtor, ūtī, ūsus sum *I use* (*e.g.* multis verbis utor)
fruor, fruī (perf. not used) *I enjoy* (*e.g.* libertate fruor)
fungor, fungī, functus sum *I perform* (*e.g.* officio fungor)
potior (4) *I take possession of, capture* (*e.g.* oppido potior)
vescor, vescī (no perf.) *I feed on* (*e.g.* pane vescor)

An abl. of the instrument appears also in these idioms:

I cross the river *on foot* pedibus flumen transeo
I ride *a horse* equo vehor (vehī, vectus sum)
(so also *nave vehor, curru vehor, &c.*)
I need money mihi pecuniā opus est[2]

183. An abl. is used with these adjectives:

dignus *worthy* (*of*)   indignus *unworthy* (*of*)
fretus *relying* (*on*)   praeditus *endowed* (*with*)
contentus *satisfied* (*with*)

---

[1] **Nātu**, in *natu maior* (older), *&c.*, is abl. of respect.
[2] Literally 'there is work *for* me to do *with* money'. If the literal meaning is kept in mind, the idiom is easily understood.

Exercise 18A

1. Do you hope to finish the task in a few days?
2. When shall we again enjoy peace? I do not know why we are waging war.
3. No-one slept that night for[1] joy.
4. The Britons are accustomed to use iron as[2] money.
5. He is so stupid that he cannot even write his own name.
6. My father has threatened not to take me with him to the sea.
7. Britain is somewhat larger than Sicily: we shall not easily take possession of the whole island.
8. Who knows the reason for the change in our plans?
9. We have brought so much wine that we need no water.
10. They said that no-one would be accused; but we thought they were not telling the truth.
11. Relying on the enemy's panic, we advanced with the greatest speed into their territory.
12. Don't you perceive how he is deceiving us?
13. I asked him whether the house had been repaired in my absence.
14. Sailing in a fast ship, we reached Asia in 12 days.
15. They had gone away without our knowledge, and we did not know when we should see them again.
16. It is said that our ancestors had long beards.
17. Do you think that such a custom deserves praise?
18. We left Troy ten years ago; we have been living on this island for six months.
19. Why do you wish to discover the height of that tree?
20. On the advice of the guide we started at the ninth hour, so as to arrive in the evening.

[1] Here *for* denotes a 'preventing circumstance': Latin uses **prae** (+abl.) to express this.
[2] *pro*.

Exercise 18B

1. I have received scarcely any letters from you in the last six months.
2. I am sorry you have been ill: when do you hope to return to your friends?
3. It is related that the birds brought leaves and covered up the boy and girl as they slept.
4. It was uncertain how many of the enemy's ships[1] had been sunk on the previous day.
5. The ambassadors demanded that a hundred hostages should be handed over to them within three days.
6. It seems that either you are trying to deceive us or you have yourself been deceived by others.
7. The Romans, whose ships are much smaller than those of the Gauls, are accustomed to use oars.
8. Suspecting that we had recognized him, he took refuge in the nearest temple.
9. Can old men enjoy many pleasures? My grandfather says that they cannot.
10. They asked me on what date I was born and if I was older than my sister.
11. The Cyclopes feed on bread and milk; yet they are much more fierce than men are.
12. You cannot make me promise, against my will, to follow you.
13. How much money shall we need? I do not know our destination.
14. Some soldiers rode into the city on horseback; others entered on foot.
15. Have you forgotten that in your mother's lifetime we had more slaves?

[1] 'how many ships of the enemy.'

19

PLACE EXPRESSIONS

191. ADVERB PHRASES OF PLACE require a preposition:

in campo pugnant   ad urbem veniunt   sub muro stant

192. EXCEPTIONS: (i) with *names* of towns[1] no preposition is used to express *at, motion to,* or *motion from.*

to Rome Romam   *at Rome* Romae (*locative*[2])   *from Rome* Romā

Similarly with the three common nouns **domus, rus, humus:**

home domum	*to the country* rūs (*acc.*)
at home domī (*loc.*)	*in the country* rūrī (*loc.*)
from home domō	*from the country* rūre
	on the ground humī (*loc.*)

(ii) *Place where* expressions need no preposition if they include *either* the noun **locus** (*e.g.* hoc loco; isdem locis) *or* the adjective **totus** or **medius** (*e.g.* totā urbe). There is also the phrase **terrā marīque** *by land and sea.*[3]

(iii) *The road by which one goes* is treated as the instrument, and so has no preposition.

    Ibam forte **Viā Sacrā**   **Omnibus portis** egressi sunt

---

[1] Also with *names* of small islands (that is, roughly, islands small enough to be thought of as single city-states).

[2] The form of the locative is:

1st and 2nd declension, sing.: like the gen. (Romae, Brundisii); *3rd declension sing. and all plurals:* like the abl. (Karthagine, Athenis). (Forms in -ī for 3rd decl. sing. (*e.g.* Karthagini) are also used.)

Note these locative usages: (i) *at my home:* domi meae; (ii) *in the very rich city of Rome:* Romae, in urbe opulentissima.

[3] With *names* of towns, **ad** means *in,* or *to, the neighbourhood of;* **ab** means *from the neighbourhood of.*

    Caesar a Gergovia discessit   Hostes ad Ilerdam castra ponunt.

193. ADVERBS OF PLACE. The *chief*[1] of these are:

hic *here*	huc *hither*	hinc *hence*
ibi *there*	eo *thither*	inde *thence*
ubi *where*	quo *whither*	unde *whence*
ubique *everywhere*		undique *from everywhere*
	eodem *to the same place*	

194. If the verb expresses, or implies, *motion to*, take great care in Latin not to use a *place where* adverb or phrase.

Where are you going? **Quo is?**
They assembled in the temple **In templum convenerunt**

If there are two place-phrases, *both* must indicate motion; and in Latin the *wider* place-phrase comes *before* the other:

He came to Caesar in the camp **In castra ad Caesarem venit**

195. There are some *place where* expressions, found mainly in military language, in which **ab** is used: *e.g.*

a fronte *in the front*	a latere (sinistro) *on the (left) flank*
a tergo *in the rear*	
ab ea parte *on that side*	a cornu (dextro) *on the (right) wing*
ab utraque parte *on both sides*	

196. DIMENSIONS (with adjectives *longus, latus, altus*) and DISTANCES are expressed by the acc. of extent of space.

After marching ten miles, they reached a river 200 feet wide
Decem milia passuum progressi, ad flumen pervenerunt **ducentos pedes latum**[2]

The new country house is 17 miles away from Rome
Villa nova **xvii milia passuum a**[3] Roma abest

---

[1] Another column could be added, thus: hāc *by this way*; eā *by that way*; quā *by what way*; these arose from *hāc viā, &c.* (§ 192 (iii).)
N.B. Do not use these words to translate *here, there, where*.

[2] Take care that the adj. agrees with the noun that it qualifies: a wide *river*, a deep *ditch, &c.* Many mistakes are made over this.

[3] In expressing *distance from* (which is not the same as *motion from*) a preposition is used even with *names* of towns.

Exercise 19A

1. The envoys were sent back from Corinth to their own city.
2. We would rather live in London than in the country.
3. Caesar ordered a large fleet to assemble at Brundisium.
4. After advancing thirteen miles, the thirteenth legion pitched camp near Ravenna.
5. On that side of the town they made[1] a ditch 15 feet deep.
6. The country-house I have bought is 20 miles from Antium.
7. We shall send this wine to our friends in the city.
8. Although he is going to the same place, he will travel by another road.
9. The River Tiber is 250 miles long.
10. Come here. Why have you left home? There are dangers everywhere to-day.

Exercise 19B

1. Although we hurried along the Appian Road, we have arrived here too late.
2. The cavalry were drawn up on the left flank, while the legions stood[2] in the centre.[3]
3. Issuing from the other side of the camp, they fell upon the enemy in the rear.
4. How can we cross a river ten feet deep on foot?
5. Many ships full of soldiers have left Carthage for Spain.
6. The Romans, having defeated their enemies by land and sea, were at last enjoying peace.
7. There were so many fires throughout the city that the inhabitants were fleeing by every gate.
8. I intend to send these gifts to my brothers in Athens.
9. Caesar's opponents thought they would be safe in the well-fortified town of Corfinium.
10. That city is surrounded by walls twenty feet high (and) ten feet thick.

---

[1] *duco.*
[2] Perfect stem of *consisto* ('I have taken my stand').
[3] No conjunction is used in Latin between two contrasted facts.

20

QUESTIONS (II): 'NUM QUIS', 'UTRUM ... AN'

201. There remain two points to explain about questions. First: ANY in a question is **num quis**.

> *Is there anyone there?* Num quis adest?
>
> *They asked whether I had lost anything*
> Rogaverunt num quid amisissem

This *indefinite* pronoun (**quis** *anyone*, **quid** *anything*, adj. form **qui qua quod** *any*) is *enclitic*: that is, it has no stress of its own, and must immediately follow the *num*, being pronounced as one word with it. Do not confuse it with the interrogative *quis, quid* (adj. form *qui* **quae** *quod*).

202. Secondly: WHETHER ... OR. There are some questions which offer a choice of alternatives: *e.g. Will you come with me or stay at home?* These are not fact-questions (§ 12); the answer to them is not *Yes* or *No*. Latin marks them clearly as **qu-**questions, by opening them with the adverb **utrum**[1]; the corresponding English word *whether* is seen only in the reported form: *I asked him whether he would come with me or stay at home*.

Utrum introduces the first alternative, **an** (*or*) the second[2]:

Utrum mecum venire vis **an** domi manere?

Eum rogavi **utrum** mecum venire vellet **an** domi manere

N.B. Or in alternative questions: **an**; *or* in other places: **aut, vel** (§ 135, *note*.)

---

[1] In origin, *utrum* is the neuter pronoun meaning *which of these two?*
[2] In Latin also, in a more informal style of speech or writing, the *utrum* could be omitted; or -ně was used instead, both in direct and reported questions, *e.g.*

Tacitus es an Plinius?
Vosne L. Domitium an vos Domitius deseruit?

But in writing exercises keep to the full formal expression.

203. OR NOT. The Latin corresponds exactly: **an non.**

Have you seen him to-day or not? Utrum hodie eum vidisti **an non?**

But in *reported* questions, *an non* is replaced by **necne.**[1]

204. Take great care in translating *whether*. *Num* and *utrum* are not interchangeable. In English the use of *whether* has spread beyond alternative questions into single ones (*e.g. I asked him whether he was coming*). But in Latin *utrum* is used in alternative questions *only*.

Always put the emphatic words next to the *utrum* and *an*:

> *Was it in Rome or at his country house that he died?*
> Utrum Romae an in villa sua mortuus est?

205. The expressions **nescio an, haud scio an,** + subjunctive, make a modest assertion, '*I rather think*'.

I am inclined to think you are wrong Haud scio an erres[2]

206. Quotations to study:

(*The morale of Caesar's troops is doubtful*) Quam primum intellegere voluit utrum apud eos pudor (*sense of shame*) atque officium an timor valeret.

(*Praise of a farmer's life*) Num igitur horum vita miserabilis fuit, qui agros colebant? Meā quidem sententiā, haud scio an nulla beatior (*happier*) possit esse.

Apud Germanos ... matres familiae sortibus (*by casting lots*) declarabant utrum proelium committi ex usu (*advantageous*) esset necne.

---

[1] Good Latin, though rarely found—outside examination papers.

[2] The expression seems to have arisen from something like 'I don't know (*whether I am mistaken*) *or* so-and-so is true'. The first of the two alternatives came to be left out.

In Latin of a later period it came to be used more literally, meaning 'I don't know whether ...' Do not use it in this way.

Exercise 20A

1. Have the scouts found anything out?
2. Did you buy the horse or find it?
3. Do you wish to send him a gift or not?
4. No-one asked whether the slave was a Gaul or a Briton.
5. I almost think you are telling the truth at last.
6. Do you prefer to hear the opinions of old men or young men?
7. We did not know whether he would undertake the task or not.
8. Do you intend to fish in the river or in the sea?
9. They did not tell me whether anyone had brought the news before me.
10. Tell me whether you sailed to Asia in winter or summer.

Exercise 20B

1. Was the ship wrecked by unexpected rocks or by the violence of the wind?
2. The soldiers were uncertain whether it was Sabinus or Cotta who commanded the legion.
3. I rather think, sailors, that we have discovered a new island, much larger than Sicily.
4. Are the mountains of Spain or those of Gaul the higher?
5. Does anybody know why our allies have threatened to desert us?
6. Although he shouted again and again, he did not know whether anyone heard.
7. The jury will decide whether the defendant is innocent or not.
8. I am inclined to believe that our ancestors were much more fortunate than we are.
9. Shall we be sent back home from here by land or by sea?
10. Do you consider that the Romans or the Carthaginians were more deserving of victory?

21

FINAL CLAUSES AND COMMANDS: FURTHER POINTS

211. ANY after a negative is **quisquam** (adj. **ullus**), as was explained in § 132. There is one important exception. After **nē**, *any* is the indefinite pronoun **quis** (used also after **num**: § 201).

This applies wherever *nē* is used: in direct or reported commands, in final clauses, and in other uses to be met later. The *quis* must immediately follow the *ne*.

> *Let no-one depart from here* Ne quis hinc discedat
>
> *I kept silent so as not to tell any lies*
> Tacui ne qua falsa dicerem

212. We have now two sets of words translating *any*:

	WITH NE	WITH OTHER NEGATIVES (§ 132)
anybody	ne quis	nec . . . quisquam
anything	ne quid	nec . . . quidquam
any (adj.)	ne qui, qua, quod[1]	neque . . . ullus
anywhere	nēcubi[2]	neque . . . usquam
ever	ne quando	neque . . . umquam

213. The English 'to avoid doing a thing' or 'to save or prevent a thing from happening' will usually be translated by a *negative final clause*.

> I write this *to prevent anyone from worrying*
> Hoc scribo ne quis anxius sit
>
> *To avoid being cut off*, they marched over the hills
> Ne intercluderentur, trans montes iter fecerunt

---

[1] But a masc. noun denoting a *person* has **quis** not *qui*. This applies to *quis* indefinite and *quis* interrogative:
　　　quis miles . . .?　　ne quis civis . . .
[2] *i.e.* nē-cubi. *Ubi* was originally a *qu-* word. *Cf.* si-cubi.

214. Just as *et non* is replaced by *neque*, so *et ne* is replaced by nēve (as already explained in § 82).

He urged us not to weep or despair
Nos cohortatus est ne ploraremus neve desperaremus

*215. A final clause may be 'signposted' by a word or phrase in the main clause, *e.g.*

eo consilio ut . . . *on purpose to* . . .
idcirco ut . . .⎱
ideo ut . . . ⎰ *for this reason, to* . . .[1]

216. Quotations to study:

Caesar ad Lingones litteras nuntiosque misit, ne Helvetios frumento neve alia re iuvarent.

Milites cohortatus est uti suae pristinae (*traditional*) virtutis memoriam retinerent neu perturbarentur animo, hostiumque[2] impetum fortiter sustinerent.

(*To distinguish friend from foe*) Ne quo errore milites caperentur (*deceive*), edicunt consules ne quis extra ordinem contra hostes pugnaret.

(*Fight to a finish*) Germani omnem aciem suam raedis et carris (*carts, wagons*) circumdederunt, ne qua spes in fuga relinqueretur.

(*Those were our war-aims*) Quae ut fierent idcirco pugnatum esse arbitror.

Exploratores dispositi sunt necubi effecto ponte Romani copias traducerent.

---

[1] Throwing the emphasis on the *purpose* more than on the action.
[2] Where English uses *but* after a negative statement, Latin has *and*.

Exercise 21A

1. Let nobody try to leave the city after sunset.
2. He warned the centurions that nobody was to draw his sword before the signal.
3. To avoid being punished, the boys hid in the garden.
4. I warned them not to say anything about my arrival.
5. Lest the natives should ever invade the province, a huge fortification was constructed.
6. To prevent the prisoners from escaping we closed all the gates.
7. They advised us not to disembark from the ship or enter the harbour.
8. I came here with the intention of killing King Porsena.
9. I urged that no-one should avoid the battle or fear the danger.
10. To save you from wasting time, I promise to hurry.

Exercise 21B

1. To avoid capture, the conspirators went secretly out into the country.
2. So as not to be awakened by any noise, he usually sleeps in the middle of the house.
3. Lest the enemy should surround our men from the rear or cut them off from the water, Caesar stationed three cohorts on the left flank.
4. My object in warning you is to save you from being deceived by any trickery.
5. To prevent disclosure of the plot, they swore that they had done nothing contrary to the laws.
6. Let us neither give up hope nor yield to threats.
7. That you may never ask in vain for help, choose your allies with great care.
8. He begged us not to blame him, nor to think him foolish.
9. Caesar was advancing by forced marches with the intention of overtaking the enemy in four days.
10. Let no-one neglect the words of this experienced man.[1]

[1] Latin: 'this so experienced man'.

22

CLAUSES OF REPORTED SPEECH: FURTHER POINTS

221. There are some verbs which can introduce more than one kind of reported speech clause; and care is needed to avoid mistakes. *Think back to the original words.*

A **statement** or a **command** may follow

(te) moneo, admoneo *I warn, advise*
(tibi) persuadeo *I persuade, convince*

> He warned me *that I could not escape*
> Me monuit **me non posse effugere**
>
> He warned me *to flee at once*
> Me monuit **ut statim fugerem**

222. A **statement** or a **question** may follow most verbs of *saying* and *knowing*: observe how the lists in § 76 and § 167 overlap.

We did not know *what he had found*   Nescivimus **quid invenisset**

We did not know *that he had found a large sum of money*   Nescivimus **eum magnam pecuniam invenisse**

223. A **question** or a **command** may follow verbs meaning *ask*. With reported commands (*He asked me to go; he asked that it should be done*) use **peto** or **rogo** for *ask*; with reported questions, use **rogo, interrogo** or **quaero**.

Me rogavit ⎱ **ut irem**
A me petivit ⎰

Me rogavit ⎫
Me interrogavit ⎬ **quid haberem**
A me quaesivit ⎭

224. There is no difficulty about these points, only need for care. *Think back to the original words.* Be careful, in particular, over the English word *tell*. It is often used to mean *order*; but *dico, certiorem facio* are never so used. When *tell* means *order*, say *order*: use **iubeo** or **veto**.

He told me that he had lost the books
Mihi dixit (me certiorem fecit) se libros amisisse

He told me how many books he had lost
Mihi dixit (me certiorem fecit) quot libros amisisset

He told me to look for the books
Me iussit libros petere

He told me the same story
Mihi eandem fabulam narravit

225. *I hope that they will come* {Spero eos venturos esse / Spero fore ut veniant

Instead of a *future infin.* in a reported statement, we may use an expression made up of **fŏre** (fut. infin. of *sum*) and an **ut** clause. The literal meaning of the example above is *I hope that it-will-be-the-case that they come*. Note that the infin. *fore* is impersonal, and the verb in the *ut* clause is present or imperfect subjunctive, according to the sequence.

This expression *may* be used instead of *any* future infin.; and if the verb to be used has no supine stem (and so no fut. infin. act. or pass.), it *must* be used.

They knew that the slaves would soon learn the language
Sciebant fore ut servi brevi linguam discerent

I thought that that law would be abolished
Arbitrabar fore ut ea lex tolleretur[1]

*226. If a clause of reported speech has a subordinate clause depending on it, the verb of that subordinate clause must be in the subjunctive[2]:

'Because you have told the truth I shall not punish you'
'Quod vera dixisti, te non puniam'
Quod vera *dixissem*, negavit se me puniturum esse

[1] Literally: they knew that *it-would-be-the-case* that the slaves soon learnt the language; I thought that *it-would-be-the-case* that that law was abolished.
[2] This is known as a *sub-oblique* subjunctive.

Exercise 22A

1. The deserters were warned by the messenger to wait for nightfall.
2. No-one will convince me that this law is fair.
3. Your wife has told me to write you a letter.
4. Our allies hoped that we should resist more bravely.
5. Tell the slaves to bring in the dinner at once.
6. Tell me whether Gaul or Britain is the larger province.
7. First he asked me what I had in my hand; then he asked me to give it to him.
8. Persuade your brother to stand for the consulship.
9.[1] I do not believe that all his slaves will be set free.
10.[1] The consul declared that he would beat the enemy before the winter.

Exercise 22B

1. How will you persuade the jury that the defendant committed such a crime?
2. When I asked him to come with me, he asked me where I was going, and at what hour I should return here.
3. Although we knew that our father was vexed at our trick, we did not know whether he would punish us.
4. We have been told not to tell anyone what happened.
5. If your wife is ill, I advise sending for a doctor at once.
6. Cicero summoned the senate and warned it that the state was in grave danger.
7. In this book Ovid tells how Jupiter decided to destroy the human race.
8. He was endowed with such[2] ability that he hoped to learn the Greek language in three months.
9.[1] Apollo had told the Athenians that they would be saved by wooden walls.
10.[1] My companions declared that we should arrive before night at the robbers' cave.

[1] These sentences (taken from Exercise 7) are to be done with *fore*.
[2] Not *talis*.

23

FEAR CLAUSES

231. The chief verbs of fearing are: **timeo** (2); **metuo** (3); **vereor** (2). Translate *fearing* by **veritus**, not by *timens* or *metuens*.

232. These verbs, in English and Latin, can have as object:
(i) a **noun**: *I fear death* Mortem timeo
(ii) an **infin.**: *I fear to stay longer* Diutius manere timeo
(iii) a **noun-clause**: *I fear that he will die* Timeo ne moriatur

233. A FEAR CLAUSE, in English, is introduced by the conjunction *that* (sometimes *lest*). In Latin the conjunction is **nē**.[1] The verb is present subjunctive in primary sequence, and imperfect subjunctive in historic sequence.

They were afraid {*that their friends would depart*
lest their friends might depart}
Timebant **ne** amici discederent

234. If there is a *negative* in the fear clause, it appears in its normal place in the clause.[2]

Fearing is a kind of thought; therefore **se** and **suus** are used, as in reported speech, to refer to the thinker (§ 74).

They were afraid that their friends would not find them
Timebant ne amici (**sui**) **se** non reperirent

---

[1] It is easy to see how this use of *ne* arose. Originally, the 'fear clause' had been a separate sentence: *e.g.*
Timeo: ne moriatur! *I am afraid: may he not die!*
The subjunctive expressed a *command*, or (more precisely) a *wish*. Gradually it came to be felt that the wish *depended* on the verb of fear; *ne* was therefore regarded as a conjunction, and no longer as a negative adverb. *Cf.* § 8.

[2] In place of *ne* . . . *non*, **ut** may be used; it is commonest with *vereor*:

We feared that reinforcements would not arrive
Verebamur **ut** novae copiae advenirent

But *ne non* is always correct; and if the main verb is negatived (*e.g.* **I am not afraid** . . .), *ut* is never used.

*235. The expression *afraid of doing* calls for thought. It usually equals a *that* clause; occasionally an infinitive:

They were afraid *of being heard* Timebant *ne audirentur*
He was afraid *of telling the truth* Metuebat *vera loqui*

236. Fear clauses naturally refer to the *future*: we fear what we think is going to happen. But the same form of words is often used, both in English and in Latin, with reference to the *present* or the *past*:

I fear that you are wrong Timeo ne erres[1]
I was afraid he had already left Timui ne iam profectus esset

The verb will still be subjunctive; but any tense may be used: follow the tense used in the English. But when translating the English simple past, take care of the sequence (compare the footnote to § 166).

He was afraid that they knew Timebat ne **scirent**
I am afraid they left yesterday Timeo ne heri **discesserint**

237. A fear clause may depend on a noun such as *timor, metus, periculum*: e.g.

There is very great danger that the defendant will get off
Ne reus elabatur summum periculum est

238. SUMMARY—FEAR

Fear to—Infinitive.

Fear that—CONJUNCTION: Engl. that, lest; Latin nĕ.
        VERB: *Mood:* Subjunctive.
                Tense: primary sequence—present;
                           historic sequence—imperfect.

But in fear about the *present* or *past*, tense corresponds to the English (but see that sequence is observed).

---

[1] The Latin is therefore ambiguous: *Timeo ne veniat* may mean *I fear that he is coming* or *I fear that he will come* (and similarly with *Timebam ne veniret*). In practice, the context almost always makes the meaning unmistakable.

Exercise 23A

1. I am not afraid that we shall be defeated.
2. I am afraid that we shall not be able to defeat the enemy.
3. Being afraid to enter the wood, they halted.
4. There is a risk that he will not return in time.
5. He feared that his companions might desert him.
6. I am afraid the citadel has already been captured.
7. Fearing that the enemy had seen them, the scouts withdrew.
8. You aren't afraid to tell the truth, surely?
9. We were afraid that our friends were not at home.
10. The slave, fearing his master's anger, ran away the following day.
11. We were afraid it would rain all night.
12. The boys feared lest the master might suddenly open the door.

Exercise 23B

1. I fear that it may seem to you I am more imprudent than my companions.
2. He feared that the others would think he was boasting.
3. There was grave danger that the new bridges would be broken down by the force of the water.
4. Fearing that the ship would not withstand the huge waves, the sailors were afraid to weigh anchor.
5. The old man, abandoned by his sons and daughters, feared that he would perish of hunger.
6. I am afraid thieves took away all the gold yesterday.
7. At first the Gauls were afraid to enter the deserted city.
8. They feared lest there might be some ambush in the streets.
9. The senators feared that Papirius would reveal their plans without his father's knowledge.
10. Surely the gladiator is not afraid of being called a coward by his opponent?

24

REVISION EXERCISES

Exercise 24A

1. I cannot tell you how I arrived here yesterday.
2. Find out whether the natives feed on corn or fish.
3. The infantry marched by a longer route to surround the enemy from the rear.
4. The citizens feared that Catiline would be made consul.
5. The young man did this on purpose to avenge his father.
6. I do not believe that the war will be finished this summer.
7. You have hardly sent any letters lately to your son in Athens.
8. I am sure that you will very easily learn to swim.
9. Defeated by land and sea, the Athenian sailors were afraid that they would never see their homeland.
10. Do you prefer to live in a city or in the country?
11. I rather think that he is worthy of a larger reward.
12. After routing the enemy we captured and destroyed their town.
13. Ask him whether he is afraid to cross a river five feet deep.
14. The body was lying on the ground all day and no-one saw it.
15. It is uncertain whether they will attack us on the flank or not.
16. The shepherd warned us that night was at hand and told us to hurry home.
17. I beg you to tell no-one about this crime.
18. Tell me when you hope to return that money to me.
19. We were afraid that the consul had fallen from his horse.
20. To prevent them from hearing anything, close all the windows.

Exercise 24B

1. To stop the enemy from foraging in this district, order the cavalry to seize the nearest high-ground.
2. I fear that I shall not be able to perform these duties any longer.
3. The citadel was protected on both sides by a rampart twenty feet high.
4. I warn you that the water is twelve feet deep in many places: take care not to fall in.
5. The fourteenth legion, which was stationed on the left flank, was attacked in the rear.
6. Tell me whether I can reach home from here in one day or not.
7. There was a risk that our friends had not foreseen our intentions.
8. Let no-one follow the example of these traitors.
9. I am afraid that the nearest mountains are thirty miles away.
10. We prefer to enjoy leisure at Baiae this summer, rather than remain longer in Rome.
11. They feared that they would be prevented by the cold from sleeping well.
12. I have lived for the last twelve years in the beautiful city of Athens.
13. Guards have been posted at the gates to prevent anyone from entering secretly.
14. He feared that he[1] would incur the danger, while[2] others would gain the glory.
15. I do not know whether anybody has noticed the mistake.
16. I rather think no-one has noticed who is sitting there.

[1] Emphatic: use *ipse*.
[2] 'He' and 'others' are contrasted: *cf. p.* 63, *n.* 3.

25

DATIVE CASE WITH VERBS

251. The following verbs are intransitive, and govern a *dative*; their English equivalent is (in most cases) transitive. Some have a transitive synonym (given in brackets).

tibi appropinquo (1) *I approach you* (te adeo)
tibi confīdo, -ĕre, confīsus sum[1] *I trust you*
tibi diffīdo, -ĕre, diffīsus sum *I mistrust you*
tibi crēdo, -ĕre, crēdidi, crēditum *I believe you*
tibi faveo, -ēre, fāvi, fautum *I support you*
tibi ignosco, -ĕre, ignōvi, ignōtum *I forgive you*
tibi invideo, -ēre, invīdi, invīsum *I envy you, am jealous*
tibi īrascor, īrascī, īrātus sum *I am angry with you*
tibi noceo (2) *I harm you* (te laedo)
tibi nūbō (3) *I marry you* (woman as subject) (uxorem duco)
tibi parco, -ĕre, peperci, —[2] *I spare you* (te conservo)
tibi pāreo (2)[2] *I obey you*
tibi persuādeo, -ēre, persuāsi, persuāsum *I persuade you*
tibi placeo (2) *I please you*
tibi displiceo (2) *I displease you*
tibi resisto, -ĕre, restiti, — *I resist you*
tibi studeo (2) *I am devoted to you; I am keen on; I study*[3]

252. Many verbs compounded with prepositions, esp. **in-**, **sub-**, **ob-**, and **prae-**, have a dative depending on them, *e.g.*

with **in**: hostibus bellum indico *I declare war on the enemy*
hostibus bellum infero *I make war on the enemy*

with **sub** (meaning *to help*):
tibi subvenio, tibi succurro *I help you*
tibi auxilium submitto *I send help to you*

---

[1] The simple verb *fido*, with the same meaning, is used chiefly in poetry. For 'trusting', 'distrusting', use *confisus, diffisus*.
[2] The supine stem is not to be used.
[3] Do not use *studeo* alone (only later writers did so, as when Pliny wrote 'Studesne?' *Do you go to school?*).

with ob (meaning *to hinder*):
> tibi aliquid obicio *I put something in your way*
> tibi occurro *I meet you (accidentally)*[1]

with prae:
> te legioni praeficio *I put you in command of the legion*

253. Compounds of **sum** govern a dative (exceptions: *possum, absum, insum*[2]).

> nuptiis adsum *I am present at the wedding*
> pecunia deest mihi *I lack money* (note change of idiom)
> proelio intersum *I take part in the battle*
> legioni praesum *I am in command of the legion*
> ars mihi prodest *skill is useful to me, benefits me*
> fratri supersum *I outlive my brother*

254. Note the dative used with these verbs:

quieti vaco (1) *I have leisure for rest*
  (*but:* labore vaco *I am free from work*)
tibi timeo, tibi metuo *I fear for you, I am anxious for you*
  (*contrast* te timeo, te metuo *I fear you*)
tibi consulo, -ĕre, consului, consultum *I take thought for you*
  (*contrast* te consulo *I consult you*)
tibi mortem minor (1) *I threaten you with death*

*255. These verbs, less frequently used, also govern a dative:

> indulgeo, -ēre, indulsi, -ltum *I indulge, give rein to*
> gratulor (1) *I congratulate*
> immineo (2) *I overhang, menace*
> obsto, -āre, obstiti, — *I oppose, stand in the way of*

---
[1] *Contrast* te convenio *I meet you by arrangement.*
[2] A dative with *insum* is rare.

Exercise 25A

1. Boys ought always to obey their fathers.
2. The enemy resisted our cavalry long and bravely.
3. His words displeased all those who were at the council.
4. Fresh troops came to the help of those who were hard pressed.[1]
5. Why, mother, did you not marry a richer husband?
6. Caesar was asked to spare all the prisoners.
7. I happened to meet Horatius yesterday on the bridge.
8. A faithful friend considers the interests of others, not his own.
9. I shall not support Pompey, for he lacks good sense.
10. They were afraid to threaten the hostages with death.
11. Caesar made war on that tribe because they had harmed the province.
12. In his youth he had taken part in many battles.

Exercise 25B

1. Mistrusting their guides, the Romans refused to advance into the heart of the mountains.
2. Because she would not marry me, I married her younger sister.
3. I almost think my mother is willing to forgive me.
4. In the previous summer the Veientines had declared war on Rome.[2]
5. Few men are devoted to liberty; the majority like[3] to consider their own interests.
6. I met Pompey's envoys, as arranged, outside the camp.
7. I replied that scarcely anyone now supported him; but they refused to believe me.
8. It is obvious that they will resist us less keenly.
9. I do not know when our allies will come to our aid.
10. For the last six months Afranius has been[4] in command of that army.

[1] § 55.
[2] *i.e.* the Romans.
[3] Use *placet*.
[4] Tense: *cf.* § 152.

26

PASSIVE OF INTRANSITIVE VERBS

261. Latin (unlike English) can use the passive voice of intransitive verbs—but *only impersonally*, *i.e.* in the 3rd sing. form, without any subject, even 'understood'.

Expressions like *itur, pugnatum est, concurritur* cannot be literally translated. They often correspond to the French *on* (*on va, &c.*) or the vague *one, you, people* in English. But our idiom will often be to use a *noun*, not a verb at all.

> Sic itur ad astra   *That is the way to the stars* (*i.e.* fame)
> Postquam ventum[1] est . . .   *After (our) arrival*
> Acriter pugnatum est   *A strenuous battle took place*[2]

262. Notice particularly those English *transitive* verbs whose Latin equivalents are *intransitive*. Common ones are:

(*a*) *We reach the city*   Ad urbem advenimus, pervenimus
   The city is reached   Ad urbem pervenitur, advenitur

   We left the city   Ab urbe discessimus, abiimus
   The city was left   Ab urbe discessum est, abitum est

(*b*) Many of the verbs in § 251[3]:

The consuls will be obeyed   Consulibus parebitur

We were persuaded by our friends   Nobis ab amicis persuasum est

*263. Impersonal verbs have no subject: therefore in a reported statement, the infin. will stand alone, with no

---

[1] *N.B.* Participles in impersonal verbs must be *neuter*.

[2] The idea in an impersonal passive is to focus the interest on the *action*, the *doer* being too vague or too obvious to mention. In practice, *venio, eo, curro, clamo* (with their compounds) and *pugno* are among the verbs most commonly used in this way.

[3] The deponents cannot, of course, be used passively; of the rest, those most commonly so used are: creditur, favetur, ignoscitur, invidetur, nocetur, parcitur, paretur, persuadetur, resistitur.

accusative subject. This is the *only* exception to the rule that the acc. subject of an infin. must be expressed.

I think I have been forgiven Existimo mihi ignotum esse

*264. Impersonal verbs are 3rd person in form: therefore a command is expressed by the subjunctive (§ 82).

Don't be persuaded Ne tibi persuadeatur

265. Quotations to study[1]:

Diu atque acriter ab utrisque pugnatum est.
(*The war-council cannot agree*) A Cotta primisque centurionibus acriter resistebatur.[2]
Mihi quidem ipsi nihil ab istis iam noceri potest.
(*Youthful zeal is viewed indulgently*) Non modo non invidetur illi aetati, verum (*but*) etiam favetur.

Exercise 26A

PART I (PASSIVE OF 'DATIVE VERBS' ONLY)

1. Rich men are often envied.
2. The prisoners will be spared because of their courage.
3. The guilty men will never be forgiven.
4. These tribes had been harmed by their neighbours.
5. We were easily persuaded to do this by our friends.
6. Cicero was envied for his eloquence.
7. I shall no longer be supported by the nobles.
8. We were resisted[2] by a large band of archers.
9. Why are the laws not always obeyed?
10. In olden times, the poor used to be relieved by the rich.

---

[1] *N.B.* They illustrate a further way of dealing with English abstract nouns: a long and fierce *struggle*; keen *opposition* was offered; no *harm* can be done.

[2] Remember that *resisto* has no supine stem in use. (Neither have *parco* and *pareo*.)

PART 2 (IMPERSONAL PASSIVES, INDICATIVE ONLY)

1. The battle continued until evening.
2. People flocked to the market-place from every quarter.
3. The Gauls will be spared, although they have resisted us for so long.
4. Say the same thing again: perhaps you will be believed.
5. I have been forgiven by those whom I injured.
6. A shout was raised that they should surrender the town.
7. The harbour was left at midnight; the island was reached on the following day.
8. With difficulty were the citizens persuaded to obey the magistrates.
9. Cavalry was sent out by both sides, and very fierce fighting occurred.
10. If you marry my brother, you will be envied by all women.

Exercise 26B

1. Although he had not been harmed, the king threatened the conspirators with death.
2. He issued orders that no-one was to be spared.
3. The battle raged very fiercely from dawn until the ninth hour of the day.
4. When we foretold what great danger threatened[1] Caesar, we were not believed.
5. Do not be anxious for us; for I am sure we shall not be harmed.
6. Before joining battle,[2] Caesar told the soldiers of the tenth legion that he trusted them.
7. Do not be persuaded, citizens, to give up your land and your resources.
8. I hear that you were persuaded to forgive your accusers.[3]
9. He has promised to come to our help within three days.
10. Although they had quite frequently displeased their father, they hoped to be forgiven.

[1] Not *minari*.   [2] Use future part.   [3] Use a relative clause.

27

FINAL RELATIVE CLAUSES

271. Caesar equites **qui hostes sequerentur** praemisit
Caesar sent forward cavalry *to pursue the enemy*

A RELATIVE CLAUSE may express purpose. The verb, as in any other final clause, is present or imperfect subjunctive (§ 102). *Final relative clauses* are specially common when the main verb means *send, leave* or *choose*: always use **qui**, not *ut*, in such a sentence. Think it out in English first, changing *to do it* into *who is (was) to do it*. This will give you the form of the Latin expression.

> We were sent *to set you free*
> We were sent *who were to set you free*
> Missi sumus **qui vos liberaremus**

272. Any case of the relative pronoun may be used: *e.g.*

He gave me a book *to read* (a book *which I was to read*)
Librum mihi dedit **quem legerem**

He left a bridge *for us to cross by* (*by which we were to cross*)
Pontem reliquit **quo transiremus**

I have no money *to buy food with* (*with which I am to buy food*)
Nullam pecuniam habeo **qua cibum emam**

273. The antecedent need not always be expressed: if the English uses a vague antecedent, such as *men, people, someone, somewhere*, no word is needed in Latin:

Caesar sent men to find water	Caesar misit **qui aquam peterent**[1]
I have someone to send	Habeo **quem mittam**
I had something to say	Habui **quod dicerem**
I have no reply to make	Non habeo **quod respondeam**
I have somewhere to go	Habeo **quo eam**
There is nowhere for us to live	Non est **ubi habitemus**

[1] It would be quite wrong to put in *viros, homines* or even *milites*.

274. If a final clause contains a *comparative* word, it is introduced by **quo**, not **ut**. The comparative word must immediately follow the *quo*.

They abandoned their baggage $\begin{cases} \textit{so as to march quickly} \\ \textit{so as to march more quickly} \end{cases}$

Impedimenta reliquerunt $\begin{cases} \textbf{ut celeriter contenderent} \\ \textbf{quo celerius contenderent} \end{cases}$

The **quo** is an abl. of measure of difference; the exact meaning of *quo celerius* is *so that by that much the more quickly*.

275. Final relative clauses cannot express a *negative* purpose.[1]

276. Quotations to study:

Legatos Romam, qui auxilium a senatu peterent, misere.

Postquam id animadvertit (*noticed*), copias suas Caesar in collem subducit (*led up*) equitatumque qui sustineret hostium impetum misit.

(*The treacherous schoolmaster punished*) Virgas (*rods*) pueris quibus proditorem agerent in urbem dedit.

Nec quo se reciperent nec quem ad modum oppida defenderent habebant.

Affirmabat se hortos aliquos emere velle, quo invitare amicos et ubi se oblectare (*enjoy himself*) posset.

(*Ships for shallow waters*) Carinae (*keels*) aliquanto planiores (*flat*) erant quam nostrarum navium, quo facilius vada (*shallows*) excipere possent.

(*A Gaul's excuse to Caesar*) Respondit se idcirco ab suis discedere noluisse, quo facilius civitatem in officio (*loyalty*) contineret.

---

[1] If the question arises whether these clauses are adjective or adverb clauses, the answer must be that they are adj. clauses used adverbially —just as some single-word adjectives are used adverbially in Latin: *e.g. He came unwillingly* Invitus venit.

Exercise 27A

1. I have been sent here to work with you.
2. We have something to give you.
3. Caesar left three cohorts to harass the enemy.
4. The boy laid down his toga so as to run more easily.
5. Owing to the fire, we had nowhere to sleep.
6. Give me some money to buy bread with.
7. The Athenians sent me to consult the oracle of Apollo.
8. My uncle has sent a new book for us to read.
9. The defendant had nothing to say about the crime.
10. So as to have more friends, buy the best wine.

Exercise 27B

1. Caesar sent forward patrols to reconnoitre the enemy's position.
2. Brutus, a most eloquent orator, was chosen to make a speech to the plebs.[1]
3. The rich merchant bought land on which to build a country-house for himself.
4. Ambassadors were sent to Rome by the Veientines to beg for peace.
5. I had no answer to give when he asked me where I had come from.
6. After pitching camp, Caesar sent out men in all directions to get water and wood.
7. I crossed the lake by the new bridge, so as to get home more quickly.
8. The women were afraid that there would be no-one to carry such heavy burdens.
9. There is no reason why you should be jealous of my fame.
10. The Gauls burnt their corn so that nothing would be left for Caesar's troops to live[2] on.

---

[1] *to make a speech:* orationem (contionem) habere. Translate *to*, in this context, by *apud*.
[2] Meaning?

28

CONSECUTIVE RELATIVE CLAUSES

281. Nemo tam stultus erat **qui illud crederet**
No one was so foolish *as to believe that*

A RELATIVE CLAUSE (with subjunctive verb) may express a result; not however an *actual* result but rather an *imagined* or *ideal* result.[1] As such a clause states an *idea*, not a fact, it follows the tense rule of all idea clauses: in primary sequence, present subjunc.; in historic sequence, imperf. subjunc.

282. Such relative clauses most commonly follow:
(*a*) a negative (or virtually negative) main clause with *tam*[2]:

Who is so bold as to refuse? Quis est tam audax qui neget?

(*b*) a negative (or virtually negative) main clause without *tam*:

There is no-one who asserts this Nemo est qui hoc dicat
Who is there to believe such tales? Quis est qui talia credat?

283. (*c*) **is sum qui** . . . (both positive and negative)[3]:

Caesar was the sort of man whom no-one dared to harm
Is erat Caesar quem nemo laedere auderet

Caesar was not the man to forgive a wrong
Non is erat Caesar qui iniuriae ignosceret

284. (*d*) **sunt qui, erant qui** *there are (were) some who* . . .

There were some who blamed us Erant qui nos reprehenderent

---

[1] It may well be an actual fact: as in the cases in §§ 284, 285; but, whether actual or not, it is being expressed as the *logical* consequence; so the clause is one of *thought, idea*.

[2] An 'ideal' consecutive clause *may* depend on an *affirmative* main clause; if so, *ut* (not *qui*) is used: Tam stultus erat **ut omnia crederet**. The tense must still be present or imperfect only.

[3] In this idiom (and often elsewhere) *is* replaces *talis* as a complement adjective meaning *such*. *Talis* is rarely used before *qui*.

285. (*e*) numerical expressions such as **multi sunt qui . . ., pauci sunt qui . . ., solus sum qui . . .**

286. (*f*) the adjectives **dignus** *worthy*, **indignus** *unworthy*, **idoneus** *suitable*. The infin. is impossible with these words in Latin.[1]

The boy is worthy to be punished
The boy deserves to be punished } Puer dignus est qui puniatur

These books are suitable for girls to read
Hi libri idonei sunt quos legant puellae

287. Some of these clauses—particularly those under (*b*) (*d*), (*e*)—denote a *class* or *type* of persons. They are commonly called GENERIC RELATIVE CLAUSES (genus, *a kind*).

288. After a *negative* main clause, if the relative clause is itself negative, *qui . . . non* is replaced by **quin**. (This applies only in the nom. sing. masc.[2])

There was no-one who did not praise Horatius' bravery
Nemo erat quin fortitudinem Horatii laudaret

Hardly anyone is so wise as not to make a mistake at times
Nemo fere tam sapiens est quin aliquando erret

N.B. Nemo est quin sciat: *everybody knows*.

289. Quotations to study:

Nemo est tam senex qui se annum non putet posse vivere.

Quis est tam stultus . . . cui sit exploratum (*certain*) se ad vesperum esse victurum (*live*)?

Neque is sum qui gravissime mortis periculo terrear.

In castello (*fort*) nemo fuit omnium militum quin vulneraretur.

(*Death pact of the Celtic blood-brotherhoods*) Neque hominum memoria repertus est quisquam qui, amico interfecto, mori recusaret (*objected*).

(*The elder Pliny*) Perire (*be wasted*) omne tempus arbitrabatur, quod studiis non impertiretur (*was devoted*).

---

[1] With *dignus* and *indignus* we use the abl. of a noun (worthy *of*), but *qui* + subjunc. of a verb (worthy *to*).

[2] *Quae non, quod non* are *sometimes* replaced by *quin*.

Exercise 28A

1. You are not one to blame me without cause.[1]
2. There were some who thought otherwise (*i.e.* another thing).
3. Everyone knows that Romans are braver than natives.
4. There used to be many citizens once who never learned to read.
5. Nobody is so brave as to despise all kinds of dangers.
6. He deserves to receive a large reward for his courage.
7. There was no-one who did not trust the new consul.
8. This language is suitable for you to learn.
9. Who is there to guide me across the marsh?
10. They were the kind of persons nobody held in honour.
11. My father was not the man to envy others.
12. There isn't anyone who does not long for peace.

Exercise 28B

1. There were some who denied that they had taken part in any plot.
2. Who is there to assert that life is more precious than freedom?
3. There was no-one in Rome at that time who did not favour Cicero rather than Catiline.
4. Hardly anyone is so wicked that he does not sometimes wish to act rightly.
5. It seemed that Verres was not fit to govern a province.
6. There are few in this state to whom the new laws seem fairer than the former ones.
7. Augustus was not the sort of man to allow Antony to threaten the whole nation with enslavement.
8. I believe there is no-one here who does not hate traitors.
9. The Gauls were not the people to yield easily.
10. There was no poor man to whom we did not give either money or land.

[1] *N.B.* 'The relative pronoun agrees in number, gender *and person.*'

29

PREDICATIVE DATIVE

291. Senectus mihi **impedimento** est
   Old age is *a hindrance* to me
                    as

The verb **esse** sometimes has as its complement a noun in the dative: this is called a PREDICATIVE DATIVE. In effect **impedimento** means *a source of hindrance, something serving as a hindrance*. The corresponding English idioms vary widely (as the exercises illustrate).

292. A predicative dative is always *singular*; *no adjective* can qualify it, except an adjective of quantity (*magnus, maximus, quantus, tantus*). It is usually accompanied by a *dative of advantage*, denoting the person affected.

   Traitors are hateful to us Proditores nobis odio sunt
   That was of great use to me Illud mihi magno usui erat

293. Only a certain limited number of nouns were used in this way. Among the commonest were:

auxilio esse *to be helpful*
cordi esse[1] *to be dear*
curae esse *to be an anxiety*
impedīmento esse *to hinder*
ŏdio esse *to be hateful*

praesidio esse *to protect, garrison*
saluti esse *to be the salvation*
usui esse *to be useful*
subsidio esse *to relieve, support*

*294. The following were also in fairly common use:

argumento esse *to be proof*
dēdecŏri esse *to be a disgrace*
dētrīmento esse *to cause loss*
documento esse *to be proof*
dolōri esse *to cause grief*
exemplo esse *to be an example*

exitio esse *to be fatal*
frūgi esse *to be thrifty*
honōri esse *to be an honour*
lūdibrio esse *to be laughed at, to be ridiculous*
oneri esse *to be a burden*

---
[1] From cor (*heart*). This, the only completely non-abstract noun in the list, is usually called a predic. dat., but *may* be a locative in origin.

295. Three of these datives are commonly used (especially by Caesar) with other verbs than *esse*: chiefly with verbs meaning *come, go, send, leave.*

> Unam cohortem castris praesidio reliquit
> *He left one cohort to guard (garrison) the camp*
>
> Unam cohortem legioni auxilio (sub)misit
> *He sent up one cohort to assist the legion*
>
> Novae copiae nostris subsidio venerunt
> *The fresh troops came to the relief of our men*

296. The verb ōdi, odisse, *to hate*, has no passive. **Odio esse** + dat., *to be hateful to*, is used to fill the gap.

Traitors are hated by everyone Proditores omnibus odio sunt

297. Quotations to study:
(*Extent of Etruscan rule in Italy*) Quantum potuerint, nomina (*place-names*) sunt argumento.
(*The rival centurions*) Alter alteri inimicus auxilio salutique erat.
Omnium rerum quae ad bellum usui erant summa erat in eo oppido facultas (*supply*).
Id cum animadvertisset P. Crassus, qui equitatui praeerat, tertiam aciem laborantibus nostris subsidio misit.
Itaque numquam tanto odio civitati Antonius fuit, quanto est Lepidus.
(*The enemy need humbling*) Hostes diutius in nostro conspectu gloriari (*boast*) magno nobis et dedecori et dolori est.
(*Gallic funerals*) Funera sunt—pro (*considering*) cultu Gallorum —magnifica et sumptuosa; omniaque quae vivis cordi fuisse arbitrantur in ignem inferunt, etiam animalia.

Exercise 29A

1. Caesar was hated by Brutus and Cato.
2. The shortage of food is causing me great anxiety.
3. Caesar had left three cohorts to guard the ships.
4. Through his courage, Manlius was the salvation of the city.
5. The captured corn was very useful to our men.
6. Your father's character is hateful to good citizens.
7. Our fleet has been a great protection to our allies.
8. The cavalry was sent to the help of the hard pressed legions.
9. The size of their ships was a great hindrance to the Romans in that battle.
10. The safety of this state will always be dear to the gods.

Exercise 29B

1. Let the wisdom of our ancestors always be an example to us.
2. I think the snow will hinder our pursuers and[1] help us.
3. His mother's death caused him such grief that he never afterwards laughed.
4. Why was Antony hated by all those to whom liberty was dear?
5. Caesar started out, leaving five hundred infantrymen to guard the booty and the camp.
6. The high wind was the undoing of the enemy and the salvation of our fleet.
7. Cicero believed that the consulship would be a very great honour for him.
8. What disgrace your crime has brought on your unfortunate parents!
9. To some men it seems that public offices are a burden, to others an advantage.
10. To me, at any rate, your speech is clear proof of your boldness.

[1] Contrast: no conjunction.

30

DATIVE USES. REVISION (25-29)

301. An INDIRECT OBJECT is used not only with verbs of *giving*, but also with verbs of *taking away*, where *from* would be used in English. The chief verbs concerned are:

>aufero, auferre, abstuli, ablātum *I remove*
>adimo, -ĕre, adēmi, ademptum *I take away*
>ēripio, -ĕre, ēripui, ēreptum *I snatch away, rescue*

The news robbed me of sleep Nuntius mihi somnum ademit[1]

302. A DATIVE OF ADVANTAGE is used (as in many languages, but not in English) in connection with parts of the body:

I seized *his* hand Manum **ei** comprehendi
They fell at *Caesar's* feet Se **Caesari** ad pedes proiecerunt

303. A DATIVE OF PURPOSE is used with some verbs, especially those meaning *choose, appoint*. Typical examples are:

Caesar left time *for the fortification of the camp*
Caesar **munitioni castrorum** tempus reliquit

A day was fixed *for the conference*
Dies **colloquio** dicta (constituta) est[2]

Towards evening they chose a place *for their camp*
Sub vesperum locum **castris** delegerunt (ceperunt)

The consul ordered *the retreat to be sounded*
Consul **receptui cani** (*or* canere) iussit

---

[1] But the indirect object must be *a person*; otherwise, use the abl. with a preposition:
>Fortune rescued me *from that peril*
>Fortuna me **ex illo periculo** eripuit.

[2] Remember that *dies* is fem. when it refers to a day appointed.

Exercise 30A

1. An unjust master took the book away from me.
2. Two praetors will be elected to administer the laws.
3. A javelin thrown from the wall struck the centurion's shield.
4. When this news was brought, people flocked into the forum from every direction.[1]
5. Your advice will always be most useful to your friends.
6. If you hand over all your arms,[2] you will be forgiven.
7. When a shout is raised, you will know that the citadel has been taken.
8. In order to reach the coast more quickly, we intend to travel all night.
9. These sailors were with difficulty rescued from the sea.
10. By a daring charge, the cavalry rescued the prisoners from the enemy.
11. When I met my brother, I grasped his hand and wept.
12. It was a great anxiety to me that[3] you did not arrive in time.
13. At last, at my suggestion, he asked my sister to marry him.
14. My brother and I[4] will choose a place for the new city.
15. My companion urged me to come to his rescue.
16. The senators had chosen Pompey to command the new army.
17. Always take thought for those who need your help.
18. Three warships had been left behind to guard the harbour.
19. Will not this gold be of very great use to us?
20. But the natives are not the sort of men to give gold to us willingly.

---

[1] Use adv. *undique*.

[2] Tense? Or a participle phrase may be used.

[3] Introduce the clause in Latin by *quod*.

[4] *He + I = we:* if joint subjects are in different persons, 'add them up' to determine the agreement of the verb. *N.B.* In Latin the order is *I and my brother* (1st person before 2nd or 3rd).

Exercise 30B

1. Everyone knows that Homer was a blind poet; but his birthplace is uncertain.
2. Fearing to pursue the enemy too far, the commander sounded the retreat.
3. In this great crisis neither party[1] came to the aid of the state.
4. We were envied by those whom we had benefited.
5. The battle had gone on from the fourth hour until late in the day.
6. When placed in command of the twentieth legion, Agricola showed himself a prudent commander.
7. There are many reasons why we do not dare always to tell the truth.
8. We could not persuade our allies to resist the enemy any longer.
9. I am angry with you because you have not carried out your duty.
10. I have been given a large sum of money[2] with which to bribe the other jurors.
11. The old man was afraid that he would be a burden to his grandsons.
12. Do you realize that this[3] rashness will be your undoing?
13. Our master is not the sort of man we can easily persuade to postpone the punishment.
14. The farmer says he cut down these trees in order to sow more corn.
15. Do not be persuaded to make[4] such a speech; for you will be the laughing-stock of all.

---

[1] The *plural* of *neuter* denotes 'neither side, neither party'—so with other pronouns normally used in the singular: *e.g.* utri: *which of the two sides?* utrique: *both sides.*
[2] *magna pecunia.*   [3] 'this of yours': *iste.*   [4] See *p.* 86, *n.* 1.

31

OBLIGATION: THE GERUNDIVE

311. The commonest way of expressing 'ought' or 'must' in Latin is to use the **gerundive** (or *gerundive-adjective*).

The gerundive is a verbal adjective, and is *always passive* in meaning, *even if it comes from a deponent verb*:

amo:	**amandus, -a, -um**	*to-be-loved (requiring-to-be-loved; worth loving; loveable)*
moneo:	**monendus, -a, -um**	*to-be-warned (requiring-to-be-warned)*
duco:	**ducendus, -a, -um**	*to-be-led (&c.)*
facio:	**faciendus, -a, -um**	*to-be-done (&c.)*
punio:	**puniendus, -a, -um**	*to-be-punished (&c.)*
hortor:	**hortandus, -a, -um**	*to-be-encouraged (&c.)*[1]

312. Thus in Latin, instead of saying 'the bridge must be built' or 'we ought to write some letters', one says:

SUBJECT		COMPLEMENT
The bridge	*is*	*to-be-built*
Pons	est	aedificandus
Letters	*are*	*to-be-written*
Epistolae	sunt	scribendae

Observe how the *object* in the English (*active*) sentence becomes the *subject* in the Latin (*passive*) sentence. Before translating, change the English into this passive form.

313. What happens to the *subject* of the English (*active*) sentence? 'The citizens must defend their country' becomes 'The country is to-be-defended *by the citizens*'. But in Latin a dative is used: **Civibus** patria defendenda est. This is really a dative of the person affected: (*so far as the citizens are concerned*),

---

[1] Compare: Q.E.D. (quod erat demonstrandum *which was to-be-shown*) and Q.E.F. (quod erat faciendum); also the agenda (n.plu.—*the things-to-be-done*); the dividend(um) (*the stuff-to-be-divided*).

but is called a dative of the *agent*. It is not always present in the sentence: when it is a pronoun (as in 'we must write some letters'), it need not be mentioned, unless the pronoun is emphasized:

The citizens must build the school, but I must seek the teacher
Civibus ludus aedificandus est, mihi magister quaerendus

314. The gerundive is passive: therefore the gerundive of an intransitive verb must be used impersonally (§ 261). So it is always *neuter singular*.

I shall have to go Mihi eundum erit

(Beware of trying to make *I* the subject here.) Similarly with the 'dative verbs' in § 251.

The consuls are obeyed   Consulibus paretur
The consuls must be obeyed Consulibus parendum est

315. When there is another dative in the sentence, adding a dative of the agent may cause ambiguity. If we say, 'Tribunis consulibus parendum est' or 'Pecunia nobis tibi reddenda est', which dative is which? To avoid this, the ablative of the agent is used: 'Consulibus a tribunis parendum est.'

But this is done *only* if confusion might otherwise arise; not just because there is a second dative. It is quite clear and correct to say: 'Omnibus civibus legibus parendum est.'

316. The gerundive, expressing obligation, is used only in the nom.; or in the acc. if in a reported statement, or if *esse* might be supplied: *e.g.*

I think them praiseworthy Eos laudandos (esse) puto

*****317.** It is also used, however, qualifying the object of *do, trado, mitto, &c.*, as follows:

He handed over (left, sent) the prisoners to us to be guarded

Captivos nobis **custodiendos** tradidit (reliquit, misit)
The usual English idiom is: *He handed over the prisoners to us to guard*.

318. OUGHT AND MUST. Do not overwork the verb *debeo*. **Debeo** denotes *moral duty* ('ought'): Vera dicere debemus. **Necesse est** denotes *inevitability*: Omnibus necesse est mori. **Cogor** denotes *compulsion*: Hostes se recipere coacti sunt. The gerundive may have any of these meanings, and is used more commonly than any of the other expressions.

319. Quotations to study:

Caesari omnia uno tempore erant agenda: vexillum (*flag*) proponendum, signum tubā dandum, ab opere revocandi milites, acies instruenda (*draw up*), milites cohortandi, signum dandum.

Resistendum senectuti est, eiusque vitia (*faults*) diligentiā compensanda sunt; pugnandum tamquam (*just as*) contra morbum sic contra senectutem; utendum exercitationibus modicis, ut reficiantur vires, non opprimantur (*overwhelmed*).

Unam legionem in Morinos ducendam C. Fabio legato dedit.

Adverso proelio ad Dyrrhachium facto, Caesar consolandos (*comfort*) milites magis quam puniendos esse habuit.

Censuere (*resolved*) non exspectandum iustum (*proper*) tempus, sed extemplo (*at once*) novos tribunos militum creandos esse.

Exercise 31A

1. The walls of the city must be repaired.
2. The gates should be closed before night.
3. The merchant must pay the money at once.
4. What ought *we* to do?
5. Citizens ought to defend their country.
6. I must remain here; the rest must cross the lake.
7. Hadn't we better be going?
8. We must resist his disgraceful plan.
9. Brutus ought to forgive his sons.
10. The Romans had to wage war in Africa.
11. We shall need to learn a new language.
12. The patrols had to climb a high hill.

Exercise 31B

1. The cities which have revolted ought to be besieged.
2. The cavalry had to pursue the Gauls across the plain.
3. We must not wait any longer for our companions; we must start at once.
4. In the early spring, Caesar had to lead his troops out of winter quarters.
5. We had better halt on rising ground, not on the very bank of the river.
6. The thief had to give the money back to the old man.
7. These boys thought they had better learn to swim.
8. My father has given me several books to read.
9. You will have to postpone your marriage until July.
10. Unless you live here, you will have to go away.

Exercise 31C

1. The following day I had to write another letter, to state my opinion more briefly.
2. All nations ought to seek peace and avoid war.
3. Your wife ought not to stay in this valley in summer, for fear she should fall ill.
4. Ought we not to spare those who have benefited us?
5. Caesar handed over the thirteenth legion to his deputy to lead into the territory of the Arverni.
6. I am a very noble citizen; you ought to demand a much larger ransom.
7. Such a storm sprang up that all the ships had to return to harbour.
8. Everyone knows that we should elect Cicero consul for[1] next year.
9. I don't think we should use the same plan again.[2]
10. Everyone must pay taxes; but the rich have to pay more than the poor.

---

[1] *in* + acc.
[2] As *utor* is intransitive, its gerundive will be impersonal (and similarly with *fruor*, &c.).

32

IDIOMS OF PRICE AND VALUE

321. These idioms are often thought confusing and difficult because it is not realized that there are two quite separate and distinct groups—on the one hand, *idioms of valuing*, on the other, *expressions of price*.

I. VALUE

322.

He valued honour highly	Honorem **magni** aestimabat
He thought a lot of his friends	Amicos **plurimi** faciebat
He cared more for leisure than for wealth	Otium **pluris** quam divitias faciebat (aestimabat)
He doesn't care a fig for glory	Gloriam **flocci** non facit

In these vague expressions of valuing, Latin uses the verb **aestimare** or **facere**, with the *thing valued* as the object,[1] and the *value* expressed by a word in the genitive.

Only the following words are to be used as gen. of value:

magni	parvi	tanti	nihili
pluris[2]	minoris	quanti	non flocci (lit. *not at a bit of fluff*)
plurimi	minimi		

These are locatives in origin—*cf.* the English 'to value a thing at so much'. When they were mistaken for genitives, **pluris** and **minoris** were added by false analogy.

The genitive of value is always *vague*: a definite money value would be expressed by the abl.

323. Quotations to study:

Me a te plurimi fieri sentio.

Iudices rem publicam flocci non faciunt.

Mea mihi conscientia pluris est quam omnium sermo.

---

[1] Also with the thing valued as subject to *esse*:
How much is this worth? Quanti hoc est?

[2] *N.B. Pluris* is never used except as a gen. of value; apart from this, *plus* is indeclinable.

II. PRICE: BUYING AND SELLING

324. In expressions of buying and selling, the *price paid* is treated as the instrument and put in the ablative. It may be *either* a definite sum, *or* an indefinite expression—often an adjective with the noun *pretio* understood: *e.g.*

I bought the toga for 100 sesterces[1] Togam centum sestertiis emi
This hesitation cost him dear Magno illi ea cunctatio stetit

Adjectives commonly used in this way are:

| magno | parvo | vīlī (*abl. of* vilis, |
| plurimo | minimo | *cheap*) |

325. Now comes the only 'overlapping'. Four words, and *four only*, to express price, are borrowed from the *value* list:

tanti *for so much*   pluris *for more*
quanti *for how much*   minoris *for less*

> *How much did you pay for it? 100 sesterces*
> Quanti emisti? Centum sestertiis

326. Verbs with which price expressions chiefly occur:

emo, emere, ēmi, emptum *I buy*   sto, stāre, steti   ⎫ *I cost*
vendo, -ĕre, vendidi, venditum   consto, -āre, -stiti ⎬ (+dat.)
I sell   vēneo, vēnīre, vēnii *I am sold*

327. Quotations to study:

Bona (*estates*) patris Sex. Roscii ... de L. Sulla duobus milibus nummum[1] sese dicit emisse.

Conduxit (*rented*) in Palatio (*Palatine Hill*) non magno domum.

(*The shopkeeper speaks*) Vendo meum non pluris quam ceteri, fortasse etiam minoris, cum (*whenever*) maior est copia.

Quanto detrimento (*loss*) et quot virorum fortium morte constabit victoria!

(*The sick miser*) 'Sume hoc tisanarium oryzae (*rice gruel*).' 'Quanti emptae?' 'Parvo.' 'Quanti ergo?' 'Octo assibus.'

---
[1] For Roman money, see Appendix B (*p.* 198).

Exercise 32A

1. All nations value liberty very highly.
2. My brother bought a horse for nine hundred sesterces.
3. I am forced to sell my house cheap, because it is old.
4. I do not care a fig for your opinion.
5. The new slave cost me a great deal.
6. We shall sell the rest of the land for ten thousand sesterces.
7. The Romans used to think very little of the character of the Greeks.
8. How much did you sell the wine for? 2,500 sesterces.
9. I think less highly of this book than that one.
10. The senators thought nothing of Lucullus' victories.

Exercise 32B

1. These fish, which used to cost one *as* each, are sold now for two sesterces.[1]
2. Ought not all men to value justice very highly?
3. I have bought a ship for so high a price that I have no money to hire sailors.
4. This victory cost the Romans 1,200 dead.
5. After selling my farm for 20,000 sesterces, I shall rent a small house cheap.
6. How much did you pay for the new toga? This one cost me 150 sesterces.
7. I think a great deal of Plautus' plays, but[2] more of yours.
8. I have rented a very fine house near the Forum[3] for 10,000 sesterces.
9. Why is a book of Martial sold for less than one of Virgil?
10. I value this statue so highly that I will never sell or give it to anyone.

---

[1] *i.e.* two each: Latin always uses the distributive numerals wherever *each* or *at a time* could be inserted, even if the meaning seems to us quite clear without it.

[2] *Cf. p.* 63, *n.* 3.　　　　[3] Latin says '*situated* near the Forum'.

33

THE GERUND

only use gerund with transitive verbs

331. The infinitive and the gerund are both verbal nouns. But they are not interchangeable: each has certain functions, which the other never performs. Together, they form a complete 'declension' for the verbal noun:

INFIN.:
- Nom. (*subject or complement*): **vincere** erit facile
- Acc. (*object of a verb*): **vincere** volumus

GERUND:
- Acc. (*after a preposition*): ad **vincendum**
- Gen. (*with a noun or adj.*): **vincendi** occasio
- Dat. *e.g. I do my best to win* **vincendo** operam do
- Abl. (*instrumental, or with preposition*): **vincendo** se liberabunt

The *gerund* is not used as subject, object or complement; and the *infinitive* is not used in other ways.

332. The gerund is a *neuter* noun, and has *no plural*. Being declined *amandum, -i, -o, -o*, it looks like the neuter singular of the gerundive (§ 311). Do not confuse them.

333. USES OF THE GERUND. The chief uses are these:

Acc. Used chiefly with **ad**, especially in such phrases as:

idoneus ad } *suitable for*
aptus ad

natus ad *born to*
missus ad *sent to*
creatus ad *elected to*

Gen. Usually depending on such nouns as:

facultas ⎫
occasio ⎬ *opportunity, chance*
potestas ⎭
cupīdo, studium *desire*
causa *reason*

tempus *time (for)*
ars *art*
signum *signal (for, to)*
initium *beginning*[1]
finis *end*[1]

[1] Note the useful phrases *initium facio, finem facio: I begin speaking* loquendi initium facio; *I stop speaking* loquendi finem facio.

Especially with the ablatives **causā, gratiā** to denote purpose:

> We have met *for the purpose of debating*
> **Deliberandi causā** convenimus

Note that the gerund always comes before the *causā, gratiā*.

The objective genitive which depends on certain *adjectives* may be a gerund, *e.g. skilled in writing*, scribendi peritus; *desirous of seeing*, videndi cupidus; *eager to go*, eundi studiosus.

Dat. Used with such verbs as **studeo** *I am keen on*, **operam do** *I do my best to*; also as dative of purpose. It is not common.[1]

Abl. Used mostly as abl. of instrument (or manner): *e.g.*

> *By fighting bravely* they defeated the enemy
> **Fortiter**[2] **pugnando** hostes vicerunt

Used also with the prepositions **in, de**:

> They spend the time *in discussing*
> **In disputando** tempus consumunt

334. The gerund is *not* to be used with prepositions other than those mentioned. To translate such expressions as *without working, before starting, after returning*, a gerund cannot be used.

335. Quotations to study:

Dolor nos ad perseverandum stimulat (*spurs on*).

(*Britain the headquarters of Druidism*) Et nunc qui diligentius eam rem cognoscere volunt, in Britanniam discendi causa proficiscuntur.

Equitatus noster praedandi (*plundering*) vastandique causa per agros erat dissipatus (*dispersed*).

(*Caesar's physique*) Longissimas vias incredibili celeritate confecit; flumina nando transiit (**nare** *to swim*).

Sus (*pig*) est ad vescendum hominibus apta.

---

[1] *N.B.* solvendo (non) esse *to be (in)solvent*.

[2] The gerund is part of a *verb*, and is qualified by *adverbs* (never, as sometimes occurs in English, by adjectives).

Exercise 33A

1. By working, we shall become richer.
2. At last an opportunity of departing has been given us.
3. The boys were sent out for the purpose of playing.
4. The old man was desirous of dying in Rome.
5. Few men are born to rule, many to obey.
6. We learn to write well by reading.
7. We have been sent ahead to reconnoitre.
8. The infantry were waiting for the signal to advance.
9. For the sake of staying here, he told many lies.[1]
10. By running quickly, the messenger arrived on the same day.
11. Teach me the art of singing.
12. The hostages had no chance to escape.

Exercise 33B

1. Some young men are keen on swimming, others on hunting; I used to spend many hours in fishing.
2. This paper is not suitable for writing (on).
3. Have you come here in order to complain?
4. Three cohorts were led out to plunder and ravage; the others spent the time in working.
5. Although he was skilled in fighting, Gaius was not chosen as leader because of his age.
6. Octavian is desirous of sparing the captured queen.
7. My[2] reason for promising was a desire to please you.
8. By speaking imprudently, Cicero had aroused Antony's hatred.
9. Because of the habit of reciting in a loud voice, the neighbours were often awakened by the pupils' shouts.
10. By resisting the Persians with supreme courage, the Greeks showed themselves worthy of their ancestors.

[1] Refer to § 174.
[2] *mihi;* similarly: *it was the Romans' custom:* mos erat Romanis (and *cf.* § 302).

34

GERUND AND GERUNDIVE

341. In English, a gerund may govern an object: 'By defeating *the champion*, he won the cup.' But in Latin, a gerund with a direct object is avoided. Its place is taken by a phrase made up of (*a*) the noun (or pronoun) which would have been the object, and (*b*) the gerundive, agreeing with that noun. The whole *noun + gerundive* phrase is in the case that the gerund would have been in—naturally, for it is playing the same part in the sentence. For example:

by helping our friends	not amicos iuvando	but	amicis iuvandis
for the purpose of seeing the city	,, urbem videndi causā	,,	urbis videndae causā
sent to buy the books	,, missus ad libros emendum	,,	missus ad libros emendos

In short: **not** gerund + object **but** noun + gerundive.

Caesar had done enough *to restore the morale* of the men
Caesar satis ad militum animos confirmandos fecerat

By postponing the war we run a greater risk
Bello differendo periculum maius adimus

342. When used in this way, the gerundive does *not* imply obligation. The noun + gerundive phrase can be used wherever the gerund can be used (§ 332).

343. The rule is: *Not* gerund + object *but* noun + gerundive. There are two exceptions:

(i) Suppose the object is a neuter pronoun (*e.g. id, haec, aliquid*). It cannot be put in the gen., dat., or abl. without breaking the rule that any forms which could be masc. or neuter (*e.g. eius, his, aliquo*) are used only as masc. So a gerund is allowed to govern a *neuter pronoun* object.[1] This does not arise when the phrase is accusative. Contrast:

[1] The same applies to neuter adjectives used as nouns (*e.g. multa*) and to *nihil* (which has no gen., dat. or abl.).

>*for saying these things* ad haec dicenda (*no ambiguity*)
>*by saying these things* haec dicendo (*not* his dicendis)

(ii) If, in using the gen. plu., the ending **-orum** or **-arum** would occur twice or more, this rather ugly rhyming effect is generally (not always) avoided. For this purpose, the gerund may govern an object.

>amicorum videndorum causā (*possible, but unusual*)
>amicos videndi causā   (*usual*)

Caesar almost always prefers the *gerund + object* form, and in writing Latin it should *always* be used.

*344. The genitives of the personal and reflexive pronouns (*mei, tui, nostri, vestri, sui*) always have their gerundive ending in **-i**, whatever number or gender is referred to.

>*for the purpose of seeing us* nostri videndi causā
>*a chance to retreat*   sui recipiendi facultas

*345. A noun + gerundive (*never* a gerund alone) can be the object of **curo** *I see to*, **suscipio** *I undertake*.[1]

Viam faciendam suscipit He undertakes *the building of a road*

346. Quotations to study:

Tam celeriter hostes procurrerunt ut spatium pila coniciendi non daretur.

(*The site of Rome*) Non sine causa di hominesque hunc urbi condendae locum elegerunt (*chose*). (*Dat. of purpose:* § 303.)

Turres testudinesque et alium urbium oppugnandarum apparatum (*equipment*) videtis.

Non sunt autem leniores (*gentler*) in exigendis vectigalibus (*taxes*) Graeci quam nostri publicani (*tax-collectors*).

(*Rout of the Britons*) Neque sui colligendi (*rally*) neque consistendi aut ex essedis (*chariots*) desiliendi facultatem dederunt.

Naves aedificandas veteresque naves reficiendas curant.

---

[1] *N.B. Engl:* I have the door closed; *French:* Je **fais** fermer la porte; *Latin:* (i) Ianuam claudi **iubeo**; (ii) Ianuam claudendam **curo**.

Exercise 34A

1. By reading books young men become wiser.
2. An opportunity of buying a country-house has occurred at last.
3. You have not learnt the art of writing letters.
4. The old man was very desirous of seeing his son.
5. We shall cross this river by building a bridge.
6. Three cohorts had been sent to defend the citadel.
7. Didn't they say that in order to injure us?
8. A chance to do this will never occur again.
9. The place seemed suitable for pitching camp.
10. By obeying the laws we set (give) a good example to others.

Exercise 34B

1. Those who are desirous of seeing the games are to stay here; the rest will be given an opportunity to leave.
2. Every morning[1] my freedmen come here to greet me.
3. To save themselves, a good many had hidden in the woods.
4. May the gods give us a better chance of defending ourselves.
5. By saying nothing, he managed[2] to appear wiser than he really was.
6. Oxen are considered more suitable than horses for ploughing the fields.
7. Although you are guilty, you will be given a second[3] chance to plead your case.
8. We will have the money paid to the magistrates to-day.
9. (When) sent to finish off the war, Pompey showed himself energetic in pursuing the king.
10. Marius afterwards undertook the destruction of the Cimbri; by doing that he hoped to win greater fame.

[1] 'every day in the morning'.
[2] *I manage to, I succeed in:* efficio ut (*or* nē) + subjunc.
[3] *alter* (not *secundus* unless in a longer series).

35

TRANSLATION OF 'TO' WITH INFINITIVE

A. EXPRESSING PURPOSE

351. In English, purpose is most often expressed by **to** with infin. We have now seen several Latin equivalents, both clauses and phrases.

All our friends came to greet us

CLAUSE: Amici universi venerunt **ut nos salutarent** (§ 102)
Amici universi venerunt **qui nos salutarent** (§ 271)

PHRASE: Amici universi **ad nos salutandos** venerunt (§ 333)
Amici universi **nostri salutandi** causa venerunt

Often (as in this instance) a given sentence may be translated quite well in several ways.[1]

352. There is one more way available:

Amici universi **nos salutatum** venerunt

When the verb of the sentence expresses motion (*go, come, send*), the purpose of the movement may be expressed by the supine in **-um** (or *accusative supine*).[2]

353. 'He gave me a book *to read*.' When an infin. of purpose is attached to a noun, the Latin may be a final relative clause (§ 272), or sometimes a gerundive. (§ 317).

Librum mihi dedit **quem legerem**   Librum **legendum** mihi dedit

---

[1] But for a *negative* purpose, there is only one way (clause with **nē**).
[2] In origin the supine is an acc. of the goal of motion. Most commonly used by Caesar are:

aquatum (*from* aquor) *to get water*   **lignatum** (lignor) *to get wood*
frumentatum (frumentor) *to get corn*   **pabulatum** (pabulor) *to forage*
            questum (queror) *to complain*
rogatum, petitum *to ask*

N.B. No supine meaning *to say* was in use.

B. EXPRESSING RESULT

354. In *too fat to run, fast enough to win*, the infin. has a consecutive meaning. In Latin an 'ideal' consecutive clause (§ 281) is used. To translate 'Who of you is brave enough to enter?' change *brave enough to* into *so brave that* ...

Quis vestrum **tam fortis est ut** (*or* **qui**) ineat?

Remember (§ 282) that *qui* may not be used unless the clause is negative (or implies a negative).

355. To translate 'We travelled too slowly to arrive in time' change *too slowly to* into *more slowly than so as to*:

Lentius iter fecimus **quam ut** ad tempus perveniremus

This city was *too large for the enemy to capture*
Maior erat haec urbs *quam ut ab hostibus capi posset*

356. ADJECTIVES (*eager to, anxious to*) are followed in Latin by the gen. of a gerund (or noun + gerundive) (§ 333).[1]

NOUNS, similarly, are followed by a gen., *never* by an infin. (*e.g. a chance to fight, the signal to retreat*) (§ 333).

*357. *The first to come; the last to go; the only one to know.* In Latin it would be quite wrong to use an infin. here. For 'I *was* the first *to* come' say *I the first came*: Ego primus veni.

You were the only one to believe me Tu solus mihi credebas

358. Quotations to study:

Aedui (*a tribe in Gaul*) cum se suaque ab eis defendere non possent, legatos ad Caesarem mittunt rogatum auxilium.

Ubii (*a Germanic tribe*) qui ante in deditionem (*surrender*) venerant, purgandi (*excuse*) sui causa ad eum legatos mittunt, qui doceant non ab se fidem laesam (*broken*) esse.

Decima legio se esse ad bellum gerendum paratissimam dixit.

---

[1] It is often easier to use the corresponding verb (*e.g.* laborare cupio *instead of* laborandi cupidus sum). *N.B.* **Paratus** *ready* may have an infin. or *ad* + gerund.

Exercise 35A

(Each sentence is to be translated in more than one way)

1. Caesar sent out three cohorts to forage.
2. Who gave you this book to read on the journey?
3. Ambassadors have come from Athens to ask for help.
4. The fleet will be ready to start to-morrow.
5. The enemy are advancing to attack the camp.
6. Many citizens came to greet Cicero as he disembarked.
7. As winter was approaching, we were eager to return home.
8. Pompey had left a few cavalrymen to defend the bridge.

Exercise 35B

1. Leaving three legions to besiege the city, Pompey marched to meet his opponents.
2. Leaving the third legion to guard the camp and the booty, Pompey led the rest of his forces across the river.
3. The Greeks were the first to realize that the earth moves round the sun.
4. These oxen are too weak to work hard all day.
5. We were chosen by our fellow citizens to go to Rome to complain about the taxes.
6. Though no-one was bold enough to strike the beast with his sword, I was the first to throw a spear at it.
7. We have been at war for so long that we are anxious to enjoy peace.[1]
8. Hand twenty hostages over to the centurion to guard.
9. No-one except you was kind enough to help me in my distress.
10. Pliny was very anxious to find out what was happening.
11. If you are the last to arrive at the council, you will have to be punished according to ancestral custom.
12. Three hundred others are ready to make the same attempt.

---

[1] Noun + gerundive: utor, &c. (§ 182), are treated, for this purpose, as transitive verbs. (But in expressing obligation, their gerundive is used impersonally, with the noun in the abl. Thus:

pecuniae utendae occasio *but* pecuniā utendum est).

36

REVISION EXERCISES

Exercise 36A

1. We have given up hope of seeing our sister to-day.
2. You will have to draw up the battle-line either here or in the plain.
3. When the war is finished we shall have to build very many new houses.
4. Hannibal was bold enough to invade Italy by land.
5. For how much did you buy this wine? 1,500 sesterces.
6. To preserve our liberty, we must incur many dangers.
7. After giving the signal to advance, the king himself rode forward.
8. Why does bread cost us more in Rome than in the country?
9. If you are willing to trust me, I swear to set you free.
10. Of his own accord the slave tried to rescue his master from the brigands.
11. You are not men whose friendship I value highly.
12. In the month of July you ought to send your children to the coast.
13. By defending this town, we shall prolong the war until[1] the winter.
14. You ought not to sell this horse for so much.
15. The envoys are desirous of obtaining peace on favourable terms.
16. The wind is too high for us to set sail to-night.
17. We have come to persuade you to surrender.
18. If you are unskilled in swimming, do not fall into the sea.
19. No opportunity for doing this occurred in the king's lifetime.
20. The thieves took the gold from me without my knowledge.

---

[1] *in* + acc.

Exercise 36B

1. Storms are much more to be feared by sailors in winter than in summer.
2. I wish you to see to the distributing of the corn to the poor.
3. For how much can I buy two oxen, with which to plough the new fields?
4. You should forgive their rashness, because they do not understand what they are doing.
5. By hesitating, we have lost a chance to drive out a cruel tyrant.
6. The crew were too unskilled in sailing to keep on their course.
7. It was uncertain whether our men or the enemy would be the first[1] to seize the top of the ridge.
8. I have sold for a very small sum a horse which six months ago cost me 2,000 sesterces.
9. Every year the Athenians had to send to Crete seven youths and seven maidens.
10. At last Theseus, the king's own son, undertook the task of killing the fierce bull.
11. This plan will be useful to us and disastrous to our opponents.
12. If you were the first to answer, you deserve to be praised.
13. To avoid being surrounded from the rear, we must seek safety in flight.
14. The speech which Cicero had made was not bold enough to convince the jury.
15. The conquerors must spare those who have surrendered of their own accord.

[1] Use *prior*, not *primus*, as only two parties are being spoken of.

37

USE OF RELATIVE WORDS

371. CORRELATIVES: *as large as, as many as, as often as.* In Latin each *relative* word has its own corresponding *demonstrative*: these pairs of correlatives are:

tantus ... quantus *as great as*	ibi ... ubi *in the same place as*
talis ... qualis *such as*	inde ... unde *from* ⎫ *the same*
tot ... quot *as many as*	eo ... quo *to* ⎭ *place as*
totiens ... quotiens *as often as*	eā ... quā *by the same road as*
tam ... quam *as ... as*	sic ... ut *in the same way as*

The city is no longer *as large as* it used to be
Non iam **tanta** est urbs **quanta** erat

He has come *from the place whence* arose so many consuls
Inde venit **unde** orti sunt tot consules

372. The proper correlative of the pronoun *qui* is *is*. If both the *is* and the *qui* happen to be in the same case, the *is* is usually omitted; otherwise it must be put in:

Caesar, **quos** ceperat, conservavit
Caesar **eos, qui** se dediderant, conservavit
Ei quibus pecunia deest cibum emere non possunt

This is the Latin for *he who, that which, those who, &c.* It is also the Latin for *the man who, anyone who, people who, &c.* It is quite wrong to write, for example, *homo qui, viri qui.*

The man who says that is a liar (Is) qui illud dicit mentitur

Qui may also follow **idem** translating 'the same *as*': *e.g.*

He said the same to you as to me Eadem tibi dixit quae mihi

373. When there is a noun antecedent, the *is* is optional:

Caesar started with the (those) troops which he had brought with him
Caesar cum (iis) copiis quas secum duxerat profectus est

*374. ORDER. (i) A sentence is made more emphatic if the relative clause is placed before the antecedent:

What he had once heard, he never forgot
   Quae semel audiverat, **ea** numquam obliviscebatur

Notice that when this is done, the *is* cannot be omitted.

(ii) A very short relative clause may be placed between two parts of the antecedent:

   Caesar cum iis **quas habebat** copiis profectus est

375. He gave me *the newest book that he had*
   Librum quem recentissimum habebat mihi dedit

A superlative adj., or a numeral (including *many, few, the only*), which in English qualifies the antecedent, is placed in Latin *in the relative clause*, and agrees with the *rel. pronoun*.

*376. The brigands—*what was surprising*—set him free
   Latrones eum liberaverunt—**id quod mirum fuit**

When a whole clause or idea forms the antecedent, translate *what* by **id quod**, or by **quae res**.

*377. If a *non-defining*[1] relative clause contains a *complement*, the rel. pronoun is attracted more strongly by the complement than by its antecedent, and agrees with the former:

   We came to Athens, which is the capital of Greece
   Athenas venimus, **quod** est caput Graeciae[2]

378. Quotations to study:

Quot homines, tot sententiae.

Ita quae pars civitatis Helvetiae magnam calamitatem populo Romano intulerat (*inflicted*), ea prima poenas persolvit.

Eodem quo antea modo circa munimenta (*defences*) pugnatum est.

Res non tam fuerat occulta (*secret*) quam erat occultanda.

(*Caesar has repaired his damaged ships*) Subductis (*beached*) navibus castrisque munitis, easdem copias, quas ante, praesidio navibus reliquit; ipse eodem, unde revenerat, proficiscitur.

[1] Recognizable because a pause (a comma) precedes it: *cf.* § 4, *note*.
[2] Contrast: *We came to the city which is the capital of Greece*
   Ad urbem venimus **quae** est caput Graeciae.

Exercise 37A

1. We usually hate those who have helped us.
2. The Gauls are no longer as brave as they formerly were.
3. With the money he had received he bought a larger house.
4. I have as many sisters as you.
5. My friend sent the swiftest horse he had.
6. I have seen nothing in Athens as beautiful as this statue.
7. The general gave rewards to those who had taken part in both battles.
8. Where you go,[1] we also will follow you.
9. The troubles of those dear to us[2] fill us with sorrow.
10. Remember always what I have said to-day.

Exercise 37B

1. Caesar demanded five hundred hostages from those tribes which he had most recently defeated.
2. The scouts returned by the only route that they knew.
3. Three days later we were sent back to the same place from which we had started.
4. Caesar advanced from there to the Rhine, which is the largest river in[3] Germany.
5. We have cut down the few trees which still stood in the garden.
6. The news of the defeat reached Rome on the same day as the battle was fought.
7. He was doing his best[4] to repair what they had broken.
8. The men we favoured were all elected tribunes, which was very gratifying to us.
9. Suspecting (as was the case) that I was in serious danger, Pliny launched the fastest ship that he had.
10. There is not as much snow[5] near the coast as in the heart of the mountains.

[1] Tense?
[2] 'those who are dear to us': a preposition phrase may not be used in Latin as an adjective phrase (exceptions are few).
[3] Latin: 'the largest river of Germany'.
[4] *to do one's best:* operam dare ut ... (+ subjunc.).
[5] *tantum* + part. gen.

38

IDIOMS OF THE COMPARATIVE AND SUPERLATIVE

381. Than. Remember that the abl. of comparison is only to be used in simple, direct comparisons of the type *A is bigger than B*. It is specially common when the subject is a negative word (*e.g. nemo, nihil*) or an implied negative:

For what is pleasanter than a peaceful old age?
Quid enim est iucundius senectute tranquilla?

N.B.—sooner than (anyone) expected spe (omnium) celerius; *larger than was thought (by him)* opinione (eius) maior.

382. More than ten, less than ten. When used with numbers, **plus, amplius** (*more*) and **minus** (*less*) require no *than*:

We have more than 500 ships Plus quingentas naves habemus

383. More lucky than careful. In Latin *both* adjectives are comparative.

The river is deeper than it is wide
Flumen altius est quam latius

384. The more ... the more ... In ratio sentences, English says '*The harder* I work, *the richer* I get'. In Latin the abl. of measure of difference is used: literally meaning '*By what* the harder I work, *by that* the richer I get'.

Quo diligentius laboro, **eo** ditior fio

The pattern is: **quo** + compar., **eo** + compar. Note the *order* carefully. The comparatives are next to the *quo* and *eo*. Sometim s an *unstressed* word is slipped in between, particularly **quis** or **quisque** (*a man, anyone, people*) after the *quo*.[1]

The more anyone has, the more he hopes for
Quo quis plura habet, eo plura sperat

[1] **Quanto ... tanto ...** are used in the same way as *quo ... eo ...*

385. Much better, much the best. With a *comparative* (or with *ante*, *post*) use abl. of measure of difference:

>multo maior *much larger, far larger*

But with a *superlative*, use **longē**:

>longe maximus *much the largest, far the largest*

386. As much as possible: *quam* + superlative.

They came as quickly as possible Quam celerrime venerunt[1]

Note the phrase **quam primum** *as soon as possible*.

***387. Very** is translated by a superlative, *except* in a negative sentence, where it is translated by a comparative: the comparative here has its sense of *rather, considerably*.

>*Fear prevented them from advancing very far*
>Timor longius eos progredi vetuit

***388.** In complimentary (and uncomplimentary) allusions, the superlative is used:

>*M. Crassus, a distinguished and wealthy citizen*
>M. Crassus, civis amplissimus ac ditissimus[2]

N.B. (i) In *favourable* allusions, **vir** is used, in *unfavourable ones* **homo**: *e.g.* homo nequissimus.

(ii) A proper noun cannot be qualified by an adjective, nor can a common noun if used in a 'proper' way:

>*the eloquent Cicero* Cicero, vir eloquentissimus
>*our brave consul*   consul, vir fortissimus

---

[1] More fully, this would be *Quam celerrime potuerunt, venerunt*. The fuller expression is sometimes used.

[2] Commonest adjectives in these allusions are:

ditissimus *rich*	honestissimus *honourable, worthy*
fortissimus *brave*	amplissimus *distinguished*
nobilissimus *noble, high-born*	sapientissimus *wise*

nēquissimus villainous

Exercise 38A

1. The ships of the Veneti were much larger than those of the Romans.
2. London is far the largest city in[1] this island.
3. I am sure that your plan is much the best.
4. The more often you write, the more eagerly I long for your return.
5. Send me as many horsemen as you can; for I have less than a hundred whom I can trust.
6. Nothing is dearer to us than the welfare of our country.
7. Leaving Italy as soon as possible, Caesar reached the region of Alesia sooner than the Gauls expected.
8. He promised not to be away for more than three days.
9. Can anything be more disgraceful than avarice?
10. The orator's words seem more beautiful than useful.

Exercise 38B

1. The temples built by the Athenians seem to me far more beautiful than ours.
2. After advancing less than ten miles, we were compelled by the very deep snow to halt.
3. It appears that the more I blame you, the more eager you are to do the same again.
4. But—what is far the most serious point—you have never promised to behave better.
5. The brave and distinguished Cato has been elected censor.
6. The general ordered his men not to pursue the enemy very far, for fear of falling into an ambush.
7. I am unwilling to mistrust our worthy consul, or to support the scoundrel Gaius Gracchus.
8. The fewer friends a man has, the more he values them.
9. This spot seems to me by far the most suitable for building the new school.
10. The Gauls were completely routed; the more numerous they were, the greater was the slaughter.

[1] Use gen. in Latin: 'the largest *of* the island'.

39

INDEPENDENT SUBJUNCTIVES

391. A subjunctive in a simple sentence may be:
(i) JUSSIVE—expressing a *command* (§ 82);
(ii) OPTATIVE—expressing a *wish* (§ 392);
(iii) DELIBERATIVE—expressing *uncertainty* what to do (§ 393);
(iv) POTENTIAL—expressing a *possibility* (§ 395).[1]

392. OPTATIVE. For **wishes,** the tense rule is:

> For *future* time, *present* subjunctive,
> for *present* time, *imperfect* subjunctive,
> for *past* time, *pluperfect* subjunctive.

This optative sense is clearly akin to the jussive sense. The negative is **nĕ**. Wishes are usually introduced by **utinam** (in English by *if only* and *would that* . . .).

> *May you be happy!* Beatus sis!
> *I wish you hadn't said anything!* Utinam ne quid dixisses!
> *If only they would come!* Utinam veniant!

393. DELIBERATIVE questions discuss possible courses of action: *What can I do? Shall we escape? Where were they to go?* The verb in Latin is subjunctive (negative **non**):

> Quid faciam?   Effugiamus?   Quo irent?

Num and *-nĕ* are not used. *Utrum . . . an* can be used if needed.

394. In a *reported* deliberative question, *e.g. He did not know what to do,* the mood is, naturally, still subjunctive. So in appearance it is like an ordinary reported question; only the sense of the passage reveals the special meaning. Note the *infinitive* in the English—*impossible* in Latin.

We did not know where to flee Nesciebamus quo confugeremus

---

[1] For the common threads linking these uses, see § 7.

395. POTENTIAL subjunctives express what *would* or *might* happen (or have happened) in certain circumstances.

What would you have done then? Quid tu tum fecisses?

The tense rule is the same as in wishes (§ 392).

Most common are: **velim** *I should like*, **vellem, nolim, nollem, malim, mallem**. These govern an infin. (*I should like to go* Velim ire) if there is no change of subject; but if there is (as in *I should like you to go*) they have an optative subjunctive 'half-dependent' on them (with no conjunction):

(Future time) *I should like you to come*   Velim venias
(Present time) *I could wish they were here*   Vellem adessent
(Past time)   *I would rather they had gone* Mallem abissent

*396. Observe the tense (imperfect, *not* pluperfect) in these potential subjunctives: crederes, putares *you would have thought;* diceres *you would have said:*

He made no reply: you would have thought he had not heard
Nihil respondit: putares eum non audivisse.

397. Quotations to study:

(*The pleasures of gardening*) Quid ego irrigationes, quid fossiones (*digging*) agri proferam (*mention*)?
Haec cum viderem, quid agerem, iudices?
Haec habui de senectute quae dicerem—ad quam utinam veniatis!
Huic cedamus, huius condiciones audiamus, cum hoc pacem fieri posse credamus?
(*Cicero on the poet Archias*) Hunc ego non diligam, non admirer? Non omni ratione defendendum putem?
(*Unwelcome news*) Illud utinam ne vere scriberem.
Tu velim saepe ad nos scribas.

Exercise 39A

1. May you be more fortunate than your father!
2. I wish they would return home at once!
3. What are we to do? Shall we tell the truth?
4. If only I had not lied to you yesterday!
5. Am I to believe what[1] you report?
6. I wish we now had the food which we have very often scorned!
7. We did not know which of the two roads to follow.
8. I would rather you had given a different answer.
9. Would that we had been born a hundred years ago!
10. Where shall I go? Where shall I be safe?

Exercise 39B

1. Where are we to take refuge? If only we had a home to go to!
2. May you not suffer what your ancestors had to endure!
3. I wish I could run as fast as my elder brother.
4. Shall we run away or hide? They will never find us in this thick wood.
5. If only I had not used up all my money before the holidays.
6. I wish you would send me the lion you caught recently.
7. No one either spoke or moved: you would have said they were all asleep.
8. I should not like you to be away more than ten days.
9. O if only we had allies to help us!
10. How am I to convince you that I am really innocent?
11. When they asked him why he had broken his promise, he did not know what to answer.
12. I wish we had supported the other side; we should have gained far greater influence.

[1] *credo* is transitive when the object is the thing believed.

40

IMPERSONAL VERBS

401. Under the heading of IMPERSONAL VERBS come:

(i) five verbs expressing *feelings*;
(ii) a group of other truly impersonal verbs;
(iii) the impersonal use of some verbs which can also be used personally (*i.e.* with noun subjects);
(iv) weather verbs: these need no further explanation.

402. IMPERSONAL VERBS OF FEELING: the *person who feels* is in the acc., the *source of the feeling* is in the gen.

> me **miseret** captivorum *I am sorry for (I pity) the prisoners*
> me **paenitet** sceleris *I am sorry for (I regret) my crime*
> me **piget** laboris *I am bored by work; work is irksome to me*
> me **pudet** verborum *I am ashamed of my words*
> me **taedet** vitae *I am tired of life*[1]

These verbs are sometimes used with an infinitive, *e.g.*

> Me hoc dicere taedebit *I shall be tired of saying this*
> Eum venire puduit *He was ashamed to come*

403. Other impersonal verbs, mostly used with an infin.[1]:

(*a*) with *acc.* of person: replace gerund

> me ire **oportet** *it is my duty to go, I ought to go*[2]
> me ire **decet** *it befits me to go, it is proper that I go*[3]

(*b*) with *dat.* of person: two verbs beginning with *l*:

> mihi ire **libet** *it pleases me to go, I like going*
> mihi ire **licet** *it is permitted to me to go, I may go*

---

[1] All the verbs in §§ 402, 403 are regular 2nd conjugation in all tenses (except *taedet*, for the perfect of which *pertaesum est* is used).

[2] Both *oportet* and *debeo* express duty, 'ought'. The gerundive, which is commoner, can express either 'ought' or 'must': *cf.* § 318.

[3] The opposite, dedecet, is to be used only with a negative:

> non dedecet *it is not unfitting.*

404. Verbs often used impersonally include:

(*a*) *with infin.* (sometimes with an *ut clause* instead):

me ire **iuvat** } *it pleases me to*   mihi ire **videtur** } *I decide*
mihi ire **placet** } *go; I like going*   mihi ire **placet** } *to go*

(*b*) *with* **ut** *clause* (never with infin.)

    mihi **accidit** ut eam   *I happen to go* (perf. tense *accidit*)

405. Interest *it is important*[1] has various constructions; they may be summarized (with an example of each) as follows:

WHAT IS IMPORTANT	DEGREE OF IMPORTANCE	PERSON CONCERNED
neuter pron. (*hoc*); infin. (*ire*) acc. and inf. (*pontem refici*); **ut** clause (*ut pons reficiatur*); reported question (*quid fiat*).	adverb (*maxime*) neut. acc. (*nihil*); or gen. of value (*pluris; minimi*).	gen. of noun or pron. (*Caesaris; omnium; eius*); but for personal and reflexive pron. use *meā, tuā, suā, nostrā, vestrā.*

It is very important to Cicero, or rather to me, who is elected
Magni interest Ciceronis, vel potius meā, quis creetur

It is highly important to the state that the enemy forces be divided
Magnopere rei publicae interest manūs hostium distineri

406. When impersonal verbs are used in acc. and inf., the infinitive stands alone, with no acc. subject word (§ 263).

    'Me tui miseret'   Dixit se mei miserere
Here *se* is not subject but object of *miserere*.

As impersonal verbs are 3rd person in form, a command must be expressed by the subjunctive (§ 264).

    You are not sorry for us   Te nostri non miseret
    Do not be sorry for us   Ne te nostri misereat

Many mistakes are made through forgetting this point.

---

[1] *Rēfert*, similar in meaning and use, is rarer. You need not use it.

*407. With *licet, oportet* and *necesse est*, a subjunctive verb is often used instead of the infinitive; no conjunction is required to introduce the subordinate clause[1]; neither is the dative or accusative of the person needed.

> *You ought to go* Oportet eas (=Te ire oportet)
> *Everybody may leave* Licet cuncti discedant

408. Quotations to study:

(*Fidenae, surrendering, pledges good relations with Rome*) Nec vos fidei nostrae nec nos imperii vestri paenitebit.

Non me vixisse paenitet.

Sunt homines, quos libidinis infamiaeque suae (*immoral and scandalous conduct*) neque pudeat neque taedeat.

Aut non suscipi bellum oportuit aut perfici quam primum oportet.

P. Sulpicius magistratum (*office*) ineat oportet Nonis Decembribus.

(*Pliny—of all people—has been hunting*) Ridebis, et licet rideas: ego ille, quem nosti, tres apros (*boars*) ... cepi.

Tua et mea maxime interest te valere.

Exercise 40A

PART I—Verbs of Feeling

1. We all pity the slaves. 2. He pities us because we are blind. 3. They were sorry for their cowardice. 4. Are you sorry for your comrades? 5. The defendants are not ashamed of their crime. 6. This boy finds work irksome. 7. This boy says he finds work irksome. 8. I think he is really tired of discipline. 9. The consul soon regretted his speech. 10. Are you not ashamed to have said that? 11. Do not pity these men. 12. Don't be ashamed of your tears, jurymen.

---

[1] The subjunctive in these sentences is less formal than the infin., but is not merely colloquial.

PART 2—Other Impersonal Verbs

13. This law ought to be changed immediately.
14. I happened to be far away at that time.
15. It was very important to us to marry rich husbands.
16. The senate decided to recall Caesar from his province.
17. The senate decided that Caesar should be recalled as soon as possible.
18. It will matter very little to the citizens which of the two is elected consul.
19. You may leave at once; you ought not to stay longer.
20. It is fitting that you should obey your parents.

Exercise 40B

1. Soldiers, do not be ashamed of your recent defeat. 2. It ill suits me, who command you, to blame either you or myself. 3. We are all weary of the lack of supplies, and sorry for our captured comrades. 4. Moreover, we may still hope for honourable terms. 5. It will, however, make the greatest difference to us who is sent by the enemy as ambassador. 6. I shall never regret having taken part in this campaign. 7. For it was of great importance to the country to prolong the war as long as possible. 8. But yesterday the magistrates decided to cease resisting. 9. I know that they were not ashamed of their brave soldiers. 10. Let no one, therefore, say that he is ashamed to have failed.[1] 11.[2] It is open to you all to state your opinion about this matter. 12.[2] But you must needs be influenced by the advice of the envoys.

---

[1] *I fail:* rem male gero; *failure:* res male gesta. *I succeed:* rem bene gero; *success:* res bene gesta.
[2] Use the subjunctive (§ 407) in nos. 11 and 12 only.

41

TRANSLATING 'OF' IDIOMS

411. *In the middle of the river:* (in) medio fluvio. When used 'partitively' an adjective always precedes its noun. The adjectives most commonly used in this way are:

prīmus *the beginning of*　　　medius *the middle of*
extrēmus *the end of*　　　　 tōtus *the whole of*
summus *the top of*　　　　　reliquus *the rest of*
īmus, infimus *the bottom of*

Very common are such time phrases as these: primo vere *at the beginning of spring*; extrema aestate *at the end of summer*; primo statim proelio *right at the beginning of the battle*.

N.B. primum agmen *the vanguard*;
　　　extremum agmen, novissimum agmen *the rearguard*;
　　　in medio colle *half way up the hill*.

412. Adjectival (or descriptive) phrases in Latin are in *either* abl. *or* gen. They must contain a noun *and* an adj.: *e.g.*

a man of great courage　vir summae virtutis (*or* vir fortissimus)
(but *a man of courage and resolution*　vir fortis et constans)

413. (i) The **genitive** of description is used:

(*a*) when there is a number-adjective:

　　　a fleet of 100 ships　classis centum navium
　　　a boy of twelve　puer duodecim annorum[1]

(*b*) when the noun in the phrase denotes 'kind':

men of every sort homines omnium generum (*or* cuiusque generis)

Eiusmodi, huiusmodi, cuiusmodi (*of this, that, what sort*) are often used instead of *talis, qualis*.

---

[1] Equivalent to *puer duodecim annos natus* (§ 154). Similarly, fossa decem pedum (*a ten-foot trench*) is equivalent to fossa decem pedes lata (*a trench ten feet wide*).

(ii) The **ablative** of description is used:

(*a*) of physical features (English uses *of* or *with*):

> *He was of remarkable height*   Erat egregiā staturā
> *a slave with long hair*   puer promissis capillis

(*b*) of temporary states of mind: *e.g.*

> *to be of good cheer*   bono animo esse
> *to be downcast*   animo demisso esse

(iii) *either gen. or abl.* is used for a permanent quality:

a man of great daring   vir summae audaciae, vir summā audaciā

414. Quotations illustrating § 413:

Castra in altitudinem pedum xii vallo, fossāque xviii pedum, muniri iubet.

Ipse Cicero tenuissima (*feeble*) valetudine erat.

Senex frigore adducitur ut capite operto (*covered*) sit.

Magni ponderis (*weight*) saxa in muro collocabant.

C. Volusenus, tribunus militum, vir et consili magni et
Galus virtutis, ad Galbam accurrit. tanto

415. Some common expressions containing 'of':

I have heard of him (of = about: always **de**): de eo audivi.[1]
Full of: plenus + gen. or abl.—the gen. is more usual.
To die of hunger (abl. of cause): fame perire.
He is worthy of a reward: praemio dignus est (§ 183).
The city of Rome (apposition): urbs Roma (*cf.* § 192, *n.* 2).
I think a lot of him: I value him highly: magni eum aestimo.
The battle of Cannae: proelium Cannense.[2]

*416. Among less common idioms, note these:

He has deserved well of us: bene meritus est de nobis.
He reached such a pitch of folly that . . . (Usque) eo imprudentiae venit ut . . . (*i.e.* he came thither on the scale of folly).

---

[1] But use the gen. with a noun: *news of victory* victoriae nuntius.
[2] There are adjectives for a few famous battles, *e.g.* Cannensis, Marathonius. But it is always safe to write 'the battle fought at . . .'. proelium ad . . . factum.

Exercise 41A

1. The camp was fortified with a moat of great width and a ten-foot rampart.
2. He had taken his son Hannibal, a boy of nine, to Spain.
3. At the top of the hill we saw an old man with a long beard.
4. Why are you ashamed of a plan of *such* boldness?
5. At the beginning of spring, we departed to the island of Crete with a fleet of thirty-eight ships.
6. Augustus thought a great deal of Maecenas, a man of the utmost prudence and loyalty.
7. Be of good cheer; we shall soon reach the end of the road.
8. I think men of such ability are deserving of the highest honour.
9. It is said that the whole of this cave is full of gold.
10. This task was (one) of the utmost difficulty, owing to the depth of the water.

Exercise 41B

1. Learning the news of our arrival, the enemy had drawn up their battle-line at the foot of the hill.
2. Those men have deserved well of their country, and will be worthy of the highest praise.
3. Towards the end of the summer, the whole of Antony's fleet was destroyed at the battle of Actium.
4. Caesar sent for Ariovistus, a man of the greatest influence in (*apud*) his tribe.
5. At the very beginning of spring we shall have to leave the beautiful city of Athens.
6. In order to cut off the rear of the column, they were lying in ambush in the heart of the forest.
7. I think highly of the laws of Gracchus, a tribune of whom[1] most of you have heard.
8. For C. Gracchus, it seems, was a man of courage and determination, and one who[2] served his country well.

[1] Say 'of which tribune'. [2] Generic relative clause (§ 287).

42

GENITIVE USES (II). REVISION (37–41)

421. The verbs *memini* and *obliviscor* govern a genitive[1]: *I forget you*, **tui** obliviscor; *I remember you*, **tui** memini (*also* mihi **tui** in mentem venit).

422. A genitive naming the *charge* is used with:

accuso *I accuse*[2]   damno, condemno *I condemn*[2]
absolvo (3) *I acquit*   reum facio *I prosecute*

>*Many have been acquitted on charges of treason*
>Multi maiestatis absoluti sunt

423. Misereor (2) *I pity* governs a genitive, just as does its impersonal equivalent *me miseret* (§ 402):

>*Have pity on your friends* Amicorum miseremini

424. Several ADJECTIVES can govern a gen.; among them:

cupidus *desirous (of)*   peritus *skilled (in)*
avidus *greedy (for)*   imperitus *unskilled (in)*
studiosus *eager (for)*   memor *(mindful, remembering*[3]*)*
patiens *tolerant (of)*   immemor *unmindful*

With **similis** *like*, **dissimilis** *unlike*, a gen. is always correct. (A dative is also used—quite often of things, rarely of persons, never of personal pronouns.)[4]

>*He is very like his father* Patris simillimus est

---

[1] The acc. may also be used, esp. of things. Of neuter pronouns, the acc. *must* be used: *e.g.* illud memini.

[2] With these verbs, moreover, the gen. *capitis* is used to name the penalty: *to condemn to death*, capitis (*not* mortis) damnare.

The traitors were condemned to death Proditores capitis damnati sunt

[3] *Memini* having no participle, *memor* can be used instead.

[4] The gen. is always used in the expression **veri similis** *likely*.

Exercise 42A

1. He is ashamed of having written these poems.
2. Why have these citizens been accused of such a crime?
3. I advise you to come here by the shortest possible route.
4. Those who wish to eat must cultivate the fields.
5. Do not regret having asked the Romans for peace.
6. She confesses that she regrets having answered thus.
7. The few books which he had were lying on the ground.
8. We ought to pity all those who are weary of life.
9. What does it matter to you where your master has gone?
10. The new house is most unlike this one; for it is the largest in[1] the whole street.
11. I wish I could return home at the end of the summer.
12. You will be prosecuted on a charge of theft.
13. At last I am free to enjoy leisure and devote myself to literature.
14. I do not choose to live any longer in the city of Corinth.
15. We shall never forget the courage which you showed to-day.
16. The larger the camp is, the more plunder there will be.
17. Let us be of good cheer: will our enemies be able to convict us of any crime?
18. If only you had waited for us! We did not know whom to follow.
19. Shall we acquit him of bribery, because he is defended by the eloquent Cicero?
20. I fear that your plan is more bold than wise.

[1] Use gen. English idiom here differs from that of Latin, French, &c.

>   the oldest city *in* Italy
>   veterrima Italiae urbs
>   la plus ancienne ville d'Italie

Exercise 42B

1. There happened to be a young man of remarkable height among those in the ship.
2. The heat of the sun is so great in this region that we may not go[1] bare headed.
3. The longer one lives in the country, the more skilful one becomes at fishing.
4. If I could only have persuaded my brother to drink less wine yesterday!
5. I delight in training my body by running, swimming, and throwing javelins.
6. I did my best[2] to hurry, but the burden was much heavier than I had expected.
7. He said he would never forget the many kindnesses he had received among us.
8. Those who had taken part in the plot were condemned to death.
9. O if only men had wings with which to fly across the sea!
10. It is very important that you alone should undertake the bribing of the guards.
11. I would rather you had died than been accused of so dreadful a crime.
12. It is fitting that your sons especially should take part in politics.[3]
13. After advancing as far as possible, they pitched camp towards evening at the foot of a hill.
14. Shall I, who scorned Catiline's violence, be terrified by Antony's threats?
15. Shall we allow[4] those who have deserved well of us to die of starvation?

---

[1] *esse.*   [2] See *p.* 116, *n.* 4.
[3] Phrases to note: *to go in for politics* ad rem publicam accedere; *to take part in p.* rei publicae interesse; in re publica versari.
[4] When 'allow' implies 'be responsible for, be guilty of causing', the Latin idiom is *committere ut* . . .

CONDITIONS: A GENERAL SURVEY

430. If he knows, he will tell us. *If he knew, he would tell us.* He never worked unless he was made to. *If they had known, they would have told us.* Condition sentences—*i.e.* sentences containing an adverb clause of condition—are of two distinct types. In English, one type has *would* (1st person, *should*) in its *main* clause; in French it has a conditional verb in its *main* clause; and in Latin it has the subjunctive mood in *both* clauses. The other type has *no* would, *no* conditional, *no* subjunctive. In Latin, then, we can call the two types *indicative conditions* and *subjunctive conditions*.

INDICATIVE CONDITIONS	'WOULD' OR SUBJUNCTIVE CONDITIONS
If he comes, I shall see him	*If he came, I should see him*
Si venerit, eum videbo	Si veniat, eum videam
If he came, I saw him	*If he had come, I should have seen him*
Si vēnit, eum vidi	Si venisset, eum vidissem

When this difference between the two types is grasped, most of the supposed difficulties of conditions disappear. The simple test is: *Is there a* **would** (*or* **should**) *in the main clause?*[1]

---

[1] The difference in *meaning* is harder to explain. Condition sentences indicate a certain connection between two events (or states): one of them (A) being the condition, without which the other (B) cannot occur. Those without *would* leave it quite open whether A and B actually happen or not—so they are often called *open* conditions· Those with *would* express the same connection, but add the further suggestion that the whole state of affairs is *imaginary*—an *idea* suggested or assumed for 'the sake of argument'. They may be called *imaginary* or *ideal* conditions.

Now to *imagine* anything about the present or past implies that things are not, or were not, so in reality; therefore imaginary conditions referring to present or past time have been called *unfulfilled* conditions. But it is better to use a term which covers all *would* conditions—future as well as present and past. In this book they are called simply *subjunctive conditions*.

43

INDICATIVE CONDITIONS

431. TENSE. Indicative conditions may refer to any time, past, present or future; and the two clauses need not refer to the same time. The tenses required will usually be obvious; but two points need attention:

(i) If the action in the *if*-clause precedes that in the main clause (however slightly), one of the *perfect* tenses must be used: the English usually conceals this point: *e.g.*

If he helped me, I used to praise him Si me **iuverat**, eum laudabam
(but *If he was ill, he stayed at home* Si aeger **erat**, domi manebat)

(ii) If the main verb is *future*, the verb in the *if*-clause also, usually, refers to future time. English uses the present in the *if*-clause; but in Latin the future—or more likely, as shown in (i) above, the future perfect—must be used.

(a) *If you are ill (i.e. now) my doctor will cure you*
Si aeger **es**, medicus meus te sanabit

(b) *If you are ill (i.e. to-morrow) you will stay at home*
Si aeger **eris**, domi manebis

(c) *If my doctor comes, he will cure you quickly*
Medicus meus, si **venerit**, cito te sanabit[1]

432. IF NOT. English may say *if he does not do it* or *unless he does it*. In Latin **nisi** (not *si non*) must be used.[2]

If you don't pay me, I shall be bankrupt
Nisi pecuniam mihi solveris, solvendo non ero

---

[1] Notice the order (common in *if* and *when* clauses). A subject shared by both clauses is placed in the main clause; the subordinate clause follows it, and then the rest of the main clause.

[2] If the negative goes closely with a single word, *si ... non* may be used; but this rarely occurs.

433. DOUBLE CONDITIONS begin in English with *whether ... or ...*; in Latin with **sive ... sive ...** (also spelt **seu**).

> *Whether they resist or surrender, they will be killed*
> **Sive** restiterint **sive** se dediderint, interficientur

If not (omitting the verb) is translated by **si minus**. So:

> *Whether they resist or not ...* Sive restiterint sive **minus ...**

434. Remember that in English the conjunctions *if*, *whether*, *whether ... or ...* are also used to introduce *noun clauses* (reported questions). Take great care not to confuse these with conditions (*adverb clauses*): no reported question must ever start with *si* or *sive*.

435. *Any* in a condition is the indefinite pronoun **quis**: adjectival form, **qui qua quod**:

if anybody si quis	*unless anybody* nisi quis
if anything si quid	*if ever* si quando

436. The main clause may be a *command*, and therefore have as its verb an imperative or a jussive subjunctive. The *if*-clause will still have its verb in the indicative. A jussive subjunctive, of course, does not make a subjunctive condition: the reason for it is quite different.

> *If he is drunk, let him not be admitted*
> Si ebrius est, ne admittatur

*437. When a command is qualified by an *if* or *when* clause, it commonly relates to a future action; and if so, the *future imperative* (amātō, amātōte) must be used. (The subordinate verb will be future or fut. perf.: *cf.* § 431 (ii).)

If (when) the messenger arrives, send him to me at once
Si (ubi, cum) nuntius advenerit, statim eum ad me **mittito**

The future imperative is to be used in the active voice only.

Exercise 43A

1. If you come to the lake with me, I will teach you to swim.
2. Whether we travel by sea or by land, the journey will be (one) of many days.
3. Our guides do not know whether we shall travel by sea or by land.
4. If they saw anybody sad, they always tried to help him.
5. If he is asleep, let no one awaken him before dawn.
6. If any one discovers our plan, we shall never be forgiven.
7. Unless he is willing to trust us it will be very difficult to cure him.
8. Whether you believe me or not, what I say is true.
9. If he ever saw me in the street, he pretended[1] not to know me.
10. If you have not read the book you do not know what happened.

Exercise 43B

1. If you have found anything, place it under this tree.
2. We shall very easily rout the enemy if we attack them unawares in the rear.
3. If he ever asks where I am, tell him that I have been living in the country for a long time past.
4. If you do not remember the words we cannot sing that song.
5. I shall not change my opinion, whether you agree with me or with the others.
6. Do not tell the judge whether you agree with me or with the other witnesses.
7. If we pretend[1] to go away, they will perhaps reveal where the gold is hidden.
8. Whether you have determined to stand for the consulship or not, you will have to return to Rome next spring.
9. If you sent the child out alone at night, you acted so foolishly that you deserve blame.
10. No one may go out by the gates unless he tell me his reason for wishing to leave.

[1] *simulo* + acc.-inf. Engl. *pretend to* becomes *pretend that* in Latin.

44

SUBJUNCTIVE CONDITIONS [1]

441. Subjunctive conditions (*imaginary* or *ideal* conditions) may refer to past, present, or future time.

> For FUTURE time use PRESENT subjunctive
> For PRESENT time use IMPERFECT subjunctive
> For PAST time use PLUPERFECT subjunctive

If he came, he would help us Si **veniat**, nos **adiuvet**
If he were here, he would be helping us Si **adesset**, nos **adiuvaret**
If he had come, he would have helped us Si **venisset**, nos **adiuvisset**

442. The time and tense of *each* clause must be thought out separately. They *may* be different: *e.g.*

If he had come, he would be helping us Si **venisset**, nos **adiuvaret**

But this is true only of *present* and *past* time (imperf. and pluperf. subjunctive). *Future* time always runs through both clauses: *two present subjunctives always go together*.

443. In an English sentence it is often hard to tell, except from the context, whether present or future time is meant.[2] *Future* time may be indicated by using *were* + infinitive: *e.g.*

---

[1] The main verb of a subjunctive condition is a *potential* subjunctive (§ 395). The subjunctive in the *if*-clause is *optative* in origin—before the *if*-clause was regarded as dependent on the other, the thought was of the following type:

> *If only he were here! He would be helping us*
> O si adesset! Nos adiuvaret

(Similarly with the other tenses: that is why the tense rule is like that given for wishes, § 392.)

[2] It is often useful to try inserting *now* and *ever*, and see which will fit the sense better (you *may* find that either will do).

If I were to tell you, you would not believe me. The use of a *continuous* tense indicates present time: *e.g.* If we were working (now), we should be earning money. But with some verbs this tense-form is not used: *e.g.*

If you possessed so much money, you would be rich
EITHER ('ever') Si tantum pecuniae habeas dives sis
OR ('now') Si tantum pecuniae haberes, dives esses

*444. Sometimes the imperfect subjunctive is used for a *continuous* state or action in *past* time, as when Cicero said:

At tum si dicerem, non audirer
But if I had been speaking then, I should not have been listened to

But this is not common; and the rule given suffices for writing Latin.

445. SUMMARY—CONDITIONS

First make sure the clause *is* conditional, not a noun clause.
CONJUNCTION: **si; nisi; sive ... sive ...**
VERB: **Engl.**, no would—**Latin**, indicative in both clauses.
  Tense: whatever the sense requires.

  Engl., would—**Latin**, subjunctive in both clauses.

  Tense: for **future** time, **present** subjunctive;
  for **present** time, **imperf.** subjunctive;
  for **past** time, **pluperf.** subjunctive.

Two present subjunctives always go together.

446. Quotations to study:

Pacem non peterem, nisi utilem crederem.

Ego, si me Scipionis desiderio (*loss*) moveri negem, mentiar.

(*Reply to a boast*) 'Meā operā, Q. Fabi, Tarentum recepisti.' 'Certe,' inquit ridens, 'nam nisi tu amisisses, numquam recepissem.'

(*Coriolanus' mother reproaches him*) 'Ergo ego nisi peperissem (*borne a son*), Roma non oppugnaretur; nisi filium haberem, libera in liberā patriā mortua essem.'

Exercise 44A

1. I should be glad, if you were returning home with me.
2. If the reinforcements had not arrived, the Romans would have been defeated.
3. If you ran away, you would be a coward.
4. We should not laugh unless you told us to, sir.
5. I should not have written unless I had been told to.
6. They would not be playing if I had told them not to.
7. If we had money, we should buy more food for you.
8. What would you do if anyone called you a traitor?
9. If the moon were not full, the enemy would not have caught sight of us.
10. If you were to stand for the consulship, you would undoubtedly be elected.
11. You would scarcely appear more wretched if you were dying.
12. If we had not ploughed as many fields as possible, we should now be short of corn.

Exercise 44B

1. I should be ashamed if I had neglected that duty.
2. If we started from here at once, we should reach the foot of the mountain before sunset.
3. Even if Hannibal's army were ten miles from Rome, we should not be downcast.
4. You would read that book much more easily if you had learnt the words.
5. If he promised to give me half the flowers, I should gladly work in his garden.
6. If I did not think the journey safe, I should not be urging you to come here.
7. What reply would you give if anyone asked you why you opened the window?
8. If you allowed me to go alone into the camp, I would strive to kill the Etruscan king.
9. If you had not pretended to understand, I should have used shorter words.
10. We should all be injured if this tree fell.

Exercise 44C

(CONDITION SENTENCES OF ALL KINDS)

1. If the dogs hear thieves, they will wake us at once.
2. If the dogs heard thieves, they would wake us at once.
3. If thieves had tried to enter, the dogs would have begun to bark at once.
4. I shall not marry you unless you promise to dine at home every day.
5. If you do not complain, nobody will know you need money.
6. Claudia would marry me if I swore to drink less wine.
7. If he were to complain, we should willingly help him.
8. You will overtake him in two days if you start without delay.
9. If I had wounded my son, I should have killed you with the second arrow.
10. Whether you surrender now, or prolong the war, the terms of peace will be harsh.
11. If the Britons had not been vexed at their wrongs, they would not have revolted from Rome.[1]
12. If you lived in the country, you would have to work in the fields in summer.
13. Do not trust him if he ever pretends to support you.
14. If we admire our ancestors' customs, let us imitate them as often as possible.
15. If Marius had not routed the Cimbri, it would have been all over[2] with Rome.[1]
16. If the road were to get narrower, we should have to proceed on foot.
17. How much would you have paid for this house if it had been larger?
18. If you cannot find a ford, you will have to build a bridge over[3] the river.
19. You would return the money to-morrow if you were really ashamed of your trickery.
20. Had you asked me yesterday, I should have given you a chance to read the letter.

[1] Not *Roma:* the people are meant. [2] *actum est de me.* [3] *in* + abl.

45

ADVERB CLAUSES OF TIME

451. Adverb clauses of time (*temporal* clauses) are introduced mostly by these conjunctions:

when ubi[1], postquam; cum
before prius quam (ante quam)
after postquam
ever since ex quo[2]
while dum
until dum
as soon as simul atque (*or* ubi primum, cum primum)

Cum and **dum** are dealt with separately in chapters 46 and 47.[3]

452. The verb of a time clause is indicative. The tense will usually be obvious; but note these points:

(i) *When they arrived, they dined*
 or When they had arrived, they dined
{ Ubi **venerunt,** cenaverunt
  Postquam **venerunt,** cenaverunt
  Cum **venissent,** cenaverunt

When the main verb is perfect, *ubi*, *postquam* and *simul atque* require the narrative tense, the perfect.[4] But *cum*, to give the same sense, requires the *pluperf.* subjunc. (§ 463).

(ii) *Before I stop, I will say just this*
 Ante quam finem **facio,** hoc tantum dicam

This type of *before*-clause, in which **ante quam** (not *prius quam*) is used, is the only context in which Latin uses a present indic. to refer to future time. Contrast:

When I stop, you will reply Cum finem **fecero,** tu respondebis

---

[1] Ut may be used with identical meaning and construction.
[2] (For ex quo tempore *from which time:* really a relative clause.)
[3] Beware the Engl. idioms *when working, while fighting, after speaking,* &c. The Latin conjunctions must *always* have a complete clause.
[4] But if the interval is stated, a pluperf. is used with *postquam:*

Two hours after they arrived, they dined
Duabus post horis quam **venerant,** cenaverunt

453. The two words of which *prius quam, ante quam, postquam* are composed need not come together. The actual conjunction is **quam**: this must stand at the head of the time clause.

The enemy abandoned the camp before anything was detected
(*The enemy* sooner *abandoned the camp* than *anything was detected*)
Hostes **prius** castris excesserunt **quam** quidquam cognitum est

> *I left three days before he died*
> Discessi tribus **ante** diebus **quam** mortuus est

454. A SUBJUNCTIVE VERB in a time clause implies that some other idea (*e.g.* purpose or cause) is added to the idea of time. After **prius quam**, a subjunctive implies *purpose*; as the clause is final, the tense must be present or imperf.

MERE TIME: *Before night fell, the camp was captured*
> Prius quam nox **advenit**, castra capta sunt

PURPOSE: *He tried to capture the camp before night fell*
> Castra prius capere conatus est quam nox **adveniret**

455. After a *negative* main clause, *until* is translated by **prius quam** or **ante quam**: *i.e.* if, in English, *until* can be replaced by *before*, Latin says *before*. **Dum** would be wrong.[1]

He would not depart until he received the money
Noluit **prius** discedere **quam** pecuniam acciperet

456. Quotations to study:

Postridie eius diei, prius quam hostes se ex terrore reciperent, in fines Suessionum exercitum duxit.

Omnes hostes terga verterunt, neque prius fugere destiterunt quam ad flumen Rhenum pervenerunt.

Anno enim post consul fuerat quam ego natus sum.

Sic omne opus prius est perfectum, quam intellegeretur ab Afranio castra muniri.

---

[1] But naturally, *He did not wait-until-I-had-finished* is: Non exspectavit dum finem facerem. Contrast it with *He did not reply until I had finished*, *i.e.* He did not *sooner* reply *than* . . .

Exercise 45A [1]

1. After the fleet had left the harbour, a very high wind suddenly sprang up.
2. Before Caesar crossed the river, he repaired the bridge.
3. The Gauls destroyed the bridge before Caesar could lead his troops across the river.
4. The traitor will not open the gate until he receives his reward.
5. Ever since Britain became a province, we have suffered grave wrongs.
6. I shall not answer until you set me free.
7. As soon as we entered the house we greeted our father.
8. When the weary sailors realized that land was at last near, they raised a great shout.
9. Before we reached the city, the gates were closed.
10. The cavalry routed the enemy before they could draw up their battle-line.

Exercise 45B [1]

1. Five months after he was elected consul, he fell ill.
2. As soon as the Roman forces began to besiege the town, the citizens, on the queen's advice, surrendered.
3. The boy revealed the whole plan before anyone[2] was able to stop him.
4. From the time when the Tarquinii were driven out, the name of that clan was always hated by the Romans.
5. He wished to finish the campaign before winter set in.
6. Before the old man died, he divided his property among his three sons.
7. Two days before I left Rome, I sent a letter to my friends in the country.
8. Do not blame me till you hear why I failed.[3]
9. Before I tell you what I intend to do, swear to help me.
10. Ten days after capturing Rome, the Gauls were induced to withdraw by fear.

[1] No sentence in this exercise requires the use of *cum* or *dum*.
[2] *quisquam*   [3] See *p.* 126, *n.* 1.

46

THE CONJUNCTION 'CUM'

461. Cum, like other time conjunctions, has its verb in the indicative (§ 452) *if it merely denotes time*. But it acquired the added meanings of *since, although, whereas* (*i.e.* cause, concession, attendant circumstance). These meanings are indicated by a subjunctive verb (§ 454).

Moreover, in writing of past time, Roman writers hardly ever used *cum* with an indicative.[1] For practical purposes, we may adopt the rule:

> **cum** meaning *when*: indic. in primary sequence,
> subjunc. in historic sequence.
> **cum** meaning *since, although, whereas*: subjunc. always.

462. TENSES after **cum** (*when*): (i) If the main verb is *future*, the subordinate verb is likely to be *fut. perf.* (§ 452).

(ii) When the main verb is *perfect*, the subordinate verb is either *imperf.* or *pluperf.* subjunc. (*never* perfect) (§ 452).[2]

When we arrived there, we dined Eo cum **venissemus,** cenavimus

*463. A past indic. with **cum** is quite correct if there really is no connexion whatever between the events except that of time; but such a use is rare. When it occurs, the *time* connexion is often emphasized by using *tum*:

> *When I was still a boy, you were already an oldish man*
> **Cum** ego adhuc puer **eram, tum** tu iam senior **eras**

The indic. *may* also follow **cum primum** *as soon as*.

As soon as the time of year allowed, he hurried to rejoin the army
Cum primum per anni tempus **potuit,** ad exercitum contendit

---

[1] It is as if they felt that, if *A* happened when *B* happened, there must have been some connection between them; and they preferred to indicate this (by the subjunctive) even in a sentence where **cum** would be adequately translated by *when* in English.

[2] In other words these *cum* clauses obey strict sequence rules.

464. **Cum** can also mean *whenever*. The verb is then indic.; and if the sense requires, *or even permits*, the tense used must show that one of the actions precedes the other:

Whenever he calls me, I shall go	Cum me vocaverit, ibo
Whenever he calls me, I go	Cum me vocavit, eo
Whenever he called me, I went	Cum me vocaverat, ibam

This tense-pattern—*perf.* with *pres.*, *pluperf.* with *imperf.*, *&c.*—is so common that it is a good working rule, and an excellent clue to the indefinite (*whenever*) use of *cum*.[1]

Whenever the Gauls attacked the camp, they were repulsed
Galli, cum castra **oppugnaverant,** repellebantur

Contrast: Galli, cum castra oppugnassent, repulsi sunt.

For other indefinite or 'ever' clauses see *ch.* 53.

465. AN INVERTED TIME CLAUSE is one which really contains the main assertion, while the *grammatical* main clause serves to mark the time of the event: *e.g.* 'We were having our dinner when the bell suddenly rang.' 'Hardly had we reached home when the storm began.' In these sentences the clause which is subordinate in grammar is 'main' in sense. In an *inverted time clause* the verb naturally denotes an event, and is in the indic. In Latin, it is in the perfect, or—very often—historic present. The main verb will be imperf. or pluperf.

The enemy were nearing the walls, when suddenly the Romans rushed out
Hostes subibant muros, **cum repente erumpunt Romani**

Not yet had ten days elapsed, when lo! the other son is killed
Dies nondum decem intercesserant, **cum alter filius necatur**

466. CUM = SINCE. Note the common expression:

Since this is (was) the case . . .
In these circumstances . . . } Quae cum ita sint (essent) . . .

---

[1] But the meaning *may* demand the same tense in both clauses:
Whenever he was in the country, he was ill
Cum ruri erat, aeger erat

*467. CUM AS ADVERB. Cum ... tum ... (lit. *when ... then ...*) means *both ... and ...* (stronger, however, than *et ... et ...*).

Haec verba cum patriciis tum etiam plebi placuerunt

468. SUMMARY—CUM[1]

Cum = *when*: indic. of primary tenses, subjunc. of historic.
Cum = *since, although, whereas*: subjunc. always.
Cum = *whenever*: indic. (usually with a perfect-stem tense).
Cum = *when* in inverted time clause: indic.

469. Quotations to study:

Haec cum dixisset, procedit extra munitiones.
Eodem fere tempore P. Crassus, cum in Aquitaniam pervenisset, ... cum intellegeret in locis tam periculosis sibi bellum gerendum, magnam diligentiam adhibendam (*employ*) intellexit.
Caesar ipse, cum primum pabuli copia (*supply*) esse inciperet, ad exercitum venit.
Cum equitatus noster praedandi causa se in agros eiecerat, omnibus viis essedarii (*charioteers*) ex silvis emittebantur.
(*Naval battle*) Cum singulas binae ac ternae naves circumsteterant, milites transcendere in hostium naves contendebant.
Iam Sora capta erat, cum consules prima luce advenerunt.
(*Were old men useless?*) Ceteri senes, cum rem publicam consilio et auctoritate defendebant, nihil agebant? (§ 463).
Praeerat Geminus Maecius, vir cum genere tum factis inter suos clarus.

Exercise 46A

1. Although I was present, I did not dare to say anything.
2. When we arrived here, we disembarked without delay.
3. When I arrive there, I shall greet the friends whom we left behind there.

---

[1] Warning: *never* use *cum* for 'when' introducing noun clauses. 'When' in a question is always *quando*.

4. Since that is so, I dare not trust such a man as you.[1]
5. We had almost given up hope of victory when reinforcements arrived.
6. Whenever we went to Rome we climbed on to the Capitol.
7. It was noon when the army marched forth from the camp.
8. When the messenger returns, I will announce the terms of peace to all.
9. Whenever I have leisure, I will write you a long letter.
10. Since a storm has arisen, let us not attempt to set sail to-day.

Exercise 46B

1. When it was reported that the Nervii had attacked the winter camp, Caesar advanced into their territory by forced marches.
2. Although they charged with great courage, our men were repulsed by the numbers of the enemy.
3. In the circumstances, the senate was unwilling for the law to be proposed.[2]
4. Whenever I refuse to obey my father, he is angry with me.
5. The prisoners had already almost escaped when they were observed by the guards on the tower.
6. Reaching the shore, we saw bare-footed boys playing among the rocks.
7. They were swimming in the sea when suddenly a strange fish with a huge head appeared.
8. Since we cannot discover which is guilty we must acquit both of them.
9. Our men were about to climb the walls, when the besieged raised a great shout and made a sortie by every gate.
10. When I helped him, the farmer always used to give me a jar of wine to take home.
11. Both in Rome and throughout the provinces there is hardly anyone who is not glad that Antony has been defeated.
12. As you have confessed that you threw the stones yourself, you will not be allowed to depart with the others.

[1] Latin: 'to trust you, such a man'.
[2] *legem rogare* (*i.e.* to ask the assembly to approve it).

47

THE CONJUNCTION 'DUM'

471. Dum has two distinct meanings—*while* and *until*.

A. DUM MEANING 'WHILE'

472. There are two uses to note, one *literal*, and one *metaphorical*; the second grew out of the first.

(i) *Literally*, of pure time: the verb is indicative.
But *while*, and *dum*, can be used in two ways:

(*a*) *While I was away, my father died*
   Dum **absum**, pater mortuus est

Here a single event (in the main clause) is placed against a prolonged background (in the while clause). *Dum*, used thus, has its verb in the *present* indic., *whatever the tense of the main verb*. This is the normal, commonest, use.

(*b*) *While I was in Rome, I used to stroll daily in the Forum*
   Dum Romae **eram**, cottidie in Foro spatiabar

Here the two periods of time are equally long. *While* could be replaced by *as long as* or *all the time that*. In this use *dum* may have whatever tense of the indic. is required.[1]

As long as (while) I live, I shall love you Dum vivam, te amabo

473. (ii) *Metaphorically*, *dum* may be used to translate *so long as* (*i.e. provided that, on condition that, if only*). The verb is subjunctive. The negative is **nē** (not *non*).

> *You may come with me, provided that you don't say anything*
> Licet tibi mecum venire, dum **ne quid dicas**

> *Let them hate, so long as they fear* Oderint, dum **metuant**

Sometimes *dum*, in this sense, has **modo** (*only*) added to it.[2]

---

[1] **Quoad** and **donec** may be used instead of *dum* in the senses *all the time that* (A (i *b*)) and *until* (B (i)). You need not use them.

[2] Occasionally the *dum* is omitted, only the *modo* being expressed.

B. DUM MEANING 'UNTIL'

474. There are two uses to be distinguished:

(i) *literally*, of pure time: the verb is naturally indicative; any tense may be used.

> *The battle raged fiercely till darkness fell*
> Acriter pugnatum est dum nox **advēnit**

Mihi usque curae erit quid agas, dum quid egeris sciero
I shall always wonder how you are faring till I know how you have fared

(ii) oftener with the *added meaning* of purpose: the verb is subjunctive, either present or imperfect. (§ 454.)

> *They put him in prison till he paid the money*
> Eum in vincula coniecerunt dum pecuniam **solveret**

Such a clause is specially common after **exspecto**. English *to wait for it to happen* is Latin *to wait until it happens*.

> *The peasant waits for the river to flow past*
> Rusticus exspectat dum defluat amnis

475. With a *negative* main clause, *until* is to be translated by **prius quam**, not by *dum* (*cf.* § 455).

476. SUMMARY—DUM

A. WHILE. (i) *literally*, of time: indic.
    (*a*) normally, *dum* + present tense; but
    (*b*) if *while* = *all the time that*, *dum* + any tense.
  (ii) *metaphorically*, provided that: subjunc. (neg. *nē*).

B. UNTIL. (i) *literally*, of pure time: indic. (any tense).
  (ii) *time* + *purpose*: subjunc. (pres. or imperf.).

477. Quotations to study:

Dum haec in colloquio geruntur, Caesari nuntiatum est equites hostium accedere, lapides telaque in nostros coicere.

Scipionem esse natum haec civitas, dum erit, laetabitur.

Spatium intercedere voluit dum milites, quos imperaverat, convenirent.

(*Epaminondas is fatally wounded*) Ferrum usque eo retinuit, **quoad** renuntiatum est vicisse Boeotios.

Exercise 47A

1. While we were away from home, our slaves ran away.
2. The enemy attacked our men while they were fortifying their camp.
3. Do not fear so long as you are telling the truth.
4. While I was living in the country, I used to run three miles every day.
5. We remained in hiding until the signal was given.
6. Wait for the signal for advancing to be given.
7. While this was taking place in Italy, Hannibal left Spain with a huge army.
8. We kept the rest of the hostages until the enemy should set our men free.
9. Provided that we do not delay, we shall arrive in time.
10. Until they perceived who he was, he pretended[1] to be a doctor.

Exercise 47B

1. While he was standing near the altar, the priest was struck by lightning and died.
2. Provided that no one disagrees, we will try to kill Caesar on March 15th.
3. While the king lives we shall never enjoy liberty.
4. Since the water has recently become deeper, we shall have to wait till the other bridge is repaired.
5. No one dared to enter until the leader told him to.
6. While making this speech,[2] the tribune noticed the faces of those listening.
7. The poet went on[3] writing in the evening until he could no longer see the tablets.
8. We need not fear the Germani so long as they remain beyond the Rhine.
9. Whilst the fleet was leaving the bay, 150 hostile ships suddenly appeared.
10. As long as I can hunt, I shall consider that I am not yet an old man.

[1] *Cf. p.* 136, *n.* 1.   [2] Use a clause in Latin.   [3] Use *usque*.

48

REVISION EXERCISES

Exercise 48A

1. If we march a little faster, we shall easily arrive in time.
2. Whenever I approached the window, I heard his voice.
3. Do not advance farther until the rearguard has crossed the bridge.
4. The sailors may weigh anchor when they obtain a favourable wind.
5. Mind that you do not fall from the top of the wall.
6. If we had not found a spring, we should not have pitched camp at the foot of the ridge.
7. Whenever I have enough leisure, I read a new book.
8. Since they had lived in the country in their father's lifetime, they were skilled in farming.
9. We were lying in the garden, when suddenly we heard the noise of many feet.
10. If our allies were to send more corn to us, we should not die of hunger next winter.
11. Scarcely had I left home when a letter was brought to me.
12. Although I came here unwillingly,[1] I shall not leave of my own accord.
13. Pretend to be working until they close the door.
14. If you were sorry for your trick, I should gladly[1] have forgiven you.
15. While the war was being fought, the citizens were not allowed[2] to use lights in the streets.
16. Provided that you follow me, you will cross the marsh safely.[1]
17. Whether you are guilty or not, these jurors will gladly[1] convict you.

---

[1] Certain English adverbs are commonly represented in Latin by adjectives; notably: *willingly, gladly:* libens; *unwillingly:* invitus; *safely:* incolumis.   [2] Use *licet*.

18. As soon as he saw me he said he remembered my name.
19. While we were sleeping on the ground, a thief took away from us a large sum of money.
20. It was already dawn when we discovered what had happened.

Exercise 48B

1. Come down out of that tree before the branch breaks.[1]
2. Whenever we tried to advance, small bands of natives would harass us in the rear.
3. Provided that you do not lack resources, there is no reason why you should fail.
4. If a man does wrong, so long as he repents he should be forgiven.
5. As soon as the corn began to be ripe, the supply of food increased[1] in the city.
6. If you had been content with a smaller price, you would have sold the house more easily.
7. Being unable to find anywhere to sleep, we were forced to turn back.
8. When you find the lost gold, return it to me at once.
9. If you consulted your own interests, you would not be disregarding your sister's advice.
10. They had gone less than three miles when they were ordered to wait till the wind changed.[1]
11. If you do not believe that the defendant is guilty, do not condemn him to death.
12. Three years after I was born, my father perished while sailing to Britain.
13. Whether it occurred on purpose or by accident, the enemy's cavalry were worsted.[2]
14. Do not cease pursuing the fugitives until I sound the signal for retreat.
15. If it is not clear whether it was done on purpose or by accident, you ought not to accuse us of carelessness.

[1] Take care in translating this *intransitive* verb. *Cf. p.* 175, *n.* 1.
[2] Common expressions are: superior(es) discedere, *to come off best*; inferior(es) discedere, *to come off worst*.

49

IDIOMS WITH 'QUIN'

491. The *relative pronoun* **quīn** (*qui+nĕ*) was dealt with in § 288. There is also a *conjunction* **quīn**.[1] The two are alike in this respect, that they can *only* be used with a negative (or virtually negative) main clause.

492. When verbs meaning *doubt* are used negatively, they are not followed by an acc. and inf. (as would be expected), but by a clause with **quin** for conjunction and with the form of a reported question.

> *We did not doubt that the accused was guilty*
> Non dubitavimus quin reus nocens esset
>
> *Who can doubt that he has told the truth?*
> Quis dubitare potest quin vera dixerit?
>
> *There was no doubt that our side had won*
> Non dubium fuit quin nostri vicissent

N.B. **Dubium** is not a noun, but the neuter of the adj. **dubius** *doubtful*. The Latin expression is *It was not doubtful.*[2]

493. The conjunction **quin** may also introduce consecutive clauses of the generic type. *Quin* can replace *ut non*, provided that the main clause also is negative.

---

[1] It arose by adding -**nĕ** (*not*) to **quī,** an earlier form of the abl. sing. of the relative pronoun. It thus meant *whereby not*. But in the idioms of § 492 little trace of the original meaning remains.

[2] Caesar occasionally extends the use of this type of clause to other expressions than doubt. Once the basis of it is understood, it is easy to follow such a sentence as:

Neque abest suspicio quin ipse sibi mortem consciverit
There is some ground for supposing that he committed suicide

Livy and later writers also use *quin* clauses after (negatived) verbs of *denial*. But for writing Latin, the rule given is sufficient.

> Numquam eum video quin tui in mentem veniat
> *I never see him without recalling you*

(literally, *in such a way that I do not recall you*)

> Nullum diem intermittebant quin aliquid discerent
> *They let no day pass without learning something*

(literally, *in such a way that they did not learn something*)

These clauses occur especially after the words **omitto, praetermitto, intermitto** *I let pass*; **intercedo** *I pass by*.[1]

494. Study these expressions: (*a*) *Non possum facere quin:*

> *I cannot help fearing him*
> **Non possum facere quin** eum timeam

(*b*) the impersonal expressions with *potest fieri*:

(i) *It may be that you are wrong* — Potest fieri **ut** erres
It may be that you are not wrong — Potest fieri **ut** non erres

(ii) *It cannot be that you are wrong* — Non potest fieri **ut** erres
It cannot but be that you are wrong; you are bound to be wrong } Non potest fieri **quin** erres

Remember that all the expressions with *fieri* are *impersonal*. In all these consecutive *quin* clauses, the tense must be present or imperfect according to the sequence. (*Cf.* § 281.)

495. Quotations to study:

Non erat dubium quin totius Galliae plurimum Helvetii possent.

Si id acciderit, non dubitat quin brevi Troia sit peritura.

Nemo est tam fortis quin novitate (*strangeness*) rei perturbetur.

Neque ullum fere totius hiemis tempus sine sollicitudine (*anxiety*) Caesaris intercessit, quin aliquem de consiliis ac motu Gallorum nuntium acciperet.

Treveri totius hiemis nullum tempus intermiserunt quin trans Rhenum legatos mitterent.

Facere non possum quin cottidie litteras ad te mittam.

Quorum nulli ex itinere excedere licebat, quin ab equitatu Caesaris exciperetur (*pounced on*).

[1] This gives us one translation for *without* + gerund: *cf. ch.* 50.

Exercise 49A

1. We no longer doubted that our ships had been wrecked.
2. He never comes to dinner without bringing a gift.
3. The Etruscans could not help admiring Horatius' courage.
4. There is no doubt that all these boys will receive rewards.
5. It may be that you have told the truth about this.
6. Not a year passed without our going to the country in the month of July.
7. The guilty are bound to be punished at last.
8. No one could doubt that the dog belonged to the farmer.
9. I cannot but praise this poet's newest poems.
10. I do not let any day go by without exercising my body.

Exercise 49B

1. I had no doubt that you would willingly undertake the management of the business.
2. You cannot possibly have finished the whole task alone.
3. My son never greets me without demanding money from me.
4. Pompey hardly let any day pass without challenging Caesar to battle.
5. Who can doubt that all men must die some time?
6. The others could not help hoping that I alone should be accused of the crime.
7. There can be no doubt that the laws of C. Gracchus were harmful to the state.
8. No one is so wise that he does not make a mistake now and then.
9. Not even Augustus is so wise that he does not make a mistake now and then.[1]
10. You may well now be regretting your goodwill towards us.[2]

---

[1] This sentence refers entirely to a *particular case*; there is nothing *generic* about it; therefore *quin* is not to be used.

[2] Towards (when used of feelings): either *ergā* or *in*, both with acc. These phrases of feeling are among the few prepositional phrases which may be used as adjective phrases in Latin. (Use *ergā* chiefly for friendly feelings, *in* for *any* feelings.)

50

WITHOUT, INSTEAD OF, SO FAR FROM

501. WITHOUT + NOUN. The preposition **sine** is not always to be used. Note the following expressions:

He went *without my orders* **Meo iniussu** discessit
He went *without Caesar's orders* **Caesaris iniussu** discessit

He went *without my knowledge* **Me inscio** discessit (*abl. abs.*)
He went *without anyone's knowledge* **Omnibus insciis** discessit

They tried *without success* **Frustra** conati sunt
They returned *without success* **Re infecta** regressi sunt
They returned *without loss* **Incolumes** regressi sunt
They entered *without opposition* **Nullo resistente** ingressi sunt

502. WITHOUT + GERUND (*e.g.* without waiting). **Sine** cannot govern a gerund: no preposition can do so, except those listed in § 333. There are several ways of recasting the sentence:

(i) a negatived participle-phrase:

without waiting for the cavalry equitibus non exspectatis
Without replying he departed **Nullo responso dato** discessit

(ii) a consecutive clause: *without being seen* becomes *in such a way that no one saw me.*

I have built my new house without spending too much money
Novas aedes **ita** aedificavi **ut non** nimis pecuniae impenderem

(iii) a consecutive clause with **quin** (§ 493), provided that the main clause contains a negative word.[1]

He never saw me without asking me for money
Numquam me videbat **quin** pecuniam a me peteret

---
[1] But *quin* cannot be used if the negative word is just *non.* In that case method (ii) must be used.
This use of *quin* is commonest after a time-negative (*e.g.* never, no day . . .): *cf.* § 493.

503. INSTEAD OF. The usual preposition is **pro**; but it cannot be used with a gerund, and the sentence must be recast: *instead of working* may mean either 'whereas I *could* have worked' or 'whereas I *ought to* have worked'. For example:

The weary soldiers, instead of keeping guard, slept
Milites defessi, **cum vigilare deberent**, dormiebant

Instead of returning at once, I travelled slowly
Cum statim revenire possem, lente iter feci

Another, even simpler, equivalent for this would be:

Non statim reveni, sed lente iter feci

504. SO FAR FROM. There are three Latin equivalents for *So far from recovering, they died*:

(i) *Not only did they not recover, but they (actually) died*
Non modo non sanati sunt, sed mortui sunt

(ii) *That-they-should-recover was so far away that they died*
Tantum afuit ut sanarentur **ut** mortui sint

Here the verb *abesse* is used *impersonally*, with an **ut** noun clause as subject; the second **ut** clause is consecutive.

(iii) *So completely did they fail-to-recover that they died*
Adeo non sanati sunt **ut** mortui sint

*505. Sometimes *so far from* is followed by *not even*:

So far from setting us free, they do not even feed us
Not only do they not set us free, but they do not even feed us
Non modo non nos liberant, **sed ne** cibum **quidem** nobis dant

Cf. Non modo nihil eorum fecit Roscius, sed ne potuit quidem facere.[1]

---

[1] With *non modo non, sed ne ... quidem*, it may happen that the two clauses have the verb in common. If so, omit the second *non*:

So far from sparing the young, they did not spare even the old
Non modo iuvenibus, **sed ne** senibus **quidem** pepercerunt

Cf. Assentatio (*flattery*) non modo amico, sed ne libero (*free man*) quidem digna est.

Exercise 50A

1. ¹We travelled through Africa without catching any lions.
2. No one will fight outside the ranks without the consul's orders.
3. ¹The infantry, instead of climbing to the top of the ridge, remained in the valley.
4. So far from becoming richer, you no longer have enough money.
5. ¹These boys have played all day instead of working.
6. So far from condemning you, I believe you are worthy of praise.
7. ¹Caesar entered the senate-house without reading my letter.
8. Why have my brothers been sent away suddenly without my knowledge?
9. ¹Instead of obeying me, you did what you yourself wished.
10. He feared that he could not embark without being seen.

Exercise 50B

1. Surely no one can watch this play without laughing?
2. I caught three fish without sitting long on the bank.
3. Yesterday I sat all day without catching any fish.
4. The cavalry who had been sent to surround the rearguard returned without success.
5. The wind was so strong that no ship could² leave harbour without being swamped by the waves.
6. Instead of choosing a general experienced in war, you have preferred a man of no ability.
7. So far from carrying out Caesar's orders, the magistrates welcomed his opponents into the city.
8. Although you are attacking the citadel without waiting for reinforcements, I do not doubt that you will succeed.
9. So far from loving all men, you do not even love your own relatives.
10. The guides started off without the commander's orders, and led the Romans through the woods instead of the plain.

¹ Give two versions. ² Use *licet*.

51

IDIOMS OF PREVENTION: 'QUOMINUS' AND 'QUIN'

511. *I prevent you from going* Te ire prohibeo

An *infinitive* is used with **prohibeo**; but with all other verbs of prevention a *clause* must be used.[1] The commonest are:

(i) verbs of *preventing*:

    impedio (4) *I hinder*   deterreo (2) *I deter*
    retineo (2) *I restrain*

(ii) verbs of *refraining* (only to be used negatively):

    mihi tempero (1) *I refrain*   recuso (1) *I object*
    dubito (1) *I hesitate*

512. The clause with these verbs is *final*; conjunction:

with a *positive* main clause, either **quo minus**[2] or **nē**;
with a *negative* main clause, either **quo minus** or **quin**.

Winter has so far hindered us from starting
Hiems adhuc nos impedivit **quo minus** (*or* **ne**) proficisceremur

You can never deter me from accusing you
Numquam me deterrere potes **quin** (*or* **quo minus**) te accusem

He did not object to coming with me
Non recusavit **quo minus** (*or* **quin**) mecum veniret

---

[1] This is a sound working rule. But **prohibeo** *may* have a clause; while **non dubito** and **non recuso** may have an infinitive.

[2] **Quo minus** (or, in one word, **quominus**) = *whereby not*: i.e. in origin it has the same meaning as *quin*. (For *minus* with the force of *non*, cf. *si minus*, § 433.) It is useful to distinguish these final *quin* clauses (in which *quo minus* might be used) from the consecutive *quin* clauses of §§ 493, 494; though some of the idioms of § 494 might be placed in either class.

513. There are two *impersonal* expressions to learn:

(i) *It was your fault that we did not escape*
   Per te stetit quo minus effugeremus[1]

   It was not Daedalus' fault that his son failed to fly
   Non per Daedalum stetit quo minus filius volare posset

(ii) *We almost managed to win; we were within an ace of winning*
   Non multum afuit quin vinceremus[2]

   Warning: these phrases are *impersonal.*

514. Quotations to study:

Iure iurando se obstrinxerunt (*bound*) se non recusaturos quo minus sub Sequanorum imperio essent.

Remi ne Suessiones quidem, consanguineos (*kinsmen*) suos, deterrere potuerunt quin cum Germanis consentirent.

Nec aetas impedit quo minus et ceterarum rerum et imprimis (*especially*) agri colendi studia teneamus usque ad ultimum tempus senectutis.

(*Gallic invasion feared*) Neque sibi homines feros (*wild*) ac barbaros temperaturos existimabat, quin in Provinciam exirent atque inde in Italiam contenderent.

Veientes legatos nostros haud procul afuit quin violarent.

Vix temperavere animis (= sibi) quin extemplo (*at once*) impetum facerent.

Caesar cognovit per Afranium (*the opposing general*) stare quominus proelio dimicaretur (*a pitched battle was fought*).

---

[1] In this idiom, **quo minus** (never *quin*) is used. The literal meaning is 'Through him it comes to a standstill, so that so-and-so does not occur'. It always implies *fault*: it would translate 'Thanks to you we did not win' but not 'Thanks to you we did not lose'.

[2] Also, *paullum abest, minimum abest.*

Exercise 51A

1. The storm prevented us from setting sail yesterday.
2. My opponents did not hesitate to accuse me of treason.
3. The arrow came very near to wounding the horse.
4. The terrified soldiers were with difficulty restrained from fleeing.
5. It was due to Crassus that the Roman army did not defeat the Parthians (*Parthi*).
6. No one will deter me by threats from telling the truth.
7. We tried to prevent the old man from drinking so much wine.
8. Why are we prevented by unjust laws from being happy?
9. It was not my fault that the old temples were not repaired ten years ago.
10. Pompey all but succeeded in destroying Caesar's army.

Exercise 51B

1. The Britons tried without success to prevent our legions from disembarking.
2. Not even the Etruscans could refrain from admiring the bravery of Mucius.
3. It was not the master's fault that the pupils did not understand the words.
4. By no means will you deter me from proposing just laws.
5. When the tribunes fled to him, Caesar did not hesitate to leave his province.
6. I was hindered by the very difficult journey from arriving here while my father was alive.
7. The plebeians no longer objected to taking up arms on behalf of the patricians.
8. I believe it is your fault that dinner is not yet ready.
9. Old age did not prevent Cato from taking part in politics.
10. Surely nothing stopped you from coming to the help of your comrades in their distress?

52

SOME, ANY, EACH, &c.[1]

521. The various 'indefinite' pronouns and adverbs are often thought confusing and difficult. Most of the difficulty vanishes if the *principles of formation* are grasped.

522. ali- before *interrogatives* gives words meaning *some*:

aliquis *somebody*
aliquid *something*
aliqui, -qua, -quod *some*
aliquantum *some amount of* (with partitive gen.)

alicubi[2] *somewhere*
aliquando *some time, sometimes*
aliquamdiu *for some while*

-que added to *interrogatives* gives words meaning *every*:

quisque *everybody*
quidque *everything*
quisque, quaeque, quodque *each*
uterque *each of two, both*

ubique *everywhere*
undique *from everywhere*

utrimque *from both sides*

-cumque added to *relatives* = *-ever* (indefinite relative):

quicumque, quaecumque, quod-
 cumque *whoever, whatever*
qualiscumque *of whatever sort*

ubicumque *wherever*
quocumque *to wherever*
quotienscumque *whenever*

Doubled forms are also indefinite relatives:

quisquis[3] *whoever*
quidquid[3] *whatever*

quotquot *however many*
quoquo *to wherever*

523. The following paragraphs deal in turn with the translation of the English words *some*, *any* and *each*.

---

[1] Many of the words brought together here for connected treatment have not been excluded from earlier exercises.

[2] *Ubi* was originally a 'qu-' word'; its earlier form survives in *alicubi*; also in *sīcubi* (if anywhere), *nēcubi* (lest anywhere).

[3] Used only in nom. and abl. sing. For other forms *quicumque* must be used.

524. SOME.

aliquis: *someone*; vague general word.
  for some reason aliqua de causa   *some food* aliquid cibi

quidam: *someone whom I could name; a certain man*
  for a certain reason quadam de causa

nescio quis: *someone or other;* very vague. (*Nescio quis* is treated as one word, a kind of compound pronoun.[1])
  for some reason or other nescio qua de causa

aliquot (indecl. adj.): *some = a certain number.*
  for some (i.e. a number of) reasons aliquot de causis

nonnulli: *some = a good many;* stronger than *aliquot.*
  for a good many reasons nonnullis de causis

complures: *some = several;* less vague than *aliquot.*
  they advanced some miles complura milia passuum ierunt

525. SOME ... OTHERS.

(*a*) **alius** repeated in the same case:

  Some creatures are inhabitants of the water, others of the land
  Aliae bestiae aquarum sunt incolae, **aliae** terrarum

(*b*) **alius** repeated in different cases; either sing. or plu. may be used:

  Some fear one thing, some another \
  One fears this, another that } **Alius aliud timet**[2]

  Some had come from one city, some from another[3]
  Alii ex aliis urbibus venerant

If there are only two altogether, **alter** replaces *alius.*

  Alter consul mortuus est, **alter** vulneratus

---

[1] Distinguish this from *nescio quis* in a reported question:
  Nescio **quis** venerit *I don't know who has come*
  Nescio **quis** venit   *Someone or other has come*

[2] This is really a shortened form of *alius aliud timet, alius aliud.*

[3] Or, *they had come from different cities.* Note this way of translating *different.*

526. ANY.

Any you like (no matter which): **quivis, quilibet.**

You may come on any day Licet tibi **quovis** die venire

Any in a question: **num quis** (§ 201).[1]

Did you see anything? **Num quid vidisti?**

Any with negatives: **quisquam** (adj. **ullus**) (§ 132).
Any with *nē*: always **quis** (§ 211).
Any with *si, nisi* (if anyone, unless anyone): **quis.**

If anyone says that, he is a liar Si **quis** illud dicit, mentitur

Remember: *si quis, nisi quis, ne quis, num quis*. The indefinite pronoun *quis* cannot be separated from the *si*, *&c.*

527. EVERY, EACH.

Every one, each one: **quisque**. But if there are only two in all, **uterque** must be used. *Quisque* is used especially:

(*a*) with superlatives: *e.g.*
  optimus quisque (*each best man*) *all the best men*

(*b*) with ordinal numbers: *e.g.*
  decimus quisque (*each tenth man*) *one in ten*

(*c*) with *se, suus* (placed next before it if possible):
Sibi quisque consulat *Let each man take thought for himself*

528. The Latin for *each other, one another*, is **inter se.** It may be used with transitive or intransitive verbs.

  Pueri inter se amant   Galli inter se pugnant

529. Quotations to study:

Optimus et gravissimus quisque philosophus confitetur se multa ignorare.
(*The ships of the Veneti*) Naves totae factae sunt ex robore (*oak*) ad quamvis vim perferendam.
Galli omnes lingua, institutis, legibus inter se differunt.

---

[1] **Ecquis** = *num quis* in use and meaning. You need not use it.

Exercise 52A

1. Sometimes both the consuls have been absent from the city at the same time.
2. After advancing some miles from there, they halted.
3. Perhaps someone will blame my boldness.
4. For numerous reasons we must return to the same place.
5. Some of those present said one thing, and some another.
6. If any danger threatens, each man will defend his own home.
7. All the bravest soldiers have been wounded already.
8. If anyone asks for a gift, I shall refuse to give him anything.
9. After losing some ships, the enemy ceased fighting.
10. The judge prefers to hear some of the witnesses to-day, and others to-morrow.

Exercise 52B

1. When the work was finished the workmen were sent away each to his own city.
2. Someone or other has declared that the same soul is at one time that of a man, at another that of a bird or a fish.
3. I hoped to meet a certain friend of mine at noon.
4. How greatly courage and rashness differ from each other!
5. Although I am speaking to you in Latin, answer in any language.
6. Unless anyone tries to hinder us from escaping, we shall soon be free.
7. After travelling some part of the journey, owing to the heat they decided to stop for some days.
8. A poet has written that one should gladly die for one's country.
9. The scouts, when asked whether they had seen any natives in the village, replied that they had observed some from afar.
10. Scarcely one in ten of the citizens has enough determination to withstand a long siege.

53

WHOEVER, WHENEVER, WHEREVER

531. Indefinite relative clauses and indefinite adverb clauses (introduced in English by *whoever, whenever, wherever, &c.*) are often called '*ever*-clauses'.

532. In Latin, *ever*-clauses have a distinctive tense pattern, which marks them off clearly from ordinary relative or adverb clauses, even when the same words introduce them. This tense pattern has already been explained in dealing with *cum* (§ 464). The *main* verb is naturally of an *imperfect* type (*i.e.* present, future simple, or imperfect) to denote repeated action. The verb in the *subordinate* clause—unless the sense definitely forbids—will be in the corresponding *perfect-stem* tense (*i.e.* perfect, future-perfect or pluperfect).

> *Whatever he threatens, he will carry out*
> Quidquid **minatus erit**, (id) **efficiet**

> *Whenever he saw me, he asked me if I was well*
> Quotiens (cum) me **viderat**, me **rogabat** num **valerem**

533. A list of the indefinite relative words is in § 522. But observe that it is not *necessary* to express the *ever*:

> Instead of *quicumque* (*quisquis*), **qui** may be used
> ,, ,, *ubicumque* **ubi** ,, ,, ,,
> ,, ,, *quotienscumque*, **quotiens** or **cum**

The tenses of the verbs reveal the indefinite meaning:

> Quod **minatus erat**, id **efficiebat**

*534. *Any* in an *ever*-clause is translated by **quisque:**

> *Whatever anyone has, others desire*
> Quod **quisque** habet, id alii cupiunt

*535. *Ever* words may also be translated by **si quis, si quando,** &c. The sense of *if* is then quite forgotten.

Let whoever is present be favourable Si quis adest, faveat

536. Beware of thinking, 'Indefinite, therefore subjunctive'. In Latin any such idea would be fatally misleading. The verb in an *ever*-clause (unless sub-oblique) is always indicative.[1]

537. For *however* followed by adj. or adv. (with concessive meaning: *e.g.* However hard you work, you will fail), see § 564.

538. Quotations to study:

Quotiens quaeque cohors procucurrerat, ab ea parte magnus hostium numerus cadebat.
(*The Gauls ensure speedy mobilization*) Qui ex eis novissimus convēnit, in conspectu multitudinis omnibus cruciatibus (*tortures*) affectus necatur.
(*Cicero reassures his brother*) Quoscumque de te queri audivi, quacumque potui ratione, placavi (*won over*).
Cum rosam viderat, tum incipere ver arbitrabatur.
(*A bad provincial official*) Quacumque iter fecit, eius modi fuit, non ut legatus populi Romani, sed ut quaedam[2] calamitas pervadere videretur.

---

[1] Livy, however, and later writers do use the 'indefinite subjunctive'. But this departure from the rules given above should not be imitated. The same remark applies to their use of the subjunctive (in sentences where Caesar and Cicero would have used the indicative) after *donec*, *prius quam*, and *si*. Part of the reason is the influence of Greek style and syntax on these writers—so that they tended to 'write Greek grammar in Latin words'.

[2] *Quaedam calamitas* here does not mean 'a certain disaster' but 'a sort of disaster' or 'a disaster, so to speak'. When, in Latin, a noun is used in a bold or metaphorical way, it is common to apologize, as it were, for the expression, to tone down the boldness by saying 'what I might call . . .' This is often done with *quidam*; the adverbs *quasi*, *tamquam*, and *velut* are also used for the same purpose, *e.g.*:

Ipsam iracundiam fortitudinis quasi cotem esse dicebant
They used to say that anger itself was the whetstone of courage

Exercise 53A

1. Whoever saw the beast used to try to kill it.
2. Whenever he ploughs this field, the farmer will find bones and weapons.
3. Whoever wrote that book does not seem to be skilled in sailing.
4. They used to give corn to everyone who asked for it.[1]
5. Whenever your friends meet me, they ask me where you are.
6. Whatever you do, you cannot alter the will of the gods.
7. Wherever Caesar went, a large crowd of men welcomed him.
8. However[2] you relate the story, few will believe you.
9. Wherever I go, I eat the food of that region.
10. Whatever he orders, we ought to do it willingly.

Exercise 53B

1. Whenever the enemy attacked the vanguard, they were repulsed with heavy losses.
2. I know that you will gladly give whatever you can.
3. He warned all whom he saw to disregard the many false rumours which we heard during[3] those days.
4. Whenever a storm gets up, several ships are driven ashore along this coast.
5. Whatever you think, you may express your opinion without fear.
6. All whom I have heard complaining, I have helped in whatever way I could.
7. They are so foolish that they believe whatever they read.
8. I will give a reward to whoever gives the best answer.
9. Enter the city by any gate; for by whatever road you go you will reach the same spot.
10. Whenever he reached home safely, he gave thanks to the immortal gods.

[1] The relative clause should be put first in Latin.
[2] Say 'in whatever way'.   [3] *per*

54

ABLATIVE USES (II). REVISION (49-53)

541. An ABLATIVE OF MANNER consists of *noun + adjective*: *e.g.* magnā diligentiā; eodem modo; magnā vōce.[1]

The preposition **cum** must be used:

(*a*) if there is no adjective: *e.g.* cum diligentia;
(*b*) if the noun is not abstract: *e.g.* multis cum lacrimis.

542. A few nouns are used alone, without *cum*, as ablatives of manner. Those in commonest use are:

cāsu *by chance*	silentio *in silence*
fortĕ *by chance*	vi *by force*
iūrĕ *rightfully*	vi et armis *by armed force*
iniuriā *wrongfully*	

543. An ABLATIVE OF SEPARATION is used with these words; no preposition is needed[2]:

DEPRIVING	FREEING
spolio (1) *I rob*	lībero (1) *I free, I release*
nūdo (1) *I strip*	līber (adj.) *free*

LACKING	CEASING AND PREVENTING
careo (2) *I lack*	dēsisto, -ĕre, destiti, — *I cease*
egeo (2) *I lack, need*	prōhibeo (2) *I prevent, cut off*
vaco (1) *I am free of*[3]	intercludo (3) *I cut off*

N.B. *I resign my consulship* Me consulatu abdĭco (1)

Caesar had cut off his opponents from their supplies
Caesar **re frumentaria** adversarios intercluserat

---

[1] A genitive may replace the adj.: *e.g.* Romanorum more.

[2] A preposition would not be incorrect with words of *freeing*; and words denoting *motion from*, and containing the prefixes *ab*, *de* and *ex*, may be used with or without a preposition.

[3] Contrast *vaco* + dat.: *I have leisure for rest* quieti vaco (§ 254).

Exercise 54A

1. We surrounded the enemy in silence and cut them off from the shore.
2. Without declaring war, the Germans suddenly invaded the territory of the Gauls.
3. They no longer lacked stones with which to repair the bridge.
4. Fabius was not prevented by old age from commanding a huge army.
5. Citizens, you have twice been unjustly robbed of your lands.
6. I cannot help hoping that you are making a mistake.
7. Whatever he says, there is no doubt that few will believe him.
8. So far from writing every day, you rarely send me any message.
9. The dictator resigned his magistracy on the eighth day.
10. I have read the works of all the best poets.
11. If anything were to prevent you from marrying him, we should be sorry.
12. We were afraid that we might be hindered by the snow from reaching the top of the mountain.
13. Since all were present at the dinner, can anyone be free from suspicion?
14. There was hardly anyone who did not support us.
15. Every man thinks his own country the most beautiful.
16. Some of the natives lacked skill, others courage; so that they could not resist the charge of the legions.
17. I let no day go by without praying the gods to protect you.
18. We intend to attack the citadel by armed force at daybreak.
19. Someone or other has entered the garden without my orders.
20. The warships were very nearly sunk by the force of the wind.

Exercise 54B

1. After suffering some casualties, the enemy abandoned the assault towards nightfall.
2. With the greatest difficulty they were restrained from avenging the wrong by force.
3. All the best citizens are hindered by fear of this[1] from taking part in politics.
4. If I were to tell you what I have done, you would rightly be angry with me.
5. So far from becoming more powerful, the tribunes do not even keep their ancient rights.
6. Fearing that their allies would revolt, the Athenians gradually deprived them of their liberty.
7. What prevents Caesar from enrolling as many legions as Pompey has?
8. On one day in seven the city dwellers delight to roam in the country.
9. There is no doubt that the defendant has already committed many most serious crimes.
10. Was it not the fault of a few wicked jurors that he was not convicted last year?
11. Caesar came to the help of whatever ships he saw to be in difficulties.
12. It is impossible that you have not realized my goodwill towards them.[2]
13. It is one thing, it seems, to promise, and another to keep your word.
14. At the beginning of spring, both sides left their winter quarters and made all preparations for renewing the war.
15. Instead of helping me, you have done all you could[3] to hinder the work.

[1] *fear of this:* hic metus (similarly for *anger at this, &c.*).

[2] See *p.* 155, *n.* 2.

[3] Observe these expressions, either of which could be used here: *I do my best to:* operam do ut . . .; nihil non facio ut . . .

55

CAUSAL CLAUSES

Adverb clauses of reason (**causal clauses**) employ these conjunctions

>   quod, quia   *because*
>   cum (+ subjunc.)   *since, as*
>   quoniam   *inasmuch as, since*

Quod and *quia* are similar in meaning, but *quod* is much the commoner. *Quoniam* and *cum* are similar in meaning; *cum* is much the commoner. *Cum*-clauses with causal meaning have already been explained in §§ 461, 466; what follows does not apply to them.

552. The verb in a causal clause is normally indicative. It is, of course, *subjunctive* if the clause is *sub-oblique*. It is also subjunctive if the clause is *virtually sub-oblique*—i.e. dependent on words which *imply* reported speech or thought. Compare these sentences:

(i) *Caesar punished the soldiers because they had fought badly*
    Caesar milites punivit quod male **pugnaverant**

This gives the reason as a plain fact.

(ii) *Caesar punished the soldiers because (he said) they had fought badly*
     (or for having fought badly)
     Caesar milites punivit quod male **pugnavissent**

Here the writer is saying, in effect, 'I am quoting Caesar's reason, but I accept no responsibility for its truth. It may be true, or not, but that is what was in his mind.' This kind of clause is called an *alleged reason*. Notice carefully the English equivalent, *for having done it*. Such a clause is, naturally, common with verbs of accusing, complaining, blaming, *&c.*

> *He accused them of failure to support him*
> Eos accusavit quod sibi non subvenissent

172

553. A reason may be mentioned only to deny that it is true. This *rejected reason* will have its verb in the subjunctive.[1] It usually starts with **non quod,** or **non quo.** If the true reason follows, that begins with **sed quia.**

He stayed at home, not because he was ill, but because I did
Domi mansit, non quod aeger esset, sed quia ego mansi.

554. A *relative clause* can have causal meaning. It will show its adverbial nature by having a subjunctive verb.

The enemy, since they were unaware (or *being unaware*) *of Caesar's approach, crossed the river*
Hostes, **qui adventum Caesaris ignorarent,** flumen transierunt

N.B. (i) In a causal rel. clause, **quippe** is often placed before the relative;

(ii) An English relative clause may imply a causal idea, and if so it should be translated accordingly:

The consul, who had been forewarned, was on the look-out for this
Consul, **quippe qui praemonitus esset,** haec exspectabat

*****555.** Sometimes the emphasis is on the *reason*, not on the main clause. This is shown by **ideo quod, idcirco quod.**

It is because you are just that I praise you
Ideo te laudo quod iustus es

*****556.** Quod is used in some expressions where English has not *because* but *that.* Note especially:

(i) gaudeo quod ... *I am glad that*; doleo quod ... *I am sorry that*; aegre fero quod ... *I am annoyed that.*[2]

(ii) (Huc) accedit quod ... *there is the further fact that.*[3]

---

[1] If the reason were true in itself, but rejected as *irrelevant*, the subjunctive would *not* be used.

[2] Also miror quod ... *I am surprised that;* queror quod ... (+ subjunctive) *I complain that.* With *all* these, the acc. and inf. is commoner than a *quod* clause.

[3] This and similar *quod* clauses are really noun clauses, not adverb clauses; but it is convenient to mention them here, especially as no sharp line can be drawn.

557. SUMMARY—CAUSAL CLAUSES

With **quod, quia** (*because*), **quoniam** (*since*)—indicative.
With **cum** or **qui** used causally—subjunctive.
For *alleged reason*—**quod** + subjunctive.
For *rejected reason*—**non quod** or **non quo** + subjunctive.

558. Quotations to study:

Tum demum Titurius, qui nihil ante providisset, trepidare et concursare (*bustle*) cohortesque timide disponere.

Pugiles (*boxers*) ingemescunt (*grunt*), non quod doleant, sed quia profundenda voce omne corpus intenditur (*is tensed*) venitque plaga (*blow*) vehementior.

Tacent idcirco quia periculum vitant.

Mirari se aiebat (*said*), quod non rideret haruspex (*soothsayer*), haruspicem cum vidisset.

Multis de causis Caesar statuit sibi Rhenum esse transeundum; quarum illa fuit iustissima quod[1] Germanos ... timere voluit, cum intellegerent et posse et audere populi Romani exercitum Rhenum transire. Accessit etiam quod pars equitatus ... se trans Rhenum in fines Sugambrorum receperat seque cum eis coniunxerat.

Exercise 55A

1. The consul condemned his own son to death for having taken part in the conspiracy.
2. The guards, who had been awake all night, were tired.
3. I have come home not because I wish to see my mother but because I have no money.
4. The master was glad because his pupils had sung well.
5. The master praised the pupils for having sung so well.
6. The citizens, being unwilling to allow[2] Catiline to become consul, elected Cicero.

---

[1] This *quod*-clause, standing in apposition to *illa* (*causa*), is a noun clause of the type mentioned in § 556 (ii).
[2] Not needed in the Latin.

7. We have been unjustly blamed for deserting you in such a crisis.
8. I am very glad that your luck has changed.[1]
9. I blame you for having spoken thus, and I shall not easily forgive you.
10. As they foresaw that the lion would come down to the river, they decided to wait for him by the bank.

Exercise 55B

1. The infantry blamed the cavalry for allowing the enemy to cut them off from their camp.
2. There was the further fact that whatever corn there had been in the town had already been used up.
3. The boy was accused of theft, not because he had been seen in the orchard, but because he was ill on the following day.
4. Cicero, being anxious to return to Rome at the earliest possible moment, was waiting for a chance to sail.
5. At the beginning of winter, since the campaign against[2] the Gauls was already finished, Caesar led his troops into winter quarters.
6. The nobles were jealous of Augustus because he had taken their privileges away from them.
7. Since you have heard, jurymen, the speeches of both men, you can judge which has the juster case.
8. Pompey complained that the senators wished to decide each for himself what to do.
9. Many men thought that C. Gracchus deserved to die because he had tried to give citizenship to the allies.
10. I blame you for failing to arrive in time; I was unwise to[3] rely on you.

---

[1] *Muto* is always transitive: use its *passive* forms to translate the English intr. use. The same applies to *verto* (I turn), *moveo* (I move), *frango* (I break), *augeo* (I increase), *mergo* (I sink), &c.
[2] *bellum* with a dependent gen.   [3] Causal rel. clause.

56

CONCESSIVE CLAUSES

561. In an adverb clause of concession, what is conceded may be (*a*) a **fact** (*Although you are wrong*, I shall vote for you) or (*b*) a **possibility, a notion** (*Even though you were wrong* I should vote for you).

562. CONCESSIONS OF FACT. The conjunctions used are:

quamquam, etsi,[1] tametsi (all with indic.)
cum (with subjunc.—§ 461)

After a concessive clause, the main clause often starts with **tamen**. This is specially useful with *cum*, to define its meaning; but owing to the Latin fondness for 'signpost words', it is frequent whatever conjunction is used.

The Romans, though exhausted by the march, formed up for battle
Romani, **quamquam itinere fessi erant,** tamen aciem instruxerunt

563. CONCESSIONS OF POSSIBILITY. The Latin conjunctions are **etsi** and **etiam si** just as English uses *even if* (sometimes *even though*). In origin the clause is clearly a subjunctive condition, and it is easiest to treat it in that way.

Though (Even if) we escaped from here we should die of hunger
Etiam si hinc effugiamus, fame pereamus

564. HOWEVER. The concessive *however* with an adj. or adverb (*e.g. however long you wait* . . .) is translated by **quamvis**. The verb is subjunctive.

However hard you work, you will not finish the task in time
Quamvis strenue labores,[2] non ad tempus opus conficies

---

[1] In origin, clearly, **etsi** = *even if*. But, when used with an indicative, it has acquired the sense of *although*.

[2] Literally, 'you may work how hard you like, . . .' The same Latin would translate 'Though you may work hard . . .' But it is safer not to use *quamvis* unless it has an adj. or adv. to qualify.

*565. Another way to translate *even though* (a concession of possibility) is to use the impersonal verb **licet** as a conjunction, followed by a subjunctive (in any tense). (Similarly in English we may say *Granted that* you are right . . .)

Even though we all work, we shall never finish the task
Licet omnes laboremus, numquam opus conficiemus

566. A *relative clause* may have concessive meaning. Its verb will be subjunctive.[1]

Although Caesar suspected that, he released the hostages
Caesar, **qui illud suspicaretur,** tamen obsides dimisit

567. SUMMARY—CONCESSIVE CLAUSES

Indic. concedes *facts*: 'although it is so': **quamquam, etsi.**
Subjunc. concedes *possibilities*: 'even if it were so': **etsi, etiamsi;** also **licet.**
However: **quamvis** (+ adj. or adv.) with subjunc.
With **cum** or **qui** used concessively, subjunc.

568. Quotations to study:

Pecuniosus homo, quamvis sit nocens, damnari non potest.
Id tulit graviter Indutiomarus, et, qui iam ante inimico in nos animo fuisset, multo gravius hoc dolore (*grievance*) exarsit (*burned with anger*).
At Caesar, etsi nondum eorum consilia cognoverat, tamen fore id quod accidit suspicabatur.
Quoniam quidem semel causam suscepi, licet undique omnes immineant terrores, succurram atque subibo.

---

[1] We have now met all the possible meanings of a relative clause with a subjunctive verb. These are:
FINAL relative clauses (*ch.* 27);
CONSECUTIVE relative clauses (*ch.* 28);
CAUSAL relative clauses (§ 554);
CONCESSIVE relative clauses (§ 566).
And, of course, a relative clause, like any other subordinate clause, has a subjunctive verb if it is sub-oblique. But this is not due to *meaning*.

Exercise 56A

1. Although Hannibal routed the Romans again and again, he was defeated in the last battle.
2. Though not large, the island of Delos is very beautiful.
3. However beautiful it is, the tree must be cut down.
4. Even if the journey were shorter, we should not promise to come.
5. However short the journey is, we shall be tired, owing to the heat.
6. Even though we had sent for a doctor at once, he would have come in vain.
7. However quickly they march, they will arrive too late.
8. My father, though[1] he had been born poor, was held in honour by all his fellow citizens.
9. Even if I called the dog myself, he would not follow me.
10. Although Caesar was warned of the plot, he determined to go to the senate-house.

Exercise 56B

1. I should not believe you even if you gave the same promise a hundred times.
2. However often you threaten to punish us, we shall always tell the truth.
3. Though already an old man, Cicero did all in his power to oppose Antony's designs.
4. Though we had neither bread nor weapons left, we preferred death to surrender.
5. Though we had neither bread nor weapons left, we should fight to the last.
6. However well he has served us, I refuse to let him marry my daughter.
7. Even though you may have read the books of famous philosophers, you do not know everything.
8. Although it seemed that I was the only survivor[2], I was not downcast.

[1] Use a rel. clause.   [2] Use the verb *superesse*.

57

CONDITIONS: FURTHER POINTS

A. COULD HAVE, OUGHT TO HAVE, SHOULD HAVE

571. *I could have gone* is in Latin **ire potui**

I ought to have gone
I should have gone[1] } ...... { **ire debui**
me ire oportuit
mihi eundum fuit

In English a *perfect* infin. is used; but in Latin the infin. (where used) is *present*, and the finite verb is perfect indic.

The war should not have been begun Non suscipi bellum oportuit

572. Such expressions sometimes form the main clause of a condition. Instead of saying *If he had done this he* would *have been punished* (a normal subjunctive condition), we may say *If he had done this he* could *have been punished, he* might *have been punished, he* ought *to have been punished.* So in Latin:

Id si fecisset, puniri **debuit** (puniendus **fuit**)
Id si fecisset, puniri eum **oportuit**
Id si fecisset, puniri **potuit**

These sentences seem to break the rule that the subjunctive must be used in *both* clauses; but the spirit of the rule is kept, for these 'modal' verbs have the same sort of meaning in themselves as the subjunctive mood has—the *possibility* or *notion* of the action, as opposed to the action itself.

B. TO SEE IF, IN CASE

573. He waited *to see if they would come* (*in case they came*)
Exspectavit **si venirent**

They fought hard *in the hope of winning*
Strenue pugnaverunt **si forte vincere possent**

---

[1] Distinguish carefully between the *should* of obligation (*should* in all persons) and the *should* of subjunctive conditions (1st person only: 2nd and 3rd person form, *would*).

A *final* subjunctive (therefore present or imperfect only), introduced by **si** or **si forte**, translates *to see if, in case, in the hope that*. It is commonest after *exspecto* and *conor*.

C. THAN IF, AS IF [1]

574. There are many variations possible, but the following are among the commonest expressions, and will suffice:

(*a*) where si is used[2]:

We are here earlier than if we had walked
Maturius adsumus **quam si pedibus venissemus**

We are here as soon as if we had started with you
Tam mature adsumus **quam si tecum profecti essemus**

You are shouting just as if I were deaf
Clamas **perinde ac si surdus essem**

By inserting, mentally, the implied main clause of the condition (*e.g.* you are shouting just as *you would shout* if I were deaf), it is easy to find the correct tense of the subjunctive, according to the rule given in § 441.

(*b*) where *si* is not used, *as if* being rendered by **tamquam, quasi**: the tense rule is different:

You are shouting as if I were deaf
Clamas **quasi (tamquam) surdus sim**

Use *present* or *perfect* subjunctive in primary sequence, *imperfect* or *pluperfect* subjunctive in historic sequence.

575. Quotations to study:

Helvetii, saepius si perrumpere possent conati, telis repulsi hoc conatu destiterunt.

Deleri totus exercitus potuit, si fugientes persecuti victores essent.

(*Absence of news*) Tamquam enim clausa sit Asia, sic nihil perfertur ad nos praeter rumores.

---

[1] Introducing clauses of 'conditional comparison'.
[2] Usually in: quam si (*than if*); tam ... quam si (*as ... as if*); idem ac si; perinde ac si (*just as if*); tamquam si, velut si (*as if*).

Exercise 57A

1. You ought to have told me at once what you suspected.
2. They waited all night in the hope of hearing news of victory.
3. Are we not more fortunate than if we had been defeated by the Germans?
4. If the reinforcements had been sent in time, the citadel could have been captured.
5. You are leaning on a stick as if you were ill. (*2 ways.*)
6. We might have sold these oxen for a higher price if we had wished to.
7. The dog followed me here just as if I were its master. (*2 ways.*)
8. The boys were as tired as if they had run five miles.

Exercise 57B

1. The young Cicero wrote a letter to his father in the hope that he would send more money.
2. It would be[1] tedious to tell what took place that day.
3. You are speaking to me as if you were addressing a public meeting.
4. They ought to have waited in case anyone needed help.
5. The thieves entered the house as easily as if the door had been wide open.
6. Caesar sent five cohorts and attempted to occupy the hill, if possible, before the enemy observed it.
7. You ought to have been given a larger reward, even if you have returned without success.
8. By crossing the mountains, we have reached here two days sooner than if we had travelled by sea.
9. It would have been better[2] to confess that you did your best to cheat me.
10. You pretend to be innocent—just as if[3] we did not all know what you have done!

---

[1] Latin says *it is tedious*: **longum est.**
[2] Here too Latin uses the indic.: **melius fuit.**
[3] *quasi vero* expresses the irony.

58

ORATIO OBLIQUA (I)

581. Consider this extract from an imaginary speech:

ORIGINAL WORDS	REPORTED FORM
'... I have myself led you to this point unscathed: do you not consider my plan a good one? Therefore do not hang back, but obey me; to-morrow we shall triumph. Are our opponents better than we? ...'	... He had himself led them to that point unscathed: did they not consider his plan a good one? So let them not hang back, but obey him; the next day they would triumph. Were their opponents better than they? ...

582. We observe the following changes:

(*a*) all 1st and 2nd person words become 3rd person;
(*b*) all primary tenses of *finite* verbs become historic;
(*c*) all words of *this* and *now* type become words of *that* and *then* type.

These changes apply equally to Latin, and work out thus:

(*a*) me, nos > se[1]; meus, noster > suus;
    tu, vos > ille, illi[2]; tuus, vester > illius, illorum

(*b*) Primary finite verbs change their tense as follows:

Pres. > Imperf. (*I am going:* eo > *he was going:* iret)
Perf. > Pluperf. (*I have gone:* ivi > *he had gone:* ivisset)
Fut. > Fut.-in-the-past: (*I shall go:* ibo > *he would go:* iturus esset)[3]

Imperfect and Pluperfect, being historic, remain.

---

[1] Pronouns not expressed in the original speech need not be put in, *except* that the acc. subject of a reported statement *must* be put in (§ 74). Emphatic ego, nos > ipse, ipsi.

[2] As a *working* rule, use ille to represent original 2nd person, is to refer to original 3rd person.

[3] Of course this does not apply to verbs in main statements.

(*c*) hic > ille   iste > ille   nunc > tunc, tum
    hic (here) > ibi   istic > illic   hodie > eo die
    huc > eo   istuc > illuc   heri > pridie
    hinc > inde   istinc > illinc   cras > postridie

583. All speech consists of statements, commands, questions and exclamations. In reported speech, these take the form already familiar to us; only as they are not directly attached to a verb of saying, *no conjunction* is needed.

584. STATEMENTS become *acc. and inf.*; the acc. subject must be expressed:

'Ipse vos huc duxi'   Se ipsum illos eo duxisse

COMMANDS become *imperf. subjunc.*; negative adverb, **nē**.

'Mihi parete; nolite cunctari'   Sibi parerent; ne cunctarentur

585. QUESTIONS in speeches are usually rhetorical—that is, they are disguised statements. Questions in the 2nd person are more likely than others to be genuine questions requiring an answer; and in practice the rule in Latin is: Questions in the 2nd person become *subjunctive*; others are treated as statements, and become *acc. and inf.*

'Cur cunctamini? Nonne   Cur cunctarentur? Nonne
    omnia parata sunt? Num   omnia parata esse? Num
    timetis?'   timerent?

EXCLAMATIONS also are vivid forms of statement, and accordingly are represented by *acc. and inf.*

586. This passage illustrates the changes described:

ORATIO RECTA	ORATIO OBLIQUA
'... Ipse vos incolumes huc duxi: nonne consilium meum bonum putatis? Proinde nolite cunctari; mihi parete; cras victoriam habebimus. Num hostes superiores sunt?'	Se ipsum illos incolumes eo duxisse: nonne consilium suum bonum putarent? Proinde ne cunctarentur; sibi parerent; postridie victoriam se habituros. Num hostes superiores esse?

*587. **Se** and **suus** may quite correctly be used to refer to the subject of their own clause, and not to the speaker, as long as there is no risk of ambiguity:

'In *vestra* oppida *vos* recipite'   In *sua* oppida *se* reciperent

The use of **ipse** for an emphatic 1st person (*cf.* § 582, *n.* 1) is not confined to the nominative. It may replace *se* in any other case, when emphasis is needed.

> *Under his* ('my') *leadership they had fought and won*
> Ipso duce proelium secundum factum esse

*588. In these quotations illustrating the use of *se* and *ipse*, the English is given in direct speech form:

'*Send me one of your men*'   E suis aliquem ad se mitteret

'*No one ever fought with me except to his own undoing*'
Neminem secum sine sua pernicie contendisse

'*Do not either overrate your own courage or despise us*'
Ne aut suae virtuti tribueret aut ipsos despiceret[1]

589. You will often find in Latin authors (notably Caesar) reported speech introduced by a verb in the present tense. The finite verbs then remain primary: the changes named in § 582 (*b*) do not take place. But in working exercises, always assume that the verb introducing the speech would have been in the perfect tense, *e.g.* dixit, respondit.

Exercise 58A

Translate first as direct speech, then as reported speech[2]:

1. I have saved you. Give me a reward.
2. They have saved you. Give them a reward.
3. You have saved me. Receive this reward.
4. Do not reveal my plans to the enemy. I shall punish all traitors with death. Why are you trying to desert?

[1] Here the use of *ipse* for the speaker makes *suae* unambiguous.
[2] Refer to § 589. *N.B.* There is no need to write down the *dixit*.

5. Does anyone believe them? They promise everything, (but) perform nothing. Do not follow such men.

Turn into reported speech:

6. Omnis regio in armis est; Germani Rhenum transierunt. Nolite auxilium a Romanis sperare.
7. Contemnite minas eius; nam neque vobis neque amicis vestris nocere conabitur.
8. Mihi confide: quae causa timoris est? Ego te periculo isto liberabo.
9. Domum statim regredere: cur tam sero huc profectus es?
10. Cur igitur arma habetis? Ferro via facienda est: sequimini me, nam hodie aut vincemus aut moriemur.

Exercise 58B

Translate first as direct speech, then as reported speech:

1. The moon is rising. Is everything ready for the journey? Open the door, and do not arouse the others.
2. By this battle the war will be ended. Fight bravely; by *your* courage (and) *my* strategy the enemy will be beaten.
3. Acquit the defendant: has he not been punished enough already? He repents of his crime; I feel sorry for him.
4. Let all good citizens support me. I wish to become consul this year: do I not seem worthy of this honour?

Turn into reported speech:

5. Has naves reficiendas curate. Quomodo enim domum regredi poterimus?[1] Hoc opus statim suscipiendum est.
6. Trans flumen vos recipite: interim ego pontem meis copiis defendam. Cur hic manere mavultis?
7. Omnia ista cras reddite mihi: quid enim furto turpius esse potest? Huius diei pudere vos oportet.
8. Cur, me petente, tu consulatum petere ausus es? Nam mea gens quam tua nobilior est; nec decet te, talem virum, mecum de honoribus contendere.

[1] There is no fut. infin. of *possum*. The present infin. generally conveys the meaning with sufficient clearness.

59

ORATIO OBLIQUA (II): SUBORDINATE CLAUSES

591. Subordinate clauses which are part of reported speech are called *suboblique clauses*.[1] Their verbs are *always subjunctive*, whatever the kind of clause. (But of course an acc. and inf. which becomes suboblique remains acc. and inf.)

DIRECT SPEECH: 'Da mihi libros quos emisti'
REPORTED: Eum iussit sibi libros dare quos **emisset**

592. The rules for change of tense have been given in § 582 (*b*). But in *if* and *when* clauses, an original *future* becomes *imperf. subjunc.*, and an original *future-perfect* becomes *pluperf. subjunc.*

DIRECT SPEECH: 'Si fortiter **pugnaveritis**, hostes vincetis'
REPORTED: Eos, si fortiter **pugnavissent**, hostes victuros

593. Suboblique clauses depend on reported statements, commands or questions, or on any other kind of clause that implies *thought* or *idea*—e.g. a final or fear clause.

He was afraid of losing the money *which he had found*
Timebat ne pecuniam, **quam invenisset**, amitteret

594. They may even depend directly on the *main* verb if it is one which *implies speech or thought* (*e.g. praise, blame, accuse, promise*):

He promised a reward to the man who arrived first
Praemium pollicitus est ei qui primus **venisset**

Such clauses are called *virtually suboblique*; clauses of alleged reason (§ 552) are of this kind.

---

[1] Occasionally a relative clause is inserted into reported speech to explain some word, although it was not part of the original speech. It is then not suboblique, and its verb is indic.

'Da mihi istos libros' Libros, **quos in manu habebat**, sibi daret

*595. A clause may be virtually suboblique if it makes a statement for which the writer wants to make someone else responsible:

He showed me the house which (so he said) he had just bought
Aedes mihi monstravit **quas nuperrime emisset**

*596. CONDITIONS IN REPORTED SPEECH. The rules already given cover conditional clauses, and no more need be said about the *subordinate clause* in a condition sentence.

The *main clause* of an *indicative* condition presents no difficulty; it is not affected by what depends on it.

The only problem, therefore, is the *main clause* in a *subjunctive* condition—that is, the clause with *would* in it. In a *reported statement*[1] it must become acc. and inf.

A present subjunc. (referring to *future* time) is represented by a *future* infin.

'*I should be glad if he came*' 'Gaudeam si veniat'
... *he would be glad if he came* ... se **gavisurum si veniret**

Both the other tenses are represented by future participle + *fuisse*:

'*He would be here if he were well*' 'Adesset si valeret'
... *he would be there if he were well* ... eum, si valeret, **adfuturum fuisse**
'*He would have come if I had called*' 'Venisset si clamassem'
... *he would have come if he had called* ... eum, si clamasset, **venturum fuisse**

It is helpful to remember that, in *past* time, *would have* becomes *was going to*.

*597. Just as *facturum esse* may be replaced by its equivalent **fore ut** + subjunctive (§ 225), so *facturum fuisse* may be re-

---

[1] The expression of these clauses in reported questions, and in consecutive and other subordinate clauses, is not dealt with in this book.

placed by **futurum fuisse ut** + subjunctive. In the *passive voice* this is the only way of dealing with an original imperfect or pluperfect subjunctive.

> *They thought that the city would have been lost*
> Existimabant futurum fuisse ut urbs amitteretur

598. Quotations to study:

Ei legationi Ariovistus respondit: si quid ipsi a Caesare opus esset, sese ad eum venturum fuisse.

Ad haec Caesar respondit: se civitatem conservaturum, si, prius quam murum aries (*battering ram*) attigisset, se dedidissent.

Caesarem profectum in Italiam; neque aliter Carnutes interficiendi Tasgeti consilium fuisse capturos, neque Eburones, si ille adesset, ad castra venturos esse.

Hoc video, dum breviter voluerim dicere, dictum esse a me paullo obscurius.

Exercise 59A

Turn into reported speech:

1. Si vis ludos spectare, veni mecum hodie. Nonne felices sumus, quod otium habemus?
2. Cum regressus ero, cenabimus. Servos iube nobis cenam parare tam splendidam quam nulla ante fuit.
3. Cur e theatro disceditis? Num fabula, quam spectatis, vobis displicet? Usque ad finem manete, ut totam rem intellegatis.
4. Si haec dixi, me paenitet. Cur ea meministi quae vino adductus locutus sum? Noli cuiquam dicere quae heri audivisti.
5. Hoc supremum erit proelium: pugnate hodie fortiter, ut semper pugnavistis. Posthac vobis praemia dabo, quae pollicitus sum.
6. Si pecuniam hodie acceperimus, haec cras ememus. Mittamus nuntium qui eam pecuniam postulet. Cur cunctamini? Occasio, quam saepe petivimus, adest.

Turn into direct speech:

7. Quid faceret, quid exspectaret? Properandum esse, si vellet ad tempus eo pervenire quo irent.
8. Ne sibi irasceretur, quamquam id de industria fecisset: nam illum, cum reliqua audivisset, risurum esse.
9. Eo die se extremam partem cibi, quem secum portavissent, consumpturos: quid postridie facerent, aut quo irent? Si quis haberet quod diceret, ne cunctaretur.
10. Se illum sub eadem arbore postridie exspectaturam, et magnum dolorem sensuram nisi ille solita hora venisset. Cur tam diu nihil scripsisset?

Exercise 59B

Turn into reported speech:

1. Cur animo demisso estis? Mittite legatos qui indutias petant; nam si id feceritis, magna spes pacis erit.
2. Quod petitis nihil est; nonne cognovistis me in alios clementem esse? Et hoc et multo maiora, si vultis, libenter dabo.
3. Ego adsum; si culpa in me est, poenas a me sumite; si in civibus est, precor ne quis deorum vos puniat.
4. Oramus ut nobis parcas. Non nostra sponte bellum suscepimus, sed a sociis coacti. Noli nos hostium numero habere.
5. Heri, nisi aeger fuissem, cenatum apud te venissem. Peto ut mihi ignoscas; nam medicus me domo exire vetuit. Cum convaluero, te certiorem faciam.

Turn into direct speech:

6. Quid crederent hostibus in animo esse? Conari eos se cogere castra eo loco ponere ubi nihil aquae esset. Si id facerent, totum exercitum siti periturum esse.
7. Sese non illi auxilio venturum, quamquam in periculo esset; itaque, si qua fuisset facultas, ad se cum omnibus copiis veniret.
8. Si qua fuisset facultas, se illi auxilio venturum fuisse; sed equites se misisse, qui hostium iter impedirent.

60

GENERAL REVISION EXERCISES

Exercise 60A

1. I have tried in vain to find out where he has gone.
2. After hurling a volley of javelins, the infantry charged the enemy's centre.
3. No one is worthy of greater honour than this poet.
4. When he secured a favourable wind, Caesar set sail.
5. In his old age, he returned to the city where he had been born.
6. At the beginning of spring the ships began to be launched.
7. Making a sortie by another gate, the townsmen took our men by surprise.
8. My brothers and I[1] have promised to obey our father.
9. It was reported to Galba that very many of the citizens hated Nero.
10. The deserter begged us with many tears not to hand him over to his foes.

* * *

11. This being the case, we must leave Rome in three days.
12. It is foolish to value eloquence more highly than wisdom.
13. The man who is content with his lot never complains.
14. It is said that Caesar is hated by those whom he has recently pardoned.
15. I have been fishing for two hours and caught nothing.
16. The patrols were prevented from advancing farther by a river ten feet deep.
17. I built my new house here so that the journey should be shorter.
18. Unwillingly the exiles swore never to try to return.
19. You do not wish me to sing the same songs again, do you?
20. I am inclined to think that he will not stay here long.

* * *

[1] See *p.* 94, *n.* 4.

21. He was warned not to lose the letter nor to give it to anyone on the way.
22. Not even the priest could tell us why the gods were angry with our state.
23. Whether he is ill or tired, he has written this letter so badly that I cannot read it.
24. Have you heard whether Cicero or Antonius has been elected consul?
25. It is one thing to ask, another to get what you ask for.[1]
26. Let us not neglect such a fortunate opportunity for making money!
27. I am afraid I must return before they close the gate.
28. You will be condemned to death, although it seems that you were wrongfully accused.
29. The centurion himself was the first to climb the wall.
30. It is most important to the whole nation that you alone should command the army.

* * *

31. Since they did not know the length of the journey, they were afraid to start towards nightfall.
32. If a man is himself unskilled in speaking, he readily believes whatever he hears.
33. Everything which will be useful for assaulting the city must be prepared at once.
34. Promising not to be away for more than three days, he left home alone ten days ago.
35. If only I had known that on the first of January!
36. While the cavalry were seizing this hill, a long and fierce battle was taking place on the plain.
37. If I were to find gold or silver in my garden, I should soon be able to free myself from debt.
38. We were silently approaching the harbour when the sentry happened to observe us.
39. After climbing to the top of the ridge, we saw how far away the coast was.
40. Your brother is not the man to waste time in talking.

* * *

[1] *to get what one asks for:* one word in Latin.

41. The majority of the slaves openly complained that they had not enough food.
42. If they had not asked me why I was hiding in the wood, I should not have told a lie.
43. After returning without success, they decided that they had better make another plan.
44. Since we had been so long without sleep, we were already worn out with toil.
45. He threatened to report to his master whatever we said.
46. The farther we advance from the camp, the more difficult the road becomes.
47. Do not draw your swords until the general gives the signal to advance.
48. Pity those whom you have injured by your crime.
49. However poor he is, if he has robbed his fellow-citizens of their property, he must not be spared.
50. Surely it matters more what we do than what we say?

* * *

51. Why are you behaving as if you were mad?
52. There are some who say it was your fault that we did not sell our house for a higher price.
53. If you do not obey me faithfully, I shall take all the money away from you.
54. The prisoners asked us for water because, they said, they had drunk nothing for some hours.
55. My captors could not help fearing that I should die.
56. I have sent you my speeches, not because they deserve to be read, but because you ought to know my opinion.
57. I never see your brother without noticing that he is very like you.
58. Let us use both oars and sails so as to reach the harbour more quickly.
59. It is impossible that anyone has escaped from here unknown to us.
60. The more I realize the violence of the enemy, the more I mistrust our own strength.

Exercise 60B

1. You were the only man to realise what I was trying to accomplish.
2. This valley is so narrow that we must draw up our battle-line half way up[1] the hill.
3. Whenever I approached the garden, I was induced to withdraw by the barking of several dogs.
4. Although suffering from a serious illness he has always carried out his duties very well.
5. We shall have to return home secretly by another route, to avoid being observed by the king's soldiers.
6. Let us send for a doctor to tell us how to cure you.
7. I shall be pleased to meet a man endowed with such great ability: be sure to tell him who I am.
8. He confesses that he joined the conspirators and did his best to overthrow the government.
9. The crowd of onlookers was a great hindrance to us in our attempts to put out the fire.
10. I would gladly resign my office, if anyone else seemed suitable to command the army.

* * *

11. I should be inclined to say that no-one in living memory served the state better than your father.
12. Next day, as soon as the slave woke him, he asked what the time was.
13. The snow was so deep on January 20th that we did not dare even to go out.
14. Whereas he pretended to favour the king, he was really eager to restore the republic.
15. So far from loving me, you have not sent me any presents for the last five years.
16. If the enemy wish to surrender, let them send envoys to beg for a truce.
17. Whenever I ask him whether he is ashamed of his acts, he always gives the same answer as he gave you.

[1] §411.

18. There can be no doubt that Marius' victories were the salvation of the Roman nation.
19. You must do everything I tell you, even if you find the work boring.
20. These recruits have been sent here to learn the art of fighting from us.

* * *

21. Relying on the goodwill of his soldiers, he intends to stand for the consulship at the next election.
22. I am sure that, now that the Aedui are subdued, no other tribe will resist us for long.
23. Although we have returned without obtaining our request, do not be downcast on that account.
24. Rarely has a man of such great daring been accused of a more terrible crime.
25. If all Romans had been like Cato, no-one would ever have laughed or played.
26. It was the farmers' custom to sell cheaply any slave that[1] was no longer useful.
27. Whenever I go into the country, I am anxious to return as soon as possible to my friends in the city.
28. The cohorts which had been left to guard the town were without weapons and supplies.
29. The wretched inhabitants of that region have to live in the tops of trees, in the manner of birds.
30. As soon as the news of the loss of the fleet reached Athens, a crowd gathered in the market place.

* * *

31. I shall not begin the work until he comes: for he ought to have promised to help us of his own accord.
32. Do you demand that I take an oath, as if I were a man whom you could not trust?
33. So far from considering his interests, his brother has always done his best to harm him.

---

[1] Use *si quis*.

34. We are vexed because we have less food than if we had been defeated in the war.
35. My son, if you are too proud to work, you ought to be ashamed to ask me for money.
36. We are unwilling to give corn to our neighbours, not because we wish them to die of hunger, but because we have not enough bread ourselves.
37. I told him that, if he had sent for me earlier, I should willingly have come to his aid.
38. However unlike our customs may be, there is little difference between our views.
39. I will help them in whatever way I can, although I am inclined to think it is all over with them.
40. Let us approach the city on the other side, in the hope that we may catch the sentries off their guard.

* * *

41. Although Clodius was born of a patrician clan, he managed to be elected tribune of the plebs.
42. I am sure that they would forgive your imprudence if you explained your intentions to them.
43. It matters very much both to us and to our sons that you should sell the house for more than you paid for it.
44. The vanguard had already reached the top of the ridge when the enemy unexpectedly attacked the main body in the rear.
45. You may converse with the prisoners provided that you do not try to induce them to escape.
46. Fearing that we should not have enough timber for building new ships, we had the old ones repaired.
47. I think very highly of your advice, but it may be that both you and I are mistaken.
48. The fact that we have nowhere to live causes every one of us great anxiety.
49. Caesar complained that the Aedui had not sent the corn which they had promised, and accused them of letting him down.

50. Shall we surrender or prolong the struggle? If only our allies would come to our aid in time!

* * *

51. My clothes have been taken away, and nobody, it seems, is willing to lend me even a shirt.[1]
52. The guards seized Mucius and led him before King Porsena to be questioned.
53. Did you wish to leave without my knowledge, or did you think I knew that you had gone?
54. The loss of over three hundred ships caused the Romans to suspend hostilities till they could build a new fleet.[2]
55. He said he needed the money, but promised to return it about March 25th.
56. For how much could we have sold the largest jar of wine that we had?
57. He feared that, unless he joined them, they would do their best to banish him.
58. Finally they had reached such a pitch[3] of starvation that they gladly fed on dogs' flesh.
59. I know that we should have found more gold if we had gone on instead of turning back.
60. As long as I live, I shall remember you, even if I forget what you have taught me.

---

[1] *ne ... quidem* may be used even when a negative has preceded.
[2] Avoid the abstract subject.   [3] § 416.

APPENDIX A: THE CALENDAR

601. The names of the months were *adjectives*; those marked
* being 1st and 2nd declension, and the others 3rd.

Iānuārius*	Māius*	September
Februārius*	Iūnius*	Octōber
Martius*	Quintīlis (*later* Iūlius*)	November
Aprīlis	Sextīlis (*later* Augustus*)	December

602. In each month there were three *key days* with names of their own (all *fem. plu.* nouns): **Kalendae**, the 1st; **Nōnae**, the 5th; **Īdūs** (Iduum), the 13th. But in four months, March, May, July and October,[1] the *Nonae* were the 7th, the *Idus* the 15th.

> *on Sept. 1st*   Kalendis Septembribus
> *until Jan. 5th*   ad Nonas Ianuarias
> *The 15th of March is near*   Idus Martiae adsunt

603. All other dates in the month were given as so many days *before* one of these key days:

(a) *The day before* was expressed by **prīdiē** + acc.

> *August 31st*   pridie Kalendas Septembres[2]
> *on July 14th*   pridie Idūs Quintiles

(b) The remaining days were termed 'the *n*th day before': *e.g.*

> *July 13th*   ante diem tertium Idūs Quintiles

N.B. (i) 'The *n*th day' (singular); *not n* days; (ii) 'the *n*th day' and the key day are *both* in the acc.[3]; (iii) the order of the words, which is quite invariable.

To calculate *n*, remember that all counting was 'inclusive'—both ends were counted in. Thus July 13th was the *third* day

---

[1] A relic of the old calendar (before Julius Caesar's reform of 45 B.C.), in which only these four months had 31 days. In writing dates, you should assume the reformed calendar, still in use to-day.

[2] Take care to name the Kalends of the *next* month.

[3] The preposition really governs *Kalendas, Idus,* or *Nonas. Diem* was illogically put in the acc. because it followed *ante*.

before July 15th. Therefore the rule is 'subtract and add one'. Moreover, the Kalends are not the last day of the month, but the first of the *next* month—another day ahead. So 'when reckoning from the Kalends, subtract and add two'.

Nov. 8th (13−8+1) ante diem sextum Idus Novembres
Nov. 20th (30−20+2) ante diem duodecimum Kalendas Decembres

604. These phrases were treated as *indeclinable nouns*, *e.g.*

I came on Feb. 20th Ante diem decimum[1] Kalendas Martias veni
He stays until May 3rd Ad ante diem quartum Nonas Maias manet

605. Dates were abbreviated thus: Kal. Sept.; pr. Id. Quint.; a.d. x Kal. Mart.; a.d. iv Non. Mai.[2]

APPENDIX B: ROMAN MONEY

606. Chief coins (in the time of Caesar and Cicero):

as, assis (*m*): a copper coin (worth about 1*d.*)
sestertius, -i (*m*): '*sesterce*', silver, = 4 *asses* (about 5*d.*)
dēnarius, -i (*m*): silver, = 4 *sestertii* (about 1*s* 8*d.*)

607. Sums of money were almost always expressed in *sestertii* (gen. plu. *sestertium*), also called *nummi*, and often written HS[3]. A rough equivalent is 100 sesterces to £2: *e.g.*

quingenti sestertii (HS d)   about £10
mille sestertii (HS m)   about £20
duo milia sestertium (HS mm)   about £40

Sums over 10,000 HS were expressed, for brevity, in idiomatic ways which lie beyond the scope of this book.

---

[1] 'Leap year' would make no difference. The extra day (inserted before Feb. 24th) did not affect the names of the other days.

[2] For practice, and in examinations, write dates in full.

[3] This sign, really denoting 'two and a half'—II S(emis)—arose from the *original* meaning of *sestertius*, for in earlier times the sesterce had been worth 2½ *asses*.

APPENDIX C: NARRATIVE PROSE

608. When we turn from isolated sentences to translate a connected narrative, our aim is (speaking broadly) to tell the story as Caesar or Cicero would have done. Because their prose style—their way of telling a story—differed from that of modern English, translation will involve certain changes, in particular the *connecting* and *combining* of the English sentences.

1. CONNECTION

609. In English, although such words as *then, therefore, next, meantime,* are quite familiar, it is more usual to leave the connection between one sentence and the next to be supplied by the reader. In Latin narrative, a sentence normally begins by stating how it is related to what has gone before. Connections are expressed, not implied.

610. Sentences may be related in various ways to those which they follow—notably:

(*a*) through some PERSON (or thing or place) mentioned in both sentences: use the pronouns *hic, is, qui.*[1] (When the subject of a sentence is the same as the *subject* of the preceding sentence, it is not expressed.)

(*b*) in TIME: use *tum, deinde, interea, postea, mox* (*&c.*).

(*c*) as RESULT (actual or logical): use *itaque, igitur.*[2]

(*d*) as EXPLANATION[3]: use *nam, enim.*[2]

(*e*) as CONTRAST or QUALIFICATION: use *sed, autem,*[2] *tamen,*[2] *at* (reserving *at* for a very emphatic *but*).

(*f*) by 'MOREOVER': use *praeterea, autem,*[2] *quin etiam, atque.*

---

[1] Sometimes *idem* is used for 'he likewise' or 'at the same time he'.
[2] Not first word in sentence.
[3] Especially when, after making a statement in general terms, one proceeds to give the details: *nam, enim* (not to be translated into English) are commonly so used.

2. COMBINATION

611. Thoughts or facts may also be linked by combining them within a single sentence. English narrative, on the whole, follows the principle of 'one fact, one sentence'; Latin narrative writers normally used longer sentences, complex—that is, containing one or more subordinate clauses—and embracing in one grammatical unit several related facts. In translating such Latin sentences (or 'periods'[1]) into English they must often be broken up; and in Latin composition the process will be reversed, with the help of participles and of the various kinds of subordinate clause, especially those introduced by *cum, ut* and relative words.

612. But combination should not be a haphazard process, as though it merely meant cutting lumps of a certain length out of the paragraph. Select the *key statements* of the passage, such as the crowning event of a series, the decisive action, the point of a story; make these the main clauses, and subordinate the rest—the background, circumstances, causes, motives, minor events. But the *order* in which the events are mentioned (no matter whether by main verb, subordinate verb, or participle) should always be the order in which they happened.

*613. If possible, tell the story from one single standpoint. In English we do not mind switching from one party to another, using each in turn as subject for a sentence as may be convenient. A Roman writer would tend to tell the story from the standpoint of a single party throughout, choosing, of course, the one of greatest importance or primary interest. Some rearrangement, such as change of voice, may therefore be needed. If a sentence does require a 'different' subject, try to make it a subordinate clause.[2]

---

[1] Strictly, a *period* is a complex sentence in which the main predicate is kept till the end, so that there is a sense of incompleteness and suspense, which is lost if some of the subordinate parts follow the main assertion, as so often in English.

[2] *N.B.* This is a *tendency*, not a *rule*: do not press it too far.

*614. If all sentences were periodic, the narrative would be monotonous. There is a place for short sentences, which can indeed be all the more effective because they contrast with the normal style. They are used especially:

(i) for variety and vividness, particularly at the climax of a story, or in parts where the action is rapid. Few if any connecting words are used; moreover, to throw the emphasis on the *action*, the verbs are often put first (and may well be in the historic present, or the historic infinitive).

(ii) when clauses are *contrasted without conjunction*. This is a common Latin idiom; English usually has *while* or *but*:

> *While he liberated the allies, he detained the Romans*
> Socios dimisit, Romanos retinuit[1]

3. MISCELLANEOUS POINTS

615. ORDER. A word is emphasized by moving it from its normal position, especially to the end or to the beginning of the sentence; or by parting it from another word with which it goes closely in sense and grammar. It is better to risk being over-emphatic than to be content always with the 'standard order'. Latin throve on emphasis.

616. CONCRETENESS. Avoid abstract expressions in narrative prose: refer to chapter 17. Express the sense in plain, concrete terms—in *verbs* if possible. Whereas English puts the *meaning* into nouns, and completes the grammar with 'empty' verbs like *have*, *do*, Latin puts the *meaning* into verbs and uses neuter pronouns, or adjectives, or the 'empty' noun *res*, to complete the grammar. Typical examples are these:

He made very many promises	Plurima pollicitus est
He had no success	{ Rem male gessit Re infecta discessit

In particular, avoid making an abstract noun the *subject* of a verb denoting action. It is a sound principle to make a *person* the subject of every action.

---

[1] 'Chiasmus' or reversal of order is a very effective figure of speech in such sentences: *e.g.* Dimisit socios, Romanos retinuit.

617. PROPER NAMES. Modern names sometimes give trouble.

(i) If possible, eliminate them: *e.g.* Wellington becomes *imperator*, Manchester becomes *urbs*, or *ea urbs*.

(ii) If convenient, Latinize them. A few (*e.g.* Columbus, Victoria) need no change; others have recognized Latin forms or equivalents (*e.g.* Carolus, Henricus, Londinium, Lutetia *Paris*, Batavi *the Dutch*). In any case, however, the Romans Latinized the foreign names they met (Hannibal, Boudicca, Darius); and we may do the same with Drake or Disraeli.

(iii) If the narrative is of a general or stock type, substitute Latin names. Any names will do, but if a parallel comes to mind, take advantage of it. It is rarely easy to find a good parallel for a detailed narrative (do not commit absurdities in trying to do so); but in many a stock battle piece Caesar may stand for Clive or Montgomery, Labienus for a 'right-hand man', the Gauls for any enemy.

618. DIRECT AND REPORTED SPEECH. In Latin, as in English, either may be used; but Latin writers showed a stronger preference for reported speech, and this should be allowed for in translating. In particular, avoid isolated sentences of direct speech in historical passages.

In writing reported speech in English, it is common to insert at frequent intervals 'he said', 'he went on', *&c.* Otherwise it would often be difficult to distinguish reported speech from ordinary narrative. Latin needs no such device, and it would be wrong to insert it. Nor is such a word always needed even at the beginning of a speech; any verb which *implies* speech is sufficient introduction:

They sent a joint embassy to Crassus, informing him that, if he wished to get his own men back, he had better return their hostages.	Communem legationem ad P. Crassum mittunt: si velit suos recipere, obsides sibi remittat.

619. METAPHORS. Latin prose is not lacking in metaphors, but in narrative (with which alone these notes deal) they are used but sparingly. It would be safe to eliminate any metaphor which the English contains, however harmless and ordinary it may seem.

He ascended the throne	Rex factus est
The streets rang with cries	Viae clamoribus plenae erant
He embarked on the undertaking	Negotium (rem, opus) suscepit

When a bold or metaphorical expression *was* used, it was often 'toned down' or apologized for by *quidam, quasi, tamquam* or *velut*: refer to *page* 167, *note* 2.

CONTINUOUS PROSE PASSAGES

The arrangement of the sixty passages which follow, and their relation to the chapters of the course, is explained on page x. Nos. 4, 10, 12, 13 and 16 are taken, with permission, from General School Examination papers of the University of London.

EASIER PASSAGES

1

On the next day, Fabius sent forward five hundred cavalry to join battle and delay the enemy's march. Varus, who commanded the cavalry, overtook the enemy column, and ordered his troops to attack the rearguard. Fierce fighting then took place; for neither side was willing to yield. About midday, the legions were seen in the distance, and the enemy took to flight. Our cavalry pursued them as they fled, and slew a large number. Those who survived the battle took refuge in the neighbouring hills.

2

That night, both sides remained inside their fortifications. At dawn the enemy's cavalry rode up to the camp and joined battle with ours. So that the Gauls should think themselves victorious, Caesar ordered his cavalry to fall back deliberately and retire into the camp. The enemy were so misled by this that they brought up the remaining forces carelessly. Some began to climb the rampart, others to fill up the ditches. Then our men made a sortie from all the gates, the cavalry were launched, and they put the enemy to flight and killed very many of them.

3

Learning that the Persians had landed near the borders of Attica, the Athenian generals sent a famous runner, named Phidippides, to Sparta to warn the Lacedaemonians that reinforcements were needed, and to ask them to come at once to their help. Phidippides, it is related, ran so fast that he reached Sparta, which is 130 miles from Athens, in two days. However, his request for help was not successful; the Spartans said that they could not depart before the full moon for fear that they would displease their gods.

4

Caesar set out without delay in order to besiege the nearest city of the enemy. When Dumnorix, the commander of the garrison, was informed that the Romans were approaching, he began to fortify the citadel. But he was unable to persuade the citizens to resist Caesar; for they were unwilling to fight against such a great general, and preferred to yield to the power of the Roman people. Dumnorix, therefore, thinking that there was no longer any hope of saving the city, fled secretly during the night.

5

After a few years the Britons, fired with anger by their grievous wrongs, decided that the Romans must be driven out. Under the leadership of Boudicca, who was then queen of the Iceni, they attacked and burnt the prosperous city of Camulodunum. Meantime Suetonius, the Roman general, advanced very swiftly with two legions to save London. But being unable to defend the town, he adopted the plan of retreating. The natives, after sacking this city, pursued the Romans as they withdrew; but at last, choosing a favourable situation, Suetonius defeated the British forces in a pitched battle. To avoid capture, Boudicca killed herself.

6

Theseus was so eager to set sail that he forgot what he had promised, and did not change the sail. King Aegeus would climb every day to the top of the citadel, to see his son's ship as soon as possible. At last, after waiting there for some days in vain, he saw the ship in the distance. At first he could not tell whether the sail was white or black; but when the ship came nearer[1] he saw that it was black. So, fearing that he had lost his son, he fell from the rock on which he was sitting, and died.

[1] Use an abl. abs. phrase: 'the ship (being) now nearer'.

7

A certain farmer used to go out with his wife to plough his land, and he used to leave his faithful dog to guard his infant son. One day, when he returned home in the evening, he saw the child wounded, and the dog's mouth covered in blood. Fired with anger, he drew his sword and slew the dog instantly. But then, turning round, he caught sight of a wolf, lying dead on the ground, and realized what had really happened. He was ashamed to have mistrusted his dog, and sorry for his hasty deed. 'Would to God', he said, 'that I could restore life to the poor dog as easily as I took it from him.'

8

After encouraging his troops, Caesar joined battle. The men threw their javelins from the higher ground[1] and easily broke the enemy's line. When this was in confusion, they drew their swords and charged them. The Gauls, who were greatly hindered by the javelins stuck in their shields, resisted with great difficulty. At last, exhausted by their wounds, they began to fall back and to withdraw to the foot of the hill. Meantime tne Boii, who were protecting the rear of the column, attacked our men from behind; and the Helvetii, seeing this, themselves renewed the battle. Thus there was a long and keenly fought contest on two fronts.

[1] *locus superior*

9

The Spartans, having secretly promised to send a fleet of forty ships to raise the siege of Mitylene, put Alcidas in command of it. He started at the beginning of spring, but thinking the Athenian fleet was too strong for him to attack, he advanced as slowly as possible. After a time news reached him that the city had already been captured. He summoned a council of war, and several of those present urged that they should nevertheless continue their voyage and try to take the

Athenians by surprise. But he decided to return to the Peloponnese, fearing that the Athenians, flushed with victory, would pounce upon his fleet. Thus, through cowardice, he lost a chance of recapturing the city.

10

As he wished to make a sudden attack, Caesar sent men ahead to reconnoitre the nature of the ground. The same day he was informed by a certain prisoner that the enemy commander, fearing that he could not defend the town, had decided to withdraw his forces during the night, and, having crossed the river which was not far away, to break down the bridge: that he hoped thus to prevent[1] the Romans from following. When he learnt this, Caesar ordered Labienus to start at once with five cohorts, that he might seize the bridge before the enemy arrived there.

[1] Use *prohibeo*.

11

While travelling to Asia, Verres came to Delos, an island on which is a very famous temple of Apollo. From this temple he removed secretly one night some very beautiful and ancient statues, and had them put on board his ship. Next day, when they realized what had happened, the inhabitants were vexed; for since it is believed that Apollo himself was born there, the place is very holy. However, they dared not say anything, for fear that they might suffer worse evils. But the ship carrying the statues had scarcely put to sea when a great storm sprang up. The ship was wrecked, and the statues were found on the shore and replaced in the temple.

12

The Romans by their charge kept the barbarians from ascending the hill and gradually forced them down into the plain. There they were beginning to form their ranks again, when a great outcry arose from the rear. Marcellus had seen from the place, where he lay in ambush, that the Romans had joined battle, and hastened to bear aid to them. Attacked on both sides, the enemy turned and fled. The Romans pursuing them killed or captured about twenty thousand men, and later took possession of their camp together with much booty. The soldiers chose the best arms from the spoil and gave them to the general that they might be carried in his triumph.

13

At dawn the Roman commander led his forces out of the camp and drew them up near the walls of the town. Before he gave the signal to advance, he addressed the soldiers in these words: 'If the enemy had lacked either arms or provisions, I should have tried to take the city by blockade. Now, however, our one hope lies in a sudden attack. I will give a handsome prize to the man who first climbs the walls.' Roused by this encouragement, the soldiers ran forward so eagerly that the enemy could not withstand them. A few were killed fighting, the rest surrendered at once.

14

A good many people believed that Nero had himself arranged for the burning of the city; but there is no doubt that this accusation was false. When he received the news of the terrible fire, he was at Antium, which is over thirty miles away from Rome. On hearing it, he at once returned to Rome. When he arrived there, he found that the flames were now threatening the very Palace. In this crisis hardly anyone showed greater courage than Nero: wherever the danger was greatest, he was present in person, and as soon as the fire was checked he relieved in whatever way he could the distress of those who had lost all their belongings: which he would not have done if he had not been innocent.

15

Solon had come to the court of King Croesus in Lydia. Croesus showed him all his treasure-houses; then he asked him whom he considered to be the most fortunate of men: 'For,' said he, 'you have visited many countries and seen many famous people.' But Solon gave a different answer from that for which Croesus was hoping: he replied that of all the young men whom he knew, Tellus of Athens had been the most fortunate, seeing that he had lived in a fair city, had possessed sufficient wealth, and had died honourably fighting for his fatherland. Croesus was vexed at this; whereupon Solon said, 'I am not willing to call anyone blessed until I hear how he has ended his life. For we should always consider the end.' So far from believing Solon, Croesus considered him very foolish; but many years later he recalled his words.

16

Next day Caesar led out his men from the camp, and having advanced a little, drew up his line. When, however, he perceived that the enemy did not wish to fight, he ordered the troops to return within the rampart. Seeing this, Ariovistus at last sent out part of the cavalry to attack the Romans from the rear as they retreated. Our soldiers resisted so bravely that they killed some of the Germans and captured others. When Caesar inquired of the prisoners why Ariovistus had not joined battle, he discovered that this was the reason: the Germans believed that they could not win if they fought before the new moon.

17

In former times at Athens, if a daughter refused to marry the man whom her father chose, he might have her put to death. Relying on this law, a man named Aegeus once complained to Theseus, the King of Athens, that his daughter Hermia, whom he had commanded to marry Demetrius, a young man of noble family, refused to do so, because—she said—she loved one Lysander. When questioned by the King, Hermia confessed that this was true, and added, 'Besides, if I were to marry Demetrius it would deeply grieve Helena, the dearest friend I have, who loves Demetrius herself.' Theseus was sorry for her; but as he could not alter the laws of the state, he gave her four days in which to decide whether to obey her father or pay the penalty.

18

Since Hercules did not know where the golden apples were, he sought for them everywhere. At last he came to the place where, by order of Jupiter, Prometheus was bound to the cliff. Hercules was so sorry for him that he persuaded Jupiter to pardon him. To show his gratitude, Prometheus advised Hercules to ask Atlas, the father of the maidens who guarded the apples, where they were to be sought for. So Hercules travelled to Africa, and asked Atlas to tell him what he wanted to know. Atlas said he was not allowed to tell anyone this; 'But,' said he, 'if you will hold up the sky until I return, I will fetch the apples myself.' But when he returned, he would have left Hercules supporting the sky on his shoulders, if the latter had not employed a trick.

19

When this was accomplished, Caesar believed that Gaul was now completely subdued. So at the beginning of winter he left for Illyricum. After his departure, a sudden outbreak of war occurred in the coastal districts. P. Crassus had sent envoys to requisition more corn from the Veneti; and the leading men of the tribe hoped that, by detaining these envoys, they could recover the hostages whom they had previously given to Rome. So they sent a message to Crassus that they would not give him the corn which he demanded, and added that if he wanted to recover his envoys, he had better send their hostages back to them.

20

Meantime, the farther Scipio advanced, the higher were the hills he saw on either hand. He had by now gone about eight miles from the camp. It was reported to him through his scouts that the enemy's forces had been seen beyond the ridge; and this report had scarcely come in when a great dust-cloud was observed. Scipio had with him no infantry at all; he had not even an adequate force of cavalry. That being so, it was very important to him to hinder the enemy from coming down from the ridge into the plain. With this object, he sent ahead the cavalry and archers, of whom he had but few, with orders to conceal themselves in ambush on either side of the route by which the enemy must descend. He hoped thus to delay them until his infantry could come up.

21

When I was only a boy of nine, and my father was leaving Carthage for Spain, he gave me the opportunity to go with him. I begged him not to hesitate to take me there. He at once led me to the altar, at which he happened to be sacrificing, and bade me swear never to be on friendly terms with Rome. This oath I have kept, up to this day, so well that no-one ought to doubt that I shall always be of the same opinion as long as I live. So even though I have been driven into exile from my own country, wherever I may be I shall always do my best to destroy the nation which has twice defeated my own. Whoever tries to persuade you otherwise must be deemed either a fool or an enemy.

22

The tribe of the Treveri was by far the strongest in cavalry in the whole of Gaul. In that tribe two of the leading men were rivals; and one of them, Indutiomarus by name, began to mobilize the cavalry and infantry and make preparations for war. Meantime the other, Cingetorix, came to Caesar and promised to carry out his orders. He also told him what was going on among the Treveri. A good many others, influenced by his example, did the same; and Indutiomarus, fearing that he would be deserted by everyone, himself sent envoys to Caesar to say that he had not come to him sooner simply because he feared that, if all the nobles departed, the common people would try to revolt against Rome.

23

While this was taking place in Italy, Mago returned to Carthage to report what his brother Hannibal had accomplished. He told the senate that he had defeated six armies, slain over 200,000 soldiers, and stormed two camps. Many tribes and cities, influenced by these victories, had revolted to the Carthaginians. For these great and numerous victories one and all ought to thank the gods. Then he emptied out before the eyes of the senators some golden rings, of which there was such a large number that they filled three measures; and that they might better realize how great the defeat had been, he explained that no-one except Knights, and not all of them, used to wear such a ring.

24

Since she saw that the Rhodian fleet was too large to be defeated in a pitched battle, the Queen decided that she must employ a stratagem. So she prepared as many ships as possible and hid them in the smaller harbour; and she ordered the citizens to man the walls. The Rhodians drew up their fleet in the larger harbour; whereupon she ordered the citizens to pretend to welcome them gladly, and to promise to surrender the city to them. But as soon as the Rhodians had got within the walls, without leaving any-one to guard the ships, the Queen unexpectedly led her ships out of the smaller harbour, sailed into the larger, and towed away the empty fleet. Thus the Rhodians, having nowhere to retreat to, were slain to the last man right in the market place.

25

After the battle of Pharsalus, Pompey fled to Asia, intending to prolong the war in Syria. After being detained for two days by bad weather, he reached Cyprus; there he learnt that the people of Antioch had taken up arms to keep him out, and sent messengers in all directions to warn him and his followers not to approach Antioch; adding that if they did so they would be in great peril of their lives. In view of this, he gave up his intention of visiting Syria, took as much money as he could, and sailed to Egypt. He begged King Ptolemy to admit him to his kingdom, and undoubtedly he would have got his way; but the king's friends (either through ill-will or because they looked down upon his wretched plight) had him murdered.

26

Gessler, the governor of the district, whose anger Tell had thus aroused, was as cruel as he was arrogant. Knowing that Tell was a very skilful archer, he contrived a plan by which both to punish Tell and amuse himself. He sent for Tell's son, a boy of ten, and ordered the wretched father to hit with an arrow an apple placed on the boy's head. Tell pleaded to be punished in any other way, but Gessler had no pity on him. Then Tell, taking two arrows, stuck one of them in his belt, while with the other he dislodged the apple, split into two pieces, without injuring the child at all. 'You have another arrow left,' said Gessler: 'how would you have used that?' 'I should have killed you,' replied Tell, 'if I had injured my son.'

27

Among the prisoners whom Scipio had taken in this battle was a remarkably handsome boy. He declared that he was of royal descent; on his father's death, he said, he had been brought up in the household of his grandfather, King Gala of Numidia. He had come over to Spain with his uncle Masinissa, who had recently brought his cavalry to the aid of Hasdrubal. He explained that, owing to his tender age, he had been forbidden to take part in the fighting, but, on the day of the battle, he had taken a horse without his uncle's knowledge and left the camp by stealth to watch the struggle. His horse had stumbled and he had been captured while trying to escape on foot. Scipio sent for him and asked him whether he wanted to return to Masinissa. He said that he did; whereupon Scipio gave him a gold ring and many other gifts, and sent him away unharmed.

28

As he had attained his object, Caesar ordered the retreat to be sounded. The troops of some of the legions failed to hear[1] the sound of the bugle, as a quite large valley lay between; their officers tried to restrain them, but, carried away by the prospect of a rapid victory, and the memory of several successes, they thought nothing too difficult for their valour to accomplish, and did not cease their pursuit until they were near the gates of the town. The townspeople, demoralized by the sudden attack, and thinking the Romans already within the gates, rushed headlong from the city. The womenfolk began to toss their clothing and other belongings from the walls, and implored the Romans to spare them, and not to put women and children to death as they had done at Avaricum.

---

[1] to catch a sound from a distance: *exaudire.*

29

The depth of the snow made progress almost impossible. One of the wounded men bade his comrades leave him behind, lest he should hinder the rest. So Xenophon ordered one of the mule-drivers to let this man ride on his mule. When they had gone some distance, Xenophon happened to see the man digging a pit, and he praised him for bestowing so much trouble on a comrade even when dead. Then, however, the man whom he thought dead moved his leg, and the bystanders exclaimed that he was alive. 'However alive he is,' replied the muleteer, '*I* shall carry him no further.' At this Xenophon, enraged, beat the man. Long after, when they reached the coast, the muleteer accused Xenophon of having treated him cruelly; whereat everyone exclaimed that he had deserved to be punished even more severely.

30

That night King Rufus dreamed that he received a serious wound, from which a mighty stream of blood flowed. He was so terrified by this dream that he cried aloud. Next morning the King and his companions went out hunting in the forest. A great stag came in view of the King; he quickly shot an arrow and wounded it. Before he could follow the injured beast, he was himself shot through the breast by an arrow. When they saw the King fall, his companions, instead of trying to help him, immediately leapt on their horses and rode away as fast as they could. No-one knows who shot the arrow; some say that the King's brother, Henry, killed him, influenced by a desire to seize the throne; others give other accounts. It is not even certain whether he was killed by accident or design. At any rate, his body was found by a peasant, who placed it in his cart and conveyed it to the nearest town.

HARDER PASSAGES

31

A man once dreamed that there was an egg hanging from his bed. In the morning, as he wished to know the meaning of this dream, he told what he had seen to an interpreter, who replied that there was treasure buried under the bed. The man returned home and dug up the ground at that spot. He found there a quantity of gold, surrounded by some silver. To express his gratitude to the interpreter, he gave him some of the silver; but the latter was not the man to be satisfied with this sort of reward: 'Why,' he asked, 'have you not sent me some of the yolk as well?'

32

The Romans had now been besieging the city of Sora for several months; but they were unable to take it by storm. At last a deserter, leaving the city by stealth, entered the Roman camp and promised to betray the city. He persuaded the Romans to move their camp six miles from the walls, so that the sentries would be less vigilant. When all preparations were complete, on the following night, he led ten picked soldiers by a steep path on to the citadel, which could be reached from the city only by a single narrow way. When they learnt that the Romans held the citadel, the citizens, not knowing how few had got in, gave up hope, broke down the gates and fled. The rest of the Romans, entering by the open gates, slew the terrified citizens as they ran aimlessly through the streets.

33

One day King Canute was sitting on the shore, surrounded by his courtiers. Hoping to please him, they said that there was nothing which he could not do in virtue of his royal power. Without replying, the king had his chair placed near the sea. Now the tide happened to be rising. Taking his seat, he loudly ordered the waves not to advance any farther. But the tide went on rising none the less; and turning to his courtiers he said, 'There are, you see, some things which not even a king can command. Take care to keep always in mind the lesson you have learned to-day. I am not the sort of man to be taken in by flattering words.'

34

Hadrian spent many years in visiting the provinces; he was so eager for travel that he wished to see with his own eyes everything he had read about. He used to travel, it is said, without pomp or display. There was hardly any province that he did not visit at some time; and wherever he went he was welcomed both by the citizens and by the soldiers. He concerned himself above all with the welfare of the legions; for now that peace was established there was a danger that the army might become less efficient. But by vigorous training he ensured that both the discipline and the loyalty of the legions increased.

35

The master who taught the sons of the leading men of Falerii had usually taken them outside the walls each day for exercise; and when the siege began he did not abandon this custom. Finally, going on farther than usual, he came to Camillus in the Roman camp; he told him that he had brought the sons of the leading men as hostages, with the intention of handing Falerii over to Rome. Camillus, however, replied, 'You have not come to a man of your own type. It is not fitting for me to take up arms against defenceless boys. We shall defeat you by the Roman qualities of courage and endurance.' Then he gave the boys sticks with which to drive the traitor into the city. The Faliscans were moved by Camillus' good faith, and agreed to ask for peace. Envoys were dispatched to Rome, and the Romans sent men to arrange for the surrender of the city.

36

A famous philosopher named Xenocrates was very dear to his pupils, not only for his teaching but also for his character. Once King Alexander, wishing to honour him, sent envoys with fifty talents, which in those days was a very large sum of money. Xenocrates invited them to dinner, and set before them an ordinary meal, without any display. Next day the envoys asked to whom they ought to pay the money which they had brought with them. But Xenocrates replied, 'What? I made it clear to you by yesterday's dinner that I do not need any wealth. Tell the king to keep his money; for he has far more people to maintain than I have.' But seeing them looking rather dejected, he accepted half a talent, to avoid seeming to despise the king's kindness.

37

Caesar took several towns; but realizing that the Veneti were invulnerable by land, he sent for his fleet. When it arrived, he told Brutus, who was in command of the whole fleet, and the military tribunes and centurions who commanded the individual ships, what they must do. For he knew that the Gallic ships were too heavy and strong to be sunk by ramming; so since they could not employ their usual tactics, he instructed them to tie sickles to long poles, with which to cut the rigging of the enemy's vessels. These orders they carried out; and whenever one of our ships came alongside one of the enemy's, it was not difficult for the soldiers to board the latter and capture it. The rest of the natives, observing this, tried to escape by flight, but at that very moment the wind happened to drop, which was of great advantage to the Romans in making their success complete.

38

I should like to know whether you believe that spirits exist or not. Personally, I am led to believe that they do by numerous facts; among which I rather think this especially deserves to be related. A friend of my father's, when a young man, had gone to the province of Africa. About noon one day, while almost everyone was asleep, he was strolling in the arcade when he saw the figure of a woman of remarkable height and beauty. She told him that she was 'Africa', and could foretell the future. He would return to Rome, she went on, hold public offices, and actually return to Africa as governor, and die there. All that she foretold came true: many years later he not only held the consulship, but returned as governor to the same province, and falling ill, he so completely gave up hope of recovery that he soon passed away.

39

Everyone knows in what great esteem Q. Fabius Maximus held the majesty of the consuls. When he was already of advanced age, and had so often held the dictatorship, his son was elected consul. The Romans were at that time still at war with Hannibal, and the younger Fabius happened to have led his troops into Apulia. His father was ordered by the senate to join him. He rode into his son's camp, and the latter came out to meet him with twelve lictors. The old man was riding past the lictors without dismounting; at last, at the consul's command, the twelfth lictor shouted to him to dismount. Then at last he said, 'I wanted to find out, my son, whether you knew clearly enough that you are the consul.' With these words he immediately dismounted.

40

While these events were taking place in Italy, Scipio had defeated Hasdrubal in Spain. But he had not prevented him from crossing the Alps and leading a second army into Italy to help his brother Hannibal. So the Romans were within a very little of being defeated; for if both brothers' forces had been united, they could have swiftly concluded the war. As it happened, however, both the consuls of that year were men of exceptional ability. C. Claudius Nero had pursued Hannibal into Bruttium, when the news arrived that Hasdrubal had already crossed the mountains and was besieging Placentia. Nero at once led a picked force secretly across Italy and joined his colleague Livius. Together they annihilated Hasdrubal's army at the River Metaurus; thus Hannibal, so far from being helped by his brother's arrival, realized that this defeat would mean the doom of Carthage.

41

Blaesus, a very wealthy man, was seriously ill, and no-one expected him to live. He wanted to alter his will. Regulus hoped to receive something from the new will, since he had recently begun to make up to the old man; so he pretended to feel great anxiety for his welfare; whenever he thought Blaesus was listening, he begged the doctors to do all they could to prolong his life. But no sooner was the new will signed than he changed his tone, and asked the doctors how long they were going to keep the poor man in torment. Since they could not cure him, why did they begrudge him the death for which he longed? A few days later Blaesus died, and—just as if he had heard all that Regulus said—when the will was opened Regulus did not get even a penny! I wish he suffered that fate more often! Yet so far from being ashamed of his unscrupulous tricks, he openly boasts of them.

42

After this battle, Edward led his army to the city of Calais and began to besiege it. For a whole year the citizens resisted, though their sufferings were terrible; when all their food was consumed, they were forced to live on the flesh of horses and dogs. They hoped to hold out until another army came to their rescue; but though the French forces did approach, they feared the English so much that they withdrew again without fighting. At last the governor of the town, to save the citizens from dying of hunger, offered to surrender if Edward would let them depart unharmed. The king promised to spare the rest of the citizens on condition that six of the leading men were handed over to him as hostages; but when he received them he would have broken his promise had not the Queen persuaded him to spare them.

43

Five cohorts had been sent out in various directions to collect corn; and the Germans, seizing the opportunity to attack the camp, suddenly rushed out of the woods all round and approached the rampart. Panic spread throughout the camp, all the more because the reason for it was not clear. Such was the demoralization that the natives thought the camp had no garrison at all. Left behind in the camp, among the sick, was the centurion P. Sextius Baculus. Fearing that it was all over with himself and every one of them, he came out of his tent, unarmed as he was; he saw that the foe was upon them and the situation very critical. He seized weapons from the bystanders and took his stand in the nearest gate, followed by the centurions of the cohort on outpost duty. The respite thus gained enabled the rest to rally and man the ramparts.

44

Meantime our troops, while on their way back to the camp, heard the noise from a distance. The cavalry galloped ahead and discovered the gravity of the situation. Hardly anyone was so brave as not to be alarmed. When the natives caught sight of the legionary standards, they gave up their attack on the ramparts, thinking that all the legions were returning. But when they saw how few our men were, they fell on them from all directions. Some of our troops, led by C. Trebonius, broke through the thick of the enemy and reached the camp unscathed; others, being less experienced soldiers, tried to follow their example but were prevented from reaching the ramparts. However, the Germans, seeing that enough men were now available to defend the camp, abandoned the assault and withdrew across the Rhine with the booty they had captured.

45

Pyrrhus, king of Epirus, had made war on Rome, and twice already defeated her armies with heavy losses. Although the Romans refused to discuss peace until he had left Italy, it seemed scarcely possible that he could be driven out by armed force. Now a deserter came from his army into the camp of the consul Fabricius, and promised, if a suitable reward were given him, to return to Pyrrhus' camp secretly and poison him. But Fabricius, who set honour before expediency, was unwilling to employ treachery, however great a peril might threaten the state. He asked the fellow why he thought so lightly of the honour of a Roman commander. He then had him taken back to Pyrrhus, informing the latter what had occurred, and this action on his part met with the approval of the Senate.

46

After the battle of Cannae, Hannibal released without ransom all the allies whom he held as prisoners, and promised to free the Romans also on receiving a ransom. The latter decided to choose ten of their number to convey these terms to the Senate at Rome; these swore to return to the Carthaginian camp. One of them, however, to fulfil his oath, pretended to have forgotten something, and returned to the camp; before nightfall he overtook his companions. The senators, on hearing what they had to say, refused to accept such terms, fearing that if they ransomed these men others might fight less bravely in future. 'Roman soldiers,' they said, 'must either conquer or die.' The envoys departed; but one of them went to his home, as if he had, by his return to the camp, already fulfilled his oath. When this was known, the Senate decreed that he should be arrested and sent back to Hannibal.

47

Caesar reached the mainland without the loss of a single ship, before the report of his approach could reach Bibulus, who was in command of Pompey's fleet. When the soldiers had been landed, the ships were sent back to Brindisi the same night so that the rest of the legions and the cavalry could be brought over more speedily. But they put to sea too late, and failing to take advantage of the night breeze they ran into danger in the course of their return. Bibulus, vexed that he had failed to prevent Caesar from crossing to Greece, met the returning ships, burnt those he caught (some thirty in number) and slew all their crews, in the hope of deterring the rest by this cruel punishment from attempting a second crossing.

48

The robbers rode into our yard, just as if they had been invited, opened the stable doors,[1] turned our horses out, and put their own in place of them. At this I was deeply grieved; for you know how much we think of our horses. By this time I could see our men, waiting in the shadow by the house till they should be given the order to fire; but Jeremy ordered them not to fire until the enemy should advance upon them. Presently two young men came to the rick in which I was hiding; one of them would have set fire to the straw, had I not struck him with my club with all my force. Down he fell, and the other man stood amazed at this, not having yet gained sight of me; till I snatched his firebrand from him unawares, and then by a sudden attack threw him down so that he lay, with his arm broken, on top of his comrade.

[1] Say 'opened the stables'.

49

That summer there happened to be a plague of snakes in Arabia. Our men used to kill about twenty every day, and the constant danger was getting on everyone's nerves. But the two boys, whose request to come with us had been granted, greatly enjoyed giving false alarms; which they did so often that Lawrence told them never again to mention snakes, on pain of dire punishment. Presently he noticed them smiling, as if they had a joke at his expense; and looking round, he saw a great snake behind him. By leaping sideways, he avoided its stroke; if he had delayed even an instant, he would certainly have lost his life. One of the men killed the snake with a stick; with which also the boys were punished for not giving warning when real danger threatened. Afterwards they were sent to collect firewood and fetch water—work which the Arabs regard as very unseemly for men.

50

Everyone knows how Hypsagoras loves to boast. The other day he happened to meet some friends from abroad,[1] to[2] whom he had often boasted that he was very rich. What was he to do? While he was greeting them, he caught sight of a house in which there was to be a party that day. He went in with his friends. 'This,' he said, 'is where I live,' and began to inspect the plate and furniture as if he were the owner. But presently one of the slaves asked him to leave, since his master would soon be home. Hearing this, Hypsagoras pretended to be going to meet his brother, and bade his friends return at the tenth hour. In the evening, when they returned, they discovered how they had been deceived. Next morning they reproached Hypsagoras for misleading them; but, so far from being ashamed of his deception, he replied that they had gone to the wrong[3] house; he had waited for them, he said, until late at night.

[1] *hospites.*   [2] *apud*   [3] *alius.*

51

When the fortification of the camp was completed, the consul, acting on the advice of C. Gallus, an officer of the second legion, paraded the troops and gave Gallus permission to address them. He said: 'To-morrow the moon will be eclipsed from eight to ten p.m. Do not be alarmed or regard this as an omen; for just as all men know when the sun or moon will rise and set, so the learned can foretell on what day and at what hour it will be eclipsed, for the simple reason that these events obey natural laws.'

On Sept. 3rd the moon was eclipsed, as Gallus had predicted, and his wisdom was thought almost superhuman by the majority of the troops. To the enemy, to whom it appeared as an omen of defeat, the eclipse caused great distress, and they did not cease their uproar and panic until the moon appeared again.

N.B. Use Oratio Obliqua.

52

After gaining the victory, de Montfort without any loss of time concentrated his forces, of which two divisions were still fresh, and exerted all his energies to take the king alive. While de Clare attacked the section of the royal army under the king's brother, de Montfort attacked the king's own forces, slaughtered them in heaps, and finally took Henry himself (whose horse had been killed) and conducted him a prisoner to a neighbouring farmhouse. Two of the king's companions made a desperate resistance, but the one, after he was severely wounded, at last saw the necessity of yielding, and the other was overpowered by force. De Montfort sent a force to seize the town of Lewes before night fell, but the resistance was so fierce that the attempt had to be abandoned.

53

Clodius knew—indeed it was not difficult to discover—that Milo had to travel to Lanuvium on the 19th of January. So he suddenly left Rome on the morning of that day, on the pretext of visiting his country house. The result was that he was absent from a public meeting which he would never have missed if he had not had some urgent business elsewhere. Milo, after attending the Senate, went home, changed his clothes, waited a little (as one does) while his wife got ready, and then towards evening started on his way. He was met by Clodius, on horseback, with no luggage, no carriage, none of his usual attendants. Several armed men instantly pounced on Milo from their hiding-place; throwing aside his overcoat, he leapt from the carriage and defended himself vigorously. Meantime, some of his slaves were killed, while others, believing that their master had perished, acted (without his orders) as any man would have wished his slaves to act in such a situation.

54

The end of summer was approaching when Agricola reached Britain, and the troops did not expect that they would have to fight that year. However, Agricola had decided that the tribe of the Ordovices ought to be punished without delay for their recent revolt; so he led a fair-sized force into their territory. After almost wiping out the tribe, he decided that the opportunity to subdue the island of Anglesey must not be lost. His lack of ships, however, made this task seem very difficult. Yet this very fact was of the greatest advantage to him, for the natives thought it impossible that he could attack them before the winter. Agricola selected the most skilful swimmers[1] from his auxiliary troops, and ordered them to swim across the strait, thus taking the enemy by surprise. So he defeated them, not because they lacked courage, but because he attacked them sooner than anyone expected.

[1] *i.e.* those most skilful in swimming.

55

Not long after, Xerxes, king of Persia, raised a huge fleet and set sail for Greece; it was said that the Athenians were the main object of his attack, since it was they who had routed the Persians at the battle of Marathon ten years earlier. In view of this, they sent a deputation to Delphi to ask what they had better do. The god replied that they should put their trust in wooden walls. No-one could understand what this reply meant, but Themistocles convinced the citizens that what the oracle counselled them to do was to take refuge in their ships; these, he said, were the wooden walls, in reliance upon which they could resist the invasion. This plan was approved, and they transferred all their movable property to the island of Salamis. Leaving the citadel and temples in the charge of the priests and a handful of elderly folk, who were too weak to go with the others, they abandoned the rest of the city.

56

On hearing this answer, Gessler, enraged, had Tell put on his boat, and set sail across the lake, intending to return home and cast him into his private dungeon. They were already in the middle of the lake when (as often happens in that region) a violent storm suddenly broke. The sailors were all terrified, and the governor entrusted the helm to Tell. The latter, knowing the shore very well, steered straight for a certain ledge[1] of rock. Reaching this, he suddenly seized his bow, leapt from the boat, and escaped into the woods before the others could follow. They had a narrow escape from death when the boat was wrecked. Later, while he was making his way homeward on foot through the woods, Gessler fell, struck by an arrow. Although there was no room for doubt whose hand shot the arrow, the guards searched in vain for him.

[1] Say 'a certain rock'.

57

Recently the power and audacity of the pirates had reached such heights that not even Roman armies dared to cross the sea except in winter; and since the import of corn was rendered impossible, there was danger that Rome would suffer from famine. In these circumstances, no-one doubted that something must be done at once. So the people chose Pompey to make war on the pirates; he was given 200 ships, very large forces, and greater powers than any Roman had ever held before. Immediately, as if the fear of famine was already removed, the price of corn, which had been very dear, became quite moderate. In three months, Pompey had rid the sea of pirates from end to end. He could never have accomplished this had he used force alone; but he promised pardon to those who surrendered, and thinking that most of them had taken to piracy more through destitution than through wickedness, he founded new cities and gave them land to cultivate.

58

Domitius sent men familiar with the region to Pompey in Apulia,[1] to beg him to come to his assistance, pointing out that if he were to do so Caesar could easily be hemmed in by the two armies and cut off from his corn supply; but if not, then Domitius' own peril would become graver every day. This letter was delivered on February 17th, and Pompey immediately sent the following reply: He could not possibly do as Domitius urged; not having sufficient confidence in the attitude of the troops he had with him, he dared not meet Caesar in a pitched battle till the men from the new levies were mobilized. Domitius was therefore to do all in his power to escape from Corfinium and join him at the earliest possible moment, before all their opponents' forces could be concentrated. Moreover, asked Pompey, whose fault was it that Domitius could not follow him? What reason had there been why he should take refuge in Corfinium?

[1] a district of southern Italy.

59

A few months after the Germans invaded our country, the 'Freedom Sender' began to be heard; and it has saved many of our lives in the last three years. There was a lawyer who went whispering about among the young men, telling them he could arrange for them to cross to England in small boats to continue the resistance. Many trusted him, supposing that the money which was needed for providing boats was being sent from England. But one night, a message came over the air through the Freedom Station, telling all good Norwegians to beware of this man, since he arranged not only for a boat but also for a German destroyer to intercept them just as they left the fiord. Not so long after this the lawyer was found dead in his bed, stabbed in several places; and it was not doubted that those responsible were the brothers of some whom he had betrayed.

60

Xenophon thus disposed of this accusation. When no-one else dared to accuse him of harsh treatment, he stood up himself and said he confessed he had flogged whoever was found setting his own profit and advantage before the general safety; for if such behaviour had been common, one and all would have perished. Others, too, he had beaten and compelled to go on when they wished to linger behind, even with the enemy close upon them. This he had done not because he was angry with them, but because there was no other means of saving them. For he knew by experience how pleasant it was to rest, when exhausted, how hard to rise, and how weary they all were of the long march. So just as parents were not blamed for punishing their children when it was necessary, so they ought to be grateful to him, however unpleasant they had found the blows at the time.

NOTES

TO THE ODD-NUMBERED PASSAGES

1. An exercise in the use of participles (§ 53). *Combination* of sentences is not needed. *Connection:* them (line 8): *quos*.
line 2. **to join ...:** § 271.
    4. **fighting took place:** § 261.
    5. **neither side:** *page* 95, *note* 1.
    7. **as they fled:** § 55.
    8. **those who:** § 372.
    9. **hills:** *montes* included hills of any considerable height.

3. *Connection:* for 'Phidippides' (line 5) use a pronoun; before 'the Spartans' (line 7) insert conjunction.
line 1. Order: The Athenian generals, when they learnt ..., sent (*cf.* § 431, *note* 1).
    4. **needed:** opus est (§ 182).
    5. **it is related:** make this personal (§ 145).
    6. **from Athens:** § 196, last example.
    7. **Spartans:** although the city was *Sparta*, the people were called *Lacedaemonii*. **request for help:** use *impetrare* (trans.), to ask successfully for.

5. *Combine* 'Meantime ... retreating' into one sentence. *Connection:* insert a conjunction in line 3. In line 8 (the natives) a small change of order brings the connecting word to the front. For abstract nouns (leadership, capture) see *ch.* 17.
line 9. **to choose a position:** locum capere, locum deligĕre.
    10. **to avoid:** § 213.

7. *l.* 2. **to guard:** § 271. **one day:** aliquando.
    4. **and:** omit; or use *autem*. **covered in:** plenus (§ 415).
    6. **turning round:** conversus—note tense and voice.
    9. **would to God:** utinam: § 392.
    10. **as easily as ...:** tam ... quam ... (§ 371).
    from him: § 301. One dative suffices for *both* verbs.

9. *Combine* into one sentence 'He summoned ... his fleet.'
line 2. **raise the siege of M.:** 'free M. from siege'.
    3. **he:** pronoun needed (§ 610 (*a*)).
    4. **too strong:** (*i.e.* too large): § 355. **thinking:** § 142, *note* 3.
    5. **as slowly as possible:** § 386.
    9. **by surprise:** *incautus, inopinans* qualify the victim (= off his

guard); *improvisus* qualifies the attacker (= unforeseen); *de improviso* is adv. phrase.

line 10. **fearing**: § 231.

11. *Combination* of sentences not needed.

line 1. **Delos** (Dēlus, -i, *f.*) is a 'small island'.
2. **an island on which**: 'on which island'.
3. **one night**: simply 'at night'.
6. **it is believed**: personal subject (§ 145).
8. **carrying**: use rel. clause.

13. The first two sentences may be combined. Use direct speech as in the English.

line 3. **addressed**: *N.B.* tibi haec loquor (*or* dico) *but* te his verbis alloquor.
6. **lies in** (depends on): the Latin metaphor is always 'is placed in'—aliquid in aliqua re positum est.
7. **the man who**: § 372. **climbs**: tense?

15. *Combine* sentences, if possible, in such a way as to make Solon the subject of all main verbs (§ 613).

line 1. **court**: say 'had come to Lydia to King C.' (§ 194).
2. **Croesus**: qui.
4. **said he**: carry on the Oratio Obliqua from the previous sentence, *without* using a verb of saying. Once any word implying reported speech has been used (here 'asked'), **no** other is required in Latin, however long the Or. Obl. continues. In English we insert 'he went on', 'he added', *&c.* at intervals; otherwise it would often not be clear that reported speech was still being used. In Latin the mood of the verbs makes it clear.
7. **knew**: I know (a person): *novi.* **of Athens**: use adj. (Atheniensis); the gen. would be quite wrong.
9. **sufficient wealth**: satis magnas divitias.
11. Use direct speech here.
12. **should**: *oportet* is best here: *cf.* § 403, *note* 2.

17. *ll.* 1, 2. Latin order: It was allowed to a father, if his daughter refused . . ., to have her put to death.
2. **have her . . .**: use *iubeo*.
4. **to Th.**: apud Thesea (acc. of *Theseus*). **of Athens**: *cf.* note on *No.* 19, *line* 8.
6. **because . . .**: § 552.
8. Keep to Oratio Obliqua throughout. *Cf.* note on *No.* 15, *line* 4.
12. **four days**: quattuor dierum spatium.

line 13. **pay the penalty**: phrases: poenas do *I pay the penalty;* poenas sumo *I exact the p.*—the noun is always *plural.*

19. *Combine* into three sentences; *connect* these suitably.

line 7. **Rome**: never use a place name as a political expression. English says, 'Germany attacked France'; Latin would name the people—Romani, populus Romanus.

9. See note on *No.* 15, *line* 4.

10. **he had better**: merely an Engl. circumlocution to show a command in reported speech (§ 584).

21. *l.* 1. **only ... nine**: 'a boy of nine years' (§ 413), or 'in my ninth year'—nonum annum agens.

2. **give an opportunity**: potestatem facere.

5. **on friendly terms**: amicus (*or* in amicitia cum).

9. **do my best**: phrases: operam dare ut ...; id agere ut ... (*cf. p.* 171, *note* 2).

11. **otherwise**: aliud (neuter acc.: a neuter pronoun may stand as the object of *persuadeo, credo, &c.*).

23. *l.* 1. Standard expression: dum haec ... geruntur.

3. **he ... he**: notice how all ambiguity vanishes in Latin.

4. **two camps**: bina (*not* duo): see grammar. **over**: § 382.

6. **these ... numerous**: 'these so great and so many'.

7. **the gods**: di immortales (conventional expression, like 'Providence' in Engl.).

9. **measures**: the Roman corn measure (about a peck): modius. **and**: *atque*, indicating that what follows is more striking or more important—'and, what is more'.

11. **except**: *nisi* (without a second verb), *e.g.* He saw no-one *except me*, Neminem nisi me vidit.

25. *l.* 1. **battle of Pharsalus** (-i, *f.*). Do not use the gen. As ex- explained in § 415, a few famous battlefields have adjectives, *e.g.* proelium Cannense, Philippense, Marathonium, Pharsalicum, *&c.* Otherwise one must say 'the battle fought at ...'—proelium ad (apud) Ilerdam factum.

3. Treat Cyprus as a *large* island.

4. Antiochēa, *f.*; its inhabitants, Antiochenses.

5. **his followers**: just *sui.*

6. **adding that**: see note on *No.* 15, *line* 4.

7. **peril**: phrases: in periculum (capitis) venire; aliquid magno cum (capitis, sui) periculo facere.

give up: (permanently) omitto, (temporarily) intermitto.

8. **much money**: magna pecunia.

line 9. **Ptolemy**: Ptolemaeus.
11. **either ... or**: in giving alternative *reasons*, sive ... sive.
12. **had him ...**: § 345.

27. *l.* 1. **remarkably handsome**: use abl. (or gen.) of description (§ 413 (iii)).
3. **of royal descent**: regii generis (gen. of description), *or* regia gente ortus (abl. of origin).
7. **he explained**: see note on *No.* 15, *line* 4. **tender**: omit.
8. **the day of the battle**: say 'the day on which ...'
9. **without ... knowledge**: § 177, 501.
11. **while trying**: *dum* cannot, of course, be followed by a participle (*cf.* § 451, *note* 3).
12. **Scipio ... he said ... Scipio**: § 613.

29. *l.* 1. Say 'owing to the deep snow they could ...' *N.B.* A 'preventing cause' may be expressed by *prae* (+ abl.) as well as by *propter*.
4. **mule**: mulus; **mule-driver**: mulio (-onis). **to let ...**: Engl. often uses *let* to make an infinitive possible, preferring infins. to clauses. Latin does not do so. Say 'he ordered A that B should ride'. *Cf. p.* 33, *note* 2.
5. **some distance**: part. gen.—aliquantum itineris.
6. **praised him for**: § 552. **bestow trouble on**: operam (tibi) praebeo.
9. **however ...**: § 564.
12. **treat cruelly**: (te) crudelitate afficio: an abl. of instrument with *afficere* is common in Latin, *e.g.* poena (supplicio) afficere *to punish*; dolore, gaudio afficere; *cf.* morbo affectus *ill*.

31. *Combine* in one sentence 'The man (line 4) ... some silver.' *Connection* to be expressed in line 4 by 'then'.
line 1. **a man**: quidam. **dreamed**: Latin idiom: so-and-so seems to me in my sleep to happen: aliquid mihi in somno fieri videtur.
2. **the meaning**: § 171.
6. **a quantity of**: aliquantum + part. gen. **some silver**: no need to translate *some*.
7. **some of**: use *pars*.
8. **not the man to**: § 283.

33. *Combine* the first three sentences thus: When C. the king, surrounded by his courtiers, was sitting ..., and they (*illi*) had ..., the king ...

line 1. **one day**: omit.
   2. **hoping**: use pres. part.
   3. **in virtue of**: relying on.
   4. **without**: § 502. **had it placed**: use *iubeo*.
   5. **now**: autem. **the tide rises**: aestus accedit, a. affluit.
   7. **and turning**: this *and* does not connect two parallel statements: make one subordinate. **turning**: conversus: note tense and voice.
   8. **there ... which**: § 284. **you see**: make this main clause.
   10. **the sort of man to**: § 283. **fl. words**: the words of flatterers (pres. part.).

35. *l.* 1. **Falerii**: its inhabitants were called *Falisci*.
   3. **for exercise**: say 'to exercise the body'. **and ... this**: rel. pron.
   4. **than usual**: solito.
   7. **Rome**: *i.e.* the people—see note on *No.* 19, *line* 8.
   12. **agreed**: use *placuit*.
   14. **arrange for**: curare (§ 345).

37. Make some of the co-ordinate clauses grammatically (as they are logically) subordinate; make use of connecting relatives.
line 2. **invulnerable**: express the idea in a verb.
   6. **too ...**: § 355. **by ramming**: 'with the beak': rostro.
   7. **tactics**: 'kind of fighting': genus pugnae, g. pugnandi.
   8. **sickles**: falces; **long poles**: longurii.
   9. **these orders ...**: note Caesar's simple expression: quod iussi sunt faciunt.
   13. **to escape by flight**: fugā salutem petere.
   14. **which**: § 376. **advantage**: use predicative dative and say 'useful for (*ad*) succeeding'.
   15. **success**: phrases: rem bene gero *I succeed*, rem male gero *I fail*.

39. Refer to § 613. Make the elder Fabius the subject of every *main* verb except 'was elected' and 'knows'.
line 5. **younger**: to distinguish father and son, Latin uses (regardless of age) *senex, adulescens*.
   6. **join**: beware of this word. *Adiungere* (trans. vb.) means to join one thing to another; when 'join' means attach oneself to, the Latin is *se adiungere* (+ dat.).
   8. **lictors** were the magistrates' attendant 'police': a consul had twelve.
   10. **shouted**: say: 'ordered in a loud voice'.
   12. **clearly enough**: satis.

41. *l.* 3. **hoped:** use causal rel. clause.
   4. **make up to** (curry favour with): *captare.*
   6. **do all they could:** omnia facere ut . . .
   7. **but:** this contrast may well be expressed by *idem* (put first for emphasis). Make *changed* the main verb.
   8. **how long:** either *quam diu* or (stronger) *quousque.*
   9. **keep in torment:** (torture) *cruciare.*
   since . . .: use a rel. clause with deferred antecedent (§ 374): quem . . . ei . . .
   14. **so far from:** § 504.
43. Combine and connect sentences, except at lines 11–13.
line 1. **various:** either *diversus* or use *alius* (§ 525).
   2. **to collect corn:** see § 352, note.
   4. **panic spread:** § 262; use *trepidare.* **throughout:** § 192 (ii).
   5. **all the more because:** eo magis quod.
   6. **demoralisation:** 'panic of all'; or avoid abstract noun.
   9. **all over with:** phrase: actum est de me.
   10. **unarmed as he was:** the adj., alone, may be used with concessive force.
   11. **the situation . . . critical:** res in summo periculo (*or* discrimine) est.
   11–13. Here (although the English does not) Latin would mark the climax, with its rapid action, by short unconnected sentences, probably in historic present, and with verbs placed first.
   13. **on outpost duty:** *N.B.* A preposition-phrase may not be used as an adjective phrase in Latin (exceptions are few: *cf. p.* 155, *note.*) Use rel. clause.
   the respite . . .: avoid abstract subject (§ 616). Make *reliqui* subject. Phrase: spatium interponere. **man:** complere; *or* consistere in (+ abl.).
45. *l.* 3. **discuss peace:** de pace agere. **until:** § 455.
   4. **possible that:** § 494.
   7. **poison him:** kill him by poison.
   8, 9. **honour . . . expediency:** the neuter adjj. *honestum* and *utile* were constantly used as nouns in this sense.
   11. **honour** (= good faith): fides.
   13. **action:** factum. The neuter participle is used as a noun (therefore, *eius* factum): *cf.* dictum, iussum.
47. *l.* 1. **without . . . ship:** 'all the ships (being) safe' (*incolumis*, not *tutus*).

line 2. **report of his approach:** could (*not* must) be expressed by verbs.
7. **take advantage of:** utor. **run** (into danger): venio. **in the course of:** *in* + abl. of gerund.
10. **some thirty in number:** ad triginta.
11. **in the hope of:** § 573. **this cruel p.:** 'this so cruel p.'

49. *l.* 1. **plague:** say 'such a large number that...'
2. **twenty:** distributive numeral (20 *each* day).
3. **getting ... nerves:** use *affligo* (in passive).
4. **request ... granted:** impetro (+ reported command).
5. **greatly enjoyed:** 'it was a great joy to them to give...' (predic. dat.) **false alarms:** express the sense.
6. **not to mention:** 'keep silent about'.
7. **on pain of:** 'threatening'.
8. **a joke at his expense:** use *ludibrio esse* (§ 294).
9. **by leaping sideways:** obliquo saltu. **stroke:** ictus, -ûs.
10. **even:** vel.
14. **Arabs:** Arabes.

51. *l.* 2. **officer:** the translation must depend on the context. Each legion was officered by six *tribuni militum*; in earlier times they were the chief and only officers, and took it in turns to command the whole legion. In Caesar's time and afterwards, each legion was usually under a *legatus* (i.e. a 'deputy' or 'delegate' of the supreme commander); the tribuni played a subordinate rôle. Officers commanding specialist troops were called *praefecti*: *e.g.* praefectus equitum, praefectus fabrum (engineers), *&c.*
4. **be eclipsed:** deficere. **from 8 to 10 p.m.:** 'from the second to the fourth hour of the night': hours were always counted from sunrise or from sunset.
9. **these events ... laws:** 'these things occur by natural order'. It would not occur to a Roman to use 'law' (a man-made rule) as a metaphor in this way.
8. **for the simple reason that:** an emphatic 'because'—propterea quod.
11. **superhuman:** divinus. **caused:** use either predic. dat. or *afficio* (explained in note on *No.* 29, *line* 12).

53. *l.* 1. **indeed ... not:** *non* + *enim* becomes *neque enim*.
5. **public meeting:** contio (an assembly of the people to hear a speech but not to vote).

line 8. **as one does:** ut fit *or* ut fieri solet.
- 10. **with:** abl. of attendant circumstance: make *nullus* the emphasized link between the phrases.
- 12. **overcoat:** paenula.
- 15. **master** (of slaves): dominus (magister = schoolmaster).
- 16. **any man ... his slaves:** suos quisque servos. *N.B.* Parts of *se* (or *suus*) and *quisque* are brought together in the sentence for mutual emphasis, the reflexive preceding.
  in such a situation: in tali re.

55. *l.* 3. **attack:** use *peto*; say 'the A. especially were being attacked'.
  since: causal rel. cl.
- 4. **battle of M.:** see note on *No.* 25, *line* 1.
- 8. **what ...:** to get this emphasis, use an anticipatory *illud*: *e.g. What I advise you to do is to go:* illud te moneo, ut eas.
- 9. **these:** hos, *not* has. A pronoun subject agrees with a complement-noun. This was mentioned so far as concerned relative pronouns in § 377.
- 12. **movable property:** 'property which could be moved'.

57. *l.* 1. **pirates:** subject. **power:** potentia, *not* potestas. **reach such heights of:** 'come to that point on the scale of'—usque eo (+ gen.) venire.
- 3. **except:** nisi.
- 4. **suffer from:** use impers. passive of *laborare*.
- 8. **greater powers than:** Latin prefers correlatives: tantum ... quantum nemo ... (*N.B.* nemo Romanus, *not* nullus R.)
- 10. **price of corn:** annona. Say 'the *annona*, from (being) very dear, became moderate (*modicus*)'. *Cf. From being poor, I became rich:* e paupere dives factus sum.
- 13. **pardon:** use a verb.
- 15. **more:** potius.
- 16. **land** (for farming): ager (collective sing.).

59. *l.* 1. **invaded:** for tense in this clause see § 452, *note.*
- 2. **the Freedom Sender** might be called 'the voice of freedom'. More precise definition is not necessary. **saved lives:** saluti esse (do not mention *vita* in 'spare life, save life').
- 4. **whispering about:** express the sense.
- 9. **good N.:** Latin uses *boni* for 'patriots' (often in Cic.).
- 11. **destroyer:** fast warship—navis actuaria.
- 12. **not so long after:** haud ita multo post.
- 14. **responsible:** auctor esse = to be the proposer of, to be responsible for. Or use *id facere*.

VOCABULARY

To avoid errors, and to obtain the greatest measure of information from the vocabulary, study these notes.

Nouns. The genitive of all 3rd, 4th and 5th declension nouns is given. *Proper nouns* are not given if the English form clearly indicates the Latin.

Pronouns, possessive adjectives and *numerals* are not given.

Adverbs formed regularly from adjectives are not given separately.

Verbs. Regular verbs of the 1st, 2nd and 4th conjugations are marked 1, 2, 4. Principal parts of other verbs are given in full; but to save repetition, compounds of common verbs whose principal parts should be familiar are merely marked with *. If their parts have to be looked up, they will be found in the list on the next page. Verbs are not marked *transitive* or *intransitive* unless the English use differs from the Latin.

Quantities of common endings, assumed to be known, are not marked; elsewhere, long vowels are marked (but the mark is not repeated each time the word is printed). A few short vowels, where special warning is needed, are also marked.

Abbreviations need no explanation, except these:
   mil. = military term or use;
   No. (in references) indicates a prose passage.

A *comma* separating two Latin equivalents implies that they are synonyms, more or less interchangeable; while a semi-colon implies different senses or different uses.

Some words are left out: they have obvious synonyms, under which the Latin is given. Sometimes a hint is given in the form (= so-and-so). For example, the entry

      as (conj.) (= since); (of manner), sicut; ut

means 'The conjunction "as" is a synonym of "since", and the Latin for it may be looked up under "since"; as may also be a word of manner—Latin *sicut* or *ut*.'

PRINCIPAL PARTS OF COMMON COMPOUND VERBS

(The sign * in the vocabulary refers to the following list)

	Simple verb	Basic meaning
-cēdo, -cēděre, -cessi, -cessum	cēdo	go; yield
-cĭdo, -cĭděre, -cĭdi, *no supine*[1]	cado	fall
-cīdo, -cīděre, -cīdi, -cīsum	caedo	cut
-cipio, -cipěre, -cēpi, -ceptum	capio	take
-curro, -currěre, -curri[2], -cursum	curro	run
-dīco, -dīcěre, -dixi, -dictum	dico	say
-do, -děre, -didi, -ditum	do (dăre)	give
-dūco, -dūcěre, -duxi, -ductum	dūco	lead
-eo, -ire, -ii, -ĭtum	eo	go
-fero, -ferre, -tuli, -lātum	fero	bear
-ficio, -ficěre, -fēci, -fectum	facio	do; make
-fugio, -fugěre, -fūgi, -fugitum	fugio	flee
-gredior, -gredi, -gressus sum	—	go; come
-icio, -icěre, -iēci, -iectum	iacio	throw
-lābor, -lābi, -lapsus sum	lābor	fall
-loquor, -loqui, -locutus sum	loquor	speak
-mitto, -mittěre, -mīsi, -missum	mitto	send
-pello, -pellere, -puli, -pulsum	pello	drive
-pōno, -pōněre, -pŏsui, -positum	pōno	put
-prehendo, -ěre, -prehendi, -nsum	prehendo	grasp; take
-rumpo, -rumpěre, -rūpi, -ruptum	rumpo	break
-scendo, -scenděre, -scendi, -scensum	—	climb
-sequor, -sequi, -secūtus sum	sequor	follow
-sisto, -sistěre, -stiti, *no supine*	sisto	stand
-spicio, -spicěre, -spexi, -spectum	—	see; look
-stituo, -stituěre, -stitui, -stitūtum	statuo	set up
-sūmo, -sūměre, -sumpsi, -sumptum	sūmo	take
-tineo, -tiněre, -tinui, -tentum	teneo	hold
-venio, -venīre, -vēni, -ventum	venio	come
-video, -viděre, -vīdi, -vīsum	video	see

[1] *except* occasum
[2] *or* -cucurri

VOCABULARY

abandon, relinquo, -ĕre, relīqui, relictum; (desert), desero, -ĕre, -ui, -tum; (leave off), dēsisto* (+*abl.*), omitto*
ability (mental), ingenium, *n.*
be able, possum, posse, potui
about (*prep.*), dē (+*abl.*); (approximately), circiter (*adv.*), ad
above all, praesertim
in absence, absens (§ 54)
be absent, absum, abesse, āfui (+ab)
accept, accipio*
by accident, cāsu
accomplish, efficio*; *see* do
of own accord, (meā, suā) sponte
account (=reason)
accusation, crīmen, -inis, *n.*
accuse, accūso 1 (§ 422)
be accustomed, soleo, -ēre, solitus sum
acquit, absolvo, -ĕre, absolvi, absolutum (§ 422)
across (*prep.*), trans (+*acc.*)
act, ago, -ĕre, ēgi, actum
act, action, factum, *n.*
address (speak to), alloquor* (*tr.*)
adequate, satis magnus
adjourn (*intr.*), (=depart)
admire, admīror 1
admit (let in), admitto*
adopt (a plan), capio, ineo* (*tr.*)
advance, prōcēdo*, prōgredior*; **advanced** (age), prōvectus
advantage, ūsus (*cf.* § 293); commodum (*in passage* 60)
adverse, adversus

advice, consilium, *n.*; **on — of**, § 177
advise, moneo, admoneo 2
from afar, prŏcul
be afraid, timeo 2, vereor 2; **be afraid of**, timeo (*tr.*)
after (*prep.*), post (+*acc.*); (*conj.*), postquam (§ 452)
afterwards, posteā
again, iterum (a second time); rursus; (afterwards), posthāc, posteā; **— and —**, iterum iterumque
against (*prep.*), contrā (+*acc.*); (*mil., with* impetus, *&c.*) in (+*acc.*)
age, aetas, aetatis, *f.*; **old age**, senectūs, -tutis, *f.*; **at age of, aged**, nātus (+*acc.*) (§ 154)
ago, abhinc (+*acc.*) (§ 155)
agree, consentio, -ire, -sensi, -sensum (cum+*abl.*); (decide), *use* placet (§ 404)
aid (=help)
aimlessly, temerē
alarm (warning cry), clāmor, -ōris, *m.*
alarm (frighten), commoveo, -ēre, -mōvi, -mōtum; perterreo 2
alive, vīvus; **be alive**, vīvo, -ĕre, vixi, victum
all, omnis, cunctus; (=whole of), totus; **one and all**, ūniversi; **it is all over with**, actum est de (+*abl.*)
all but, § 513
at all, omnīno (*before a neg.*)

241

allow, patior, -i, passus sum; sino, -ĕre, sīvi, situm[1]; **I am allowed,** mihi licet (*impers.*), § 403
ally, socius, *m.*
almost, paenĕ
alone, sōlus
along (*prep.*), per (+*acc.*)
come alongside, appropinquo 1 (+*dat.*)
aloud, magnā vōce
already, iam
also, quoque; (not only) **but also,** sed etiam
altar, āra, *f.*
alter, mūto 1
although, quamquam, etsi; cum (§ 461)
always, semper
be amazed, obstupesco, -ĕre, obstupui
ambassador, lēgātus, *m.*
ambush, insidiae, *f. plu.*
among (*prep.*), inter (+*acc.*); apud (+*acc.*)
amuse, dēlecto 1
ancestors, māiores, *m. plu.*
anchor, ancora, *f.*; **weigh —,** ancoram (or -as) tollo, navem (or -es) solvo
ancient, antīquus; vetus, veteris[2]
and, et, -que; **and not,** neque
anger, īra, *f.*
Anglesey, Mŏna, *f.*
angry, īrātus; **be angry, get —,** īrascor, -i, iratus sum
annihilate, dēleo, -ēre, -ēvi, -ētum
announce, prōnuntio 1

another, alius, alia, aliud; **at — time,** aliās (*adv.*)
answer, respondeo, -ēre, respondi, responsum (+*dat. of person*)
answer (*noun*), responsum, *n.*
Antony, Antōnius, *m.*
anxiety, cūra, *f.* (§ 293)
anxious to, cupidus (+*gen.*); **be anxious for,** timeo (+*dat.*)
any, anyone, anything (*after a neg.*), § 132; (*after* ne, si), quis (§ 211–12); (*in questions*), quis (§ 201); (= any you like), quilibet, quivis: *see also* § 526
anywhere, usquam; **not —,** nusquam
Apollo, Apollo, Apollinis, *m.*
appear (be in view, come into view), appāreo 2; (seem), videor, -ēri, vīsus sum
apple, mālum, *n.*
approach, appropinquo 1 (+*dat.*); accēdo* (ad)
approval (=praise)
approve, probo 1
arcade, porticus, -ūs, *f.*
archer, sagittārius, *m.*
arise, orior, oriri, ortus sum; coörior
arm (limb), bracchium, *n.*
armed, armatus
arms, arma, *n. pl.*; **take up arms,** arma sumo
army, exercitus, -ūs, *m.*
arouse, excito 1; (feelings), moveo
arrange for, cūro 1 (§ 345)
arrest, comprehendo*

---

[1] *patior,* merely 'not prevent'; *sino,* actually 'give consent'.
[2] *vetus,* 'old but still existing'; *antiquus,* 'former', usually implying 'no longer current'.

arrival, adventus, -ūs, *m.*
arrive, venio*, pervenio, advenio; arrive at (= come to)
arrogant, superbus
arrow, sagitta, *f.*
art, ars, artis, *f.*
as (*in comparisons*), § 371; as if, § 574
as (*conj.*) (=since); (*of manner*), sicut; ut
ascend, ascendo*, *tr. or intr.*
ascertain, cognosco, -ĕre, cognōvi, cognitum
be ashamed, pudet (*impers.*), § 402
ask, rogo 1 (*acc. of person*); (+*rep. question*), (te) rogo, (te) interrogo, (ex te) quaero; (+ *rep. command*), (te) rogo, (a te, ex te) peto; ask for, rogo, peto (*both + acc. of thing*: § 87)
be asleep, dormio 4
assault, oppugno 1
assault (*noun*), oppugnatio, -onis, *f.*
assemble (*intr.*), convenio*
assert, affirmo 1
assure, § 86, *note*
at (a town), *use loc. case;* (=near), ad; (*with* throw, shoot, *&c.*), in (+*acc.*); be at, adsum (+*dat.*)
at once (immediately), statim, confestim; (simultaneously), simul
Athenian, Athēniensis
Athens, Athēnae, *f. plu.*
Atlas, Atlas, Atlantis, *m.*
attack, oppugno 1; (persons only), aggredior*; (= pounce on), adorior, -iri, adortus sum; (in battle), impetum facio (in +*acc.*)

attack (*noun*), impetus, -ūs, *m.*
attain (an object), consequor*
attempt, cōnor 1 (+ *infin. only*)
attempt (*noun*), cōnatus, -ūs, *m.*
attend, adsum, adesse, adfui (+*dat.*)
attendant, cŏmes, comitis, *m.*
attitude (mental), voluntas, -tatis, *f.*
avarice, avāritia, *f.*
avenge, ulciscor, -ī, ultus sum
avoid, vīto 1; to avoid (*neg. purpose*), § 213
be awake, vigilo 1
awaken, excito 1
be away, absum, abesse, āfui

back (*adv.*), *prefix* re
bad, malus; badly, malĕ
band (troop), manus, -ūs, *f.*
banish, expello* (*alone or* + *abl.*)
bank (of river), rīpa, *f.*
barbarian, barbarus
bare, nūdus
bark, latro 1; barking (*noun*), clāmōres, *m. plu.*
battle, proelium, *n.*, pugna, *f.*; battle of, *see* § 415
battle-line, aciēs, -ei, *f.*
bay, sinus, ūs, *m.*
beard, barba, *f.*
beast, fera, *f.*
beat (=defeat)
beat (whip), verbero 1; concīdo*
beautiful, pulcher, -chra, -chrum
beauty, forma, *f.*, pulchritudo, -dinis, *f.*
because, quod, quia: *see ch.* 55
because of, propter (+*acc.*)
become, fio, fieri, factus sum
bed, lectus, *m.*

before (*prep.*), ante (+*acc.*); (*adv.*), ante, anteā; (*conj.*), ante quam, prius quam; (=in the presence of) cōram (+*abl.*)

beg (+*rep. command*), ōro 1; **beg for**, oro (*tr.*), peto (*tr.*)[1]

begin, incipio, -ĕre, coepi, coeptum (*only* + *infin.*); (*with object-noun*), *use* initium facio (+*gen.*)

beginning of, prīmus (§ 411)

begrudge, invideo* (id tibi)

on behalf of, prō (+*abl.*)

behave, me gero, -ĕre, gessi, gestum; *or use* ago

behind (*prep.*), post (+*acc.*)

from behind (*mil.*), a tergo

believe, crēdo, -ĕre, credidi, creditum; puto 1; (*person as object*), credo (+*dat.*)

belong to, sum (+ *possessive gen.*)

belongings, bona, *n. plu.*

belt, balteus, *m.*

benefit, prōsum, prodesse, profui (+*dat.*)

besiege, obsideo, -ēre, obsēdi, obsessum

best, optimus

betray, prōdo*

between (*prep.*), inter (+*acc.*)

beware of, caveo, -ēre, cāvi, cautum (*tr.*)

beyond (*prep.*), ultrā (+*acc.*)

bind (fetter), vincio, -ire, vinxi, vinctum

bird, avis, avis, *f.*

black, niger, nigra, nigrum

blame, reprehendo*

blame (*noun*), culpa

blessed (=fortunate)

blind, caecus

blockade (*noun*), obsidio, -onis, *f.*

blood, sanguis, sanguinis, *m.*

blow (*noun*), plaga, *f.*

board (a ship), (navem, in navem) conscendo*; (in battle), (in hostium navem) transcendo*; **put on board**, (in navem) impōno*

boast, glōrior 1

boat, nāvis, navis, *f.*; (small), nāvicula, *f.*

body, corpus, -oris, *n.*

bold, audax

boldness, audācia *f.*

bone, ŏs, ossis, *n.*

book, līber, libri, *m.*

booty, praeda, *f.*

borders, fīnes, *m. plu.*

boring, *use* me piget (*impers.*), § 402

be born, nascor, nasci, nātus sum

both (*pron. adj.*), uterque (*sing.*); **both sides** (*or* parties), utrique (*plu.*)

both ... and, et ... et; cum ... tum (§ 467)

bound to, *see* § 494

bow (weapon), arcus, -ūs, *m.*

boy, puer, pueri, *m.*

branch, rāmus, *m.*

brave, fortis

bread, panis, panis, *m.*

break, frango, -ĕre, frēgi, fractum (*tr.*); **break down** (bridge, &c.), refringo, -ĕre, refrēgi, refractum; **break out** (arise), orior, oriri, ortus sum; coörior; **break** (a battle-line), perfringo; **break one's word,**

---

[1] *oro*, like *rogo* (§ 87, *note*), with acc. of person, *or* acc. of thing asked for, but not both at once: *te oro ut venias* but *auxilium a te oro*.

fidem fallo, -ĕre, fefelli, falsum; break through (*intr.*), perrumpo*
breast, pectus, -oris, *n.*
breeze, aura, *f.*, ventus, *m.*
bribe, corrumpo*
bribery, ambitus, -ūs, *m.*
bridge, pons, pontis, *m.*
brief, brevis
brigand, latro, -onis, *m.*
bring (things), affero*; (persons), addūco*; **bring back**, reporto 1; **bring in**, infero*; **bring over**, transporto 1; **bring up** (*mil.*), addūco*; **bring up** (a child), ēdŭco 1
Britain, Britannia, *f.*
Briton, Britannus
brother, frāter, fratris, *m.*
bugle, tŭba, *f.*
build, aedifico 1; facio
bull, taurus, *m.*
burden, onus, oneris, *n.*
burn (destroy by fire), incendo, -ĕre, incendi, incensum
bury (things), dēfodio, -ĕre, defōdi, defossum
business, negōtium, *n.*; rēs, rei, *f.*
but, sed; autem (*after first word*); **cannot but**, § 494
buy, emo, emere, ēmi, emptum
bystanders, adstantes (*see* § 55)

Caesar, Caesar, Caesaris, *m.*
call (summon), voco 1; (name), appello 1; **call together**, convoco
camp, castra, -orum, *n. plu.*
campaign, bellum, *n.*
can, possum, posse, potui; **cannot but . . .**, § 494
Capitol, Capitōlium, *n.*
captor, *use* capio
capture, capio, -ĕre, cēpi, captum
care (*noun*), cūra, *f.*; **take care to**, § 84
care for, cūro 1 (*tr.*); (= value) facio (§ 322)
careful, dīligens
careless, neglegens
carelessness, neglegentia, *f.*
carriage, raeda, *f.*
carry, porto 1, fero*; **carry away**, aufero, auferre, abstuli, ablātum; **carry out** (perform), fungor, -i, functus sum (+*abl.*), facio; **carried away** (*metaphor*), ēlātus
cart, plaustrum, *n.*
Carthage, Carthāgo, -inis, *f.*
Carthaginian (*noun*), Poenus; (*adj.*) Pūnicus
case (legal), causa, *f.*; **plead case**, causam dico
in case, si, si forte (§ 573); **this being the case**, quae cum ita sint (essent)
casualties, *use* vulnero 1 (*in pass.*) *or* vulnera accipio*
catch, capio, -ĕre, cēpi, captum; **catch sight of**, conspicor 1, conspicio* (*both tr.*)
Catiline, Catilīna, *m.*
cause, causa, *f.*; see § 172
cavalry, equites, *m. plu.*
cave, spēlunca, *f.*
cease, dēsino, -ĕre (*for perf. use* dēstiti *from* desisto) (+*infin.*); finem facio (+*gen.*)
censor, censor, -ōris, *m.*
centre of, medius (§ 411); **centre** (*mil.*), media acies

centurion, centurio, -onis, *m.*
a certain, quidam, quaedam, quoddam
certainly, sine dubio (*not* certe)
chair, sella, *f.*
challenge (to battle), (proelio) lacesso, -ĕre, lacessivi, lacessitum
chance (opportunity), occāsio, -onis, *f.*, facultas, -tatis, *f.*
change, mūto 1 (*tr.*)
character (a person's), mōres, *m. plu.*
characteristic of, *see* § 63
charge (*mil.*), impetum facio (in + *acc.*)
charge (*noun*) (*mil.*), impetus, -ūs, *m.*
in **charge of**: *see* entrust
cheap (*adj.*), vīlis; (*adv.*) vili (§ 324)
cheat, decipio*, fraudo 1
check, coerceo 2
cheer: be of good —, bono animo sum
chieftain, princeps, principis, *m.*
child, puer, pueri, *m.*; (little), infans, infantis, *c.*; **children**, līberi, *m. plu.*[1]
choose, dēligo, -ĕre, delēgi, delectum; (a place), deligo, capio; **choose to** (= like to), *use* libet
Cingetorix, Cingetorix, -origis, *m.*
in the **circumstances**, quae cum ita sint (essent)
citadel, arx, arcis, *f.*
citizen, cīvis, civis, *c.*

citizenship, cīvitas, -tatis, *f.*
city, urbs, urbis, *f.*
clan, gens, gentis, *f.*
it is **clear**, appāret; **make clear**, dēmonstro 1
cliff, rūpes, rupis, *f.*
climb, ascendo* (*tr. and intr.*); (=climb over), transcendo*
close, claudo, -ĕre, clausi, clausum
closely, *see* follow
clothes, vestīmenta, *n. plu.*
club, fustis (*abl.* fusti), *m.*
coast, ōra, *f.*
coastal, maritimus
cohort, cohors, cohortis, *f.*
cold (*noun*), frīgus, frigoris, *n.*
collapse, dēlābor, -i, delapsus sum
colleague, collēga, *m.*
column (of troops), agmen, -inis, *n.*
come, venio*; **come back**, revenio*, regredior*; **come down**, dēscendo*; **come off** (best, *&c.*), discēdo*; **come up** (to help), subvenio* (+*dat.*)
command (=order), impero 1 (+*dat.*); (be commander of), praesum, praeesse, praefui (+*dat.*)
command (*noun*) (=order), *see* order; (power), imperium; **be in — of**, praesum (+*dat.*); **put in — of**, praeficio* (+*acc. and dat.*)
commander, imperātor, -ōris, *m.*; **be — of**, praesum (+*dat.*)

---

[1] *liberi* (like Engl. 'offspring') only with reference to a parent—*e.g.* his children, *liberi eius*. Latin has no word for 'children' in the sense of youngsters, but makes do with *pueri*.

commit (crime), (scelus) admitto*
common people, plebs, plēbis, *f.*, vulgus, -i, *n.*
companion, cŏmes, comitis, *c.*
compel, cogo, -ĕre, coēgi, coactum
complain, queror, -i, questus sum
completely, *use* omnis, totus; **so —**, adeo (*adv.*)
comrade, cŏmes, comitis, *c.*
conceal (=hide)
concentrate (forces), cōgo
concern oneself with, *use* curae esse (§ 293)
condemn, damno 1 (§ 422)
on **condition that**, eā condicione ut, ne
confess, confiteor, -ēri, -fessus sum
have **confidence** in (=trust)
in **confusion**, turbatus, disiectus
conquer, vinco, -ĕre, vīci, victum
conqueror, victor, -ōris, *m.*
consider (=think); (take account of), respicio*; — **the interests of**, consulo, -ĕre, consului, consultum (+*dat.*)
conspiracy, coniūratio, -onis, *f.*
conspirator, coniūratus, *m.*
conspire, coniūro 1
constant, perpetuus
construct (=make, build)
consul, consul, consulis, *m.*
consulship, consulatus, -ūs, *m.*
consult, consulo, -ĕre, -sului, -sultum; — **the interests of**, consulo (+*dat.*)
consume, consumo*

content (*adj.*), contentus (+*abl.*)
contest (*noun*), certāmen, -inis, *n.*; proelium, *n.*
continue (prolong), prōduco*; — **a journey**, pergo, -ĕre, perrexi, perrectum (*intr.*)
contrary to, contrā (+*acc.*)
converse, colloquor* (cum + *abl.*)
convict, damno 1, condemno 1 (+ *gen. of charge*)
convince, persuādeo, -ēre, -suāsi, -suāsum (+*dat.*)
Corinth, Corinthus, *f.*
corn, frūmentum, *n.*; **collect corn**, frūmentor 1
cost, sto, stare, stĕti, statum (§ 326)
council, concilium, *n.*; — **of war**, concilium
country, terra, *f.*; (fatherland), patria, *f.*; (*opp. to* town), rūs, rūris, *n.* (§ 192)
country-house, villa, *f.*
countryside, agri, *m. plu.*
courage, virtūs, virtutis, *f.*, fortitudo, -dinis, *f.*, animus, *m.*
course (ship's), cursus, -ūs, *m.*
in **course of**, in (+*abl.*)
courtier, (rēgis) amīcus
cover, tego, -ĕre, texi, tectum
coward, ignāvus
cowardice, ignāvia, *f.*
Crete, Crēta, *f.*
crew (=sailors)
crime, scelus, sceleris, *n.*
crisis, discrīmen, -inis, *n.*
critical (situation), *see note to No. 43*
cross, transeo* (*tr.*)
crowd, multitudo, -dinis, *f.*, turba, *f.* (*implies* mob); **a**

crowd gathers, concurritur (*impers.*)
cruel, crūdēlis
cry (shout), clāmo 1
cultivate, colo, -ĕre, colui, cultum
cunning (*noun*), ars, artis, *f.*
cure, sāno 1
custom, mōs, mōris, *m.* (*esp. in phrase* mos maiorum)
cut, caedo, -ĕre, cecīdi, caesum; dēcīdo*; seco, -are, secui, sectum; **cut down** (trees), caedo, excīdo*; **cut off** (from) (*mil.*), interclūdo (+*abl.*)
Cyclops, Cyclops, -ōpis, *m.*

daily (*adv.*), cottīdie
danger, perīculum, *n.*
dare, audeo, -ēre, ausus sum (+*infin.*)
daring (*adj.*), audax
daring (*noun*), audācia
dark (*noun*), nox, noctis, *f.*
date, dies, diei, *m.* or *f.*
daughter, fīlia, *f.*
dawn, prima lux
day, dies, diei, *m.*; **by day**, interdiu; **next day**, postrīdie; **every day**, cottīdie; **two days**, biduum, *n.*; **three days**, triduum, *n.*
daybreak (=dawn)
dead, mortuus
dear, cārus; *or use* cordi (§ 293); (in price), carus
death, mors, mortis, *f.*; **put to death**, interficio*; **condemn to death**, capitis damno
debt, aes aliēnum, aeris alieni
deceive, dēcipio*; fallo, -ĕre, fefelli, falsum

deception, fraus, fraudis, *f.*
decide, statuo, -ĕre, statui, statutum; constituo* (*both* + *infin. or* + ut-*clause*; *sometimes* + *rep. speech clause*); *or use* placet (*impers.*) (§ 404)
declare, affirmo 1; dico*; **declare war on**, bellum indīco* (+*dat.*)
decree (*vb.*), *use* placet (§ 404)
deed, factum, *n.*
deep, altus
defeat, supero 1, vinco, -ĕre, vīci, victum
defeat (*noun*), clādes, cladis, *f.*, adversum proelium
defenceless, inermis
defend, dēfendo, -ĕre, defendi, defensum
defendant, reus, *m.*
dejected (=downcast)
delay, moror 1 (*tr. and intr.*); (hesitate), cunctor 1 (*intr.*)
delay (*noun*), mŏra, *f.*; **without delay**, nullā morā
deliberately, consulto
delight (*vb.*), *use* me iuvat, mihi libet (§§ 403, 404)
deliver, dēfero*, reddo*
Delos, Dēlus, -i, *f.*
Delphi, Delphi, -orum, *m. plu.*
demand, postulo 1 (ab+*abl.*); (=commandeer), impero 1 (+*dat. of person*)
demoralized, perterritus, permōtus
deny, nego 1
depart, discēdo*, dīgredior*
deprive, prīvo (+*abl.*) (§ 543)
depth, altitudo, -dinis, *f.*
deputation, legati, *m. plu.*
deputy, lēgātus, *m.*

descend, dēscendo*
descent (=ancestry), gens, gentis, *f.*; genus, generis, *n.*
desert (*tr.*), dēsero, -ĕre, deserui, desertum; relinquo; (*intr.*), transfugio*
deserter, transfuga, *m.*
deserve, dignus sum (+*abl.*); **deserve to,** dignus sum (+qui-*clause*) (§ 286); **deserve well of,** bene mereor (2) de (§ 414)
deserving, dignus (+*abl.*)
design (=plan); **by —,** consulto
desire, cupio, -ĕre, cupivi, cupitum; volo, velle, volui
desire (*noun*), cupīdo, -dinis, *f.*
desirous, cupidus (+*gen.*)
despair, dēspēro 1
despise (look down on), dēspicio*; (make light of), contemno, -ĕre, -tempsi, -temptum
destitution, egestas, -tatis, *f.*
destroy, dēleo, -ēre, -ēvi, -ētum
detain, retineo*
deter, dēterreo 2
determination (will-power), constantia, *f.*
determine (=decide)
devote oneself to, be devoted to, studeo 2 (+*dat.*)
dictator, dictator, -ōris, *m.*
dictatorship, dictatura, *f.*
die, morior, mori, mortuus sum; (perish), pereo*
difference: it makes a —, interest (§ 405)
different (other), alius; (unlike), dissimilis (§ 424)
difficult, difficilis

difficulty, difficultas, -tatis, *f.*; **be in —,** labōro 1 (*esp. in pres. part.*); **with —,** aegre
dig, dig up, effodio, -ĕre, effōdi, effossum
dine, cēno 1
dinner, dinner-party, cēna, *f.*
direction, *use* pars, partis, *f.* (*e.g.* in omnes partes); **from all directions,** undique
disagree, dissentio, -ire, -sensi, -sensum
disastrous, exitio (§ 294)
discipline, disciplīna, *f.*
disclose, aperio, -ire, aperui, apertum
discover (= find *or* find out)
discuss (peace), de (pace) ago
disembark (*intr.*), (nave, e nave) ēgredior*; (*tr.*) expono*
disgrace, dēdecus, -oris, *n.*
disgraceful, turpis
dislodge, deicio*
dismount, ex equo descendo*
display (=ostentation), apparātus, -ūs, *m.*
displease, displiceo 2 (+*dat.*)
dispose of (a charge), dīluo, -ĕre, -ui, -utum
disregard, contemno, **-ĕre,** -tempsi, -temptum; neglego, -ĕre, neglexi, neglectum
in distance, from —, procul
distinguished, praeclārus, insignis
distress (=grief); (=poverty), inopia, *f.*; **be in distress,** labōro 1
distribute, distribuo, -ĕre, -ui, -utum
district, regio, -onis, *f.*; loca (*n. plu.*) (§ 192, ii)

ditch, fossa, *f.*
divide, dīvido, -ĕre, dīvīsi, dīvīsum
division (of troops), *use* legio, -onis, *f.*
do, facio, -ĕre, fēci, factum; ago, agere, ēgi, actum; gero, -ĕre, gessi, gestum[1]; **do one's best**, operam do (ut), id ago (ut); **do wrong**, pecco 1
doctor, medicus, *m.*
dog, canis, canis, *c.*
doom, exitium, *n.* (§ 294)
door, iānua, *f.*
doubt, dubito 1 (§ 492)
doubt (*noun*): **there is no doubt**, *use adj.* dubium (doubtful) (§ 492)
down from (*prep.*), de (+*abl.*)
downcast, dēmisso animo (§ 413) (*compar.* demissiore a.)
drag, traho, -ĕre, traxi, tractum
draw (sword), dēstringo, -ĕre, destrinxi, destrictum
draw up (*mil.*), instruo, -ĕre, instruxi, instructum
dreadful, atrox
dream, *use* mihi in somno videtur (*see note on No.* 31)
dream (*noun*), somnium, *n.*
drink, bibo, bibere, bibi, —; pōto 1
drive (cattle *&c.*), ago, agere, ēgi, actum; **drive out**, expello*; **drive ashore**, ēicio*; **drive back**, repello*
drop (wind) dēficio*
due to (= the fault of), *see* § 513
dungeon, carcer, carceris, *m.*

dust, dust-cloud, pulvis, pulveris, *m.*
duty, officium, *n.*

each (=every); **each other**, § 528
eager, cupidus (+*gen.*); **be eager to**, cupio, -ĕre, cupivi, cupitum
eagerness, studium, *n.*
early (spring, *&c.*), prīmus
earlier (=before)
earth, terra, *f.*
easy, facilis; **easily**, facilĕ
eat, ĕdo, ēsse, ēdi, ēsum (*irreg. present*); (=feed on), vescor, -i, *no perf.* (+*abl.*)
be eclipsed, *use* deficio*
Edward, Eduardus, *m.*
efficient, dīligens
egg, ōvum, *n.*
Egypt, Aegyptus, -i, *f.*
either ... or, aut ... aut (*or* vel ... vel: § 135, *note* 2); *sometimes* sīve ... sive (*see note on No.* 25)
elder, nātu māior
elderly, senior, natu maior
elect, creo 1
election, comitia, *n. plu.*
eloquence, ēloquentia, *f.*
eloquent, ēloquens
elsewhere, alibi
embark (*intr.*), navem conscendo*, in navem conscendo
employ (=use)
empty, vacuus
empty out, effundo, -ĕre, effūdi, effusum
encourage, hortor 1, cohortor 1

[1] *facio*, strictly, calls attention to the product of the activity, *ago* to the activity itself.

encouragement, cohortatio, -onis, *f.*
end (*noun*), fīnis, finis, *m.*; **the end of**, extrēmus (*adj.*)
end (*vb.*), finem facio (+*gen.*)
endowed, praeditus (+*abl.*)
endurance, patientia, *f.*
endure, fero, perfero*
enemy, hostis, hostis, *m.* (*usu. in plu.*); (personal), inimīcus, *m.*
energetic, strēnuus, impiger, -gra, -grum
England, Anglia *or* Britannia, *f.*
English (*plu.*), Angli *or* Britanni
enjoy (=have benefit of), fruor, -i¹ (+*abl.*); (=delight in), *see* delight
enough (*adj.*), satis (*indecl. noun*) (+*gen.*²); (*adv.*), satis; **enough to**, § 354
enquire (=ask)
enrol (*tr.*), conscrībo, -ĕre, -scripsi, -scriptum
enslavement, servitūs, -utis, *f.*
ensure that, efficio ut (+*subjunc.*)
enter, ingredior*, ineo*, intro 1 (*all can be tr.*)
enthusiasm, studium, *n.*
entreat, ōro, 1
entrust, committo* (+ *acc. and dat.*)
envoy, lēgātus, *m.*
envy, invideo* (+*dat.*)
escape, effugio*
escape (*noun*): **a narrow —**, § 513 (ii)
especially, praecipuē, imprīmīs

establish, confirmo 1 (*only w. abstract object*)
esteem (=honour, value)
Etruscan, Etruscus
even, etiam; vel; **not even**, nē ... quidem (§ 131); **even though**, etiam si
evening, vesper, vesperi, *m.*; **in evening**, vesperi (*loc.*)
every, everybody, omnes (*or more emphatic* universi); **everything**, omnia; *or use* quisque (*sing.*: see § 527); **everybody who** (=whoever); **every day**, cottidie; **— year**, quotannīs
everywhere, ubīque
evil (*noun*), malum; **worse evils**, pēiora
example, exemplum, *n.* (§ 294)
excellent, optimus
except (*prep.*), praeter (+*acc.*); *or use* nisi
exceptional, ēgregius
exclaim, clāmo 1, conclamo
exercise (*tr.*), exerceo 2
exert energies (=do one's best)
exhausted, confectus
exile (person), exsul, -ulis, *c.*; (banishment), exsilium, *n.*
exist, sum
expect, spēro 1; **than expected**, § 381
expediency, ūtile *n. adj.* (*see note on No.* 45)
experience: know by —, *perfect tenses of* experior, -iri, expertus sum
experienced (in), perītus (+*gen.*)

---

¹ If the perfect is required, use *usus sum*.
² expressing amount, *not* number: thus, enough money: *satis pecuniae*; enough strength, *satis virium*; but enough ships, *satis magnus numerus navium*.

explain to, doceo, -ēre, docui, doctum (+ *acc. of person*)
express (opinion), dīco 3
eye, oculus, *m*.; **with own eyes**, *use* ipse *or* cōram (face to face)

face, ōs, ōris, *n*.; (=expression), vultus, -ūs, *m*.
fact, rēs, rei, *f*.; **the further fact**: *see* further
fail, rem male gero, -ĕre, gessi, gestum; **fail to** (= do not)
fair, aequus; (=beautiful), pulcher; **fair sized**, satis magnus
faith, **good faith**, fides, -ei, *f*.
faithful, fidēlis
fall, cado, -ĕre, cecĭdi, cāsum; **fall down**, decĭdo*, delābor*; **fall ill** (*see* ill); **fall in, into**, incĭdo*; **fall back** (*mil.*), pedem refero* (*never* pedes); **fall upon** (*mil.*) incido* in (+*acc.*), adorior, -iri, adortus sum (*tr.*)
false, falsus
fame, fāma, *f*., glōria, *f*.
familiar with, perītus (+*gen.*)
family (=descent), gens, gentis, *f*.
famine, fames, -is, *f*.; inopia, *f*.
famous, praeclārus, nōtus
far, longe; prŏcul; (= by far), longe, multo (§ 385); **so far from**, § 504
farm, fundus, *m*.
farmer, agricola, *m*
farmhouse, villa, *f*.
farming, res rustica
fast (*adj.*), celer, vēlox; (*adv.*), celeriter
father, pater, patris, *m.*
fatherland, patria, *f*.

my fault that (not), per me stat quominus (§ 513)
favour, faveo, -ēre, fāvi, fautum (+*dat*.)
favourable, aequus; (wind, &c.), secundus
fear, timeo 2, vereor 2; **fearing**, veritus
fear (*noun*), timor, -ōris, *m*., metus, -ūs, *m*.; **for fear that**, nē
feed on, vescor, -i (*no perf.*) (+*abl*.)
fellow (contemptuous), homo
fellow-citizen (*&c*.), *use possessive adj.*: *e.g*. cives mei
fetch, peto, -ĕre, petivi, petitum
few, pauci; **a few**, pauci
field, ager, agri, *m*.
fierce, saevus, ācer (acris)
fig (in value phrase), flocci (§ 322)
fight, pugno 1 (*intr. only*); **fight a war**, bellum gero; **fight a battle**, proelium facio
figure (person's), figūra, *f*.
fill, fill up, compleo, -ēre, -plēvi, -plētum; (*with grief, &c*.), afficio*
finally, postrēmo, tandem, dēnique
find, invenio*; (by search), reperio, -ire, repperi, repertum
find out, cognosco, -ĕre, cognovi, cognitum
fine (splendid), pulcher
finish, conficio*, perficio*
fiord (=bay)
fire, ignis, ignis, *m*.; (destructive), incendium, *n*.; **set fire to**, incendo, -ĕre, -ndi, -nsum (*tr.*)
fire (=shoot), tela cŏnicere*

252

firebrand, fax, facis, *f.*
fired (with), incensus (+*abl.*)
firewood, lignum, *n.*; **collect** —, lignor 1
first (*adj.*), prīmus; **the first to**, § 357
first (*adv.*), prīmum; **at first**, primo
fish, piscis, piscis, *m.*
fish (*vb.*), piscor 1
fit (= worthy), dignus; (suitable) idōneus
be fitting, decet (*impers.*), § 403
flame, flamma, *f.*
flank, lătus, lateris, *n.* (§ 195), cornu, -ūs, *n.*
flatter, adūlor 1
flee, fugio, -ĕre, fūgi, fugitum; **flee for refuge**, confugio
fleet, classis, classis, *f.*
flesh, caro, carnis, *f.*
flight, fuga, *f.*; **take to flight**, fugio*[1]; **put to flight**, fugo, 1; in fugam verto, -ĕre, verti, versum (*tr.*)
flock, convenio*, concurro*
flog (= beat)
flow (out), effluo, -ĕre, effluxi
flower, flōs, flōris, *m.*
flushed with, laetus (+*abl.*)
fly, volo 1
follow, sequor, -i, secutus sum; **follow closely**, subsequor
following (next), proximus, (*with* dies) posterus
food, cibus, *m.*
fool, foolish, stultus, imprūdens
foot, pēs, pedis, *m.*; **on foot**, pedibus; **foot of hill** (*&c.*), īmus (*adj.*) (§ 411)

for (*prep.*), prō (+*abl.*); (*giving destination*), ad, in (+*acc.*); (= with a view to), ad; (= because of), propter (+ *acc.*)
for (*conj.*), nam; enim (*after first word*)
forage, pābulor 1
forbid, veto, -are, vetui, vetitum
force (compel), cōgo, -ĕre, coēgi, coactum (+*infin.*); **forced march**, magnum iter; **force down**, dēpello*
force, vīs, *f.*; **by armed force**, vi et armis
forces (troops), copiae, *f. plu.*
ford, vadum, *n.*
foresee, prōvideo*
forest, silva, *f.*
foretell, praedīco*
forget, oblīviscor, -i, oblītus sum (§ 421)
forgive, ignosco, -ĕre, ignōvi, ignōtum (+*dat.*)
form ranks, aciem instruo, -ĕre, instruxi, instructum
former, prior; **former times**, prisca tempora[2]
formerly, ōlim, anteā
fortification, vallum, *n.*; mūnītiones, *f. plu.*
fortify, mūnio 4
fortunate, fēlix; beatus (*of persons only*)
fortune, fortūna, *f.*
found (= establish), condo*
free (*adj.*), līber, libera, liberum; **set free**, libero 1; **be free to**, *use* licet (§ 403); **be free of**, vaco 1 (§ 543)
free (*vb.*), libero 1; dīmitto*

---

[1] also, *se fugae mandare* or *terga vertĕre*.
[2] *priscus* often implies 'good old'.

freedman, lībertus, *m.*
freedom, lībertas, -tatis, *f.*
French (*noun*), Gallus; (*adj.*), Gallicus
frequently, saepe, nonnumquam
fresh, novus; (=unwearied), integer, -gra, -grum
friend, amīcus, *m.*, amīca, *f.*
friendship, amīcitia, *f.*
from (*prep.*), ā, ab (+*abl.*); ex (+*abl.*) (*esp. with towns and countries*); (= down from), dē (+*abl.*)
from there, inde; **from here**, hinc
on two fronts, utrimque; ab utrāque parte
fugitive, fugitīvus, *m.*; *or pres. part of* fugio
fulfil (oath), solvo, -ĕre, solvi, solutum
full, plēnus (+ *gen. or abl.*)
furniture, supellex, supellectilis, *f.*
further (besides), praetereā; **there is the — fact that**, § 556
the future, futura, *n. plu.* **in future**, posteā (*in No.* 46)

gain (acquire), paro 1; quaero, -ĕre, quaesivi, quaesitum; (victory), reporto 1 (*or use* proelium secundum facio)
gallop ahead, praecurro*
games, lūdi, *m. plu.*
garden, hortus, *m.*
garrison, praesidium, *n.*
gate, porta, *f.*

Gaul, Gallia, *f.*
a Gaul, Gallus, *m.*
general (*mil.*), dux, *m.*, imperator, *m.*
German, Germānus
get (=become), fio; (=obtain), *use* peto; **get up** (=arise); **get one's way**, *use* impetro 1 (*tr.*, = get by asking)
gift, dōnum, *n.*
girl, puella, *f.*
give, do, dăre, dĕdi, dătum; **give thanks**, gratias ago; **give** (opportunity), *use* facio; **give back**, reddo*; **give up** (surrender), dēdo*; **give up** (hand over), trādo*; **give up** (abandon), omitto*; **give up hope**, spem abicio*, *or use* dēspero 1
be glad, gaudeo, -ēre, gāvīsus sum; **gladly**, libenter *or* (*adj.*) libens, laetus (*p.* 151, *note*)
gladiator, gladiator, -ōris, *m.*
glory, glōria, *f.*
go, eo, ire, īvi, ĭtum; **go away**, abeo*, discēdo*; **go back**; redeo*, regredior*; **go on** (=happen); **go out**, exeo*, ēgredior*; **go to**, adeo* (*tr.*)
god, deus, *m.*
gold, aurum, *n.*
golden, gold (*adj.*), aureus
good, bonus
good sense, prūdentia, *f.*
goodwill, benevolentia, *f.*
govern, rego 3, administro 1
government, res publica
governor, praefectus, proconsul[1]

---

[1] *proconsul* may be used for the governor of a Roman province (though not all of them had that title); in any other sense use *praefectus*.

gradually, paullātim
grandfather, avus, *m.*
grandson, nepōs, nepōtis, *m.*
grasp, comprehendo*
grateful, *see* gratitude
gratifying, grātus; *or use* placeo
gratitude, grātia, *f.*; **show —**, gratiam refero*
grave (=serious)
great, magnus; (*stronger word*) ingens; **greatest** (*with abstract nouns*), summus
Greece, Graecia, *f.*
Greek, Graecus
greet, salūto 1
grief, dolor, dolōris, *m.* (§ 294)
grieve (*tr.*), § 294
ground, humus, -i, *f.*; **on the —**, humi (*loc.*)
guard, custōdio 4; **to guard**, *use* praesidio (§ 295)
guard (*noun*), custōs, custōdis, *m.*; **off one's guard**, incautus, inopīnans (*see note on No. 9, l. 9*)
guide, dux, dŭcis, *m.*
guilty, nocens

habit, mōs, mōris, *m.*, consuētudo, -dinis, *f.*; **be in habit of**, soleo, -ēre, solitus sum; consuēvi (*perf. of* consuesco)
Hadrian, Hadrianus, *m.*
half, dīmidia pars; **half way up:** *use* medius (§ 411)
halt, consisto*
hand, manus, -ūs, *f.*; **be at hand**, adsum, adesse, adfui
hand over, trādo*
handsome (=generous), amplus; (=good-looking), pulcher

hang (*intr.*), pendeo, -ēre, pepeṛdi, pensum
Hannibal, Hannibal, -alis, *m.*
happen, fio, fieri, factus sum; accĭdo (§ 404); **as it happens**, fortĕ, cāsu; **happen to**, *use* forte, casu
happy, beatus
harass, vexo 1
harbour, portus, -ūs, *m.*
hard (=difficult)
hard (*adv.*), strēnue; **be hard pressed**, labōro 1
hardly, vix; (with difficulty), aegre; **hardly any**, § 132, *note*
harm, noceo 2 (+*dat.*), laedo, -ĕre, laesi, laesum
harm (*noun*), dētrīmento (§ 294)
be harmful, *see* harm
harsh, sevērus; **harsh treatment**, sevēritas, *f.*
Hasdrubal, Hasdrubal, -alis, *m.*
hasten, propero 1, mātūro 1 (*both may be used* + *infin.*)
hasty, imprūdens
hate, ōdi, odisse; be hated, *use* ŏdio sum (§ 296)
hateful, *use* ŏdio (§ 293)
hatred, ŏdium, *n.*
have, habeo 2; **have something done** (= cause, order it to be done), *use* curo 1 (§ 345), iubeo
head, caput, capitis, *n.*
headlong, praeceps, praecipitis
hear, audio 4; (= catch the sound of), exaudio
heart of (= middle of)
heat, calor, calōris, *m.*; (severe heat), aestus, -ūs, *m.*
heavy, gravis

height, altitudo, -dinis, *f.*; *but see* § 172; (person's), **statura**, *f.*
helm, gubernāculum, *n.*
help, adiuvo, -āre, adiūvi, adiūtum; succurro* (+*dat.*); auxilio sum (§ 293); **cannot help doing**, § 494
help (*noun*), auxilium, *n.*; **by help of**, § 177; **come to help of**, succurro* (+*dat.*); auxilio venio, subsidio venio (§ 295)
hem in (*mil.*), circumvenio* (*tr.*)
Hercules, Hercules, -lis, *m.*
here, hīc; (=hither), hūc
hesitate, cunctor 1; dubito 1 (§ 511)
be hidden, lateo 2
hide (*tr.*), cēlo 1, condo*, abdo*; (*intr.*), me celo (*&c.*); **be hiding**, lateo 2
hiding-place, insidiae, *f. plu.*
high, altus; (price) magnus; **high ground**, collis, collis, *m.*; (wind), magnus; **highest** (=greatest) summus
highly (valuing), magni (§ 322)
hill, collis, collis, *m.*, mons, montis, *m.*[1]
hinder, impedio 4; *or use* impedīmento sum (§ 293)
hindrance, impedīmentum, (*n.*) (§ 293)
hire, conduco*
hit (with missile), transfīgo, -ĕre, -fixi, -fixum
hold, teneo, 2 (*no supine*), habeo 2; (powers, office), gero; (=consider), habeo; **hold up** (support), sustineo*; **hold out** (*intr.* = resist), resisto*
holiday(s), feriae, *f. plu.*

holy, sanctus
home, dŏmus, -ūs, *f. irreg.*; *see* § 192
homeland, patria, *f.*
Homer, Homērus, *m.*
honour, honos, honōris, *m.*; **hold in honour**, in honore habeo; (= loyalty to promise), fides
honour (*vb.*), in honore habeo, honore afficio*
honourable, honestus
hope, spēro 1; **hope to**, § 143; **hope for**, spēro (*tr.*)
hope (*noun*) spēs, spei, *f.*; **in the hope of**, § 573
Horace, Horātius, *m.*
horse, equus, *m.*
on horseback, equo (§ 182); **in equo** (esse), ex equo (pugnare)
horseman, eqŭes, equitis, *m.*
hostage, obsĕs, obsidis, *m.*
hostile (=enemy's)
hour, hōra, *f.*; **at what hour**, quotā horā
house, domus, -ūs, *f. irreg.*; aedes, -ium, *f. plu.*
in household of, apud (+*acc.*)
how (*manner*), quōmodo, (*in rep. questions*), quemadmodum; (*degree, with adj. or adv.*), quam; **how great**, quantus; **how much**, quantum (+*gen.*); **how many**, quot; — — **times**, quotiens
however (=but), tamen (*not first word*); (= in whatever way), quoquo modo; (*with adj. or adv.*), quamvīs, § 564
huge, ingens
hunger, fămes, famis, *f.* (*abl.* -ē)

---

[1] Anything more than an 'eminence' or 'high ground' is *mons*.

hunt, vēnor 1
hurl a volley of, conicio*
hurry, propero 1; (travel quickly), contendo, -ĕre, -tendi, -tentum
husband, vĭr, viri, *m.*

if, si; **if not**, nisi; **if only** (*in wish*), utinam; **if** (*in rep. question*), num
ill (sick), aeger, aegra, aegrum; **be ill**, aeger sum, aegrōto 1; **fall ill**, morbo afficior*, in morbum incĭdo*
illness, morbus, *m.*
ill-will, invidia, *f.*
imitate, imitor 1
immediately, statim, confestim
immortal, immortalis
import, importo 1
be important, interest (*impers.*), § 405
it is impossible (that), non potest fieri (§ 494)
imprudence, imprūdentia, *f.*
imprudent, imprūdens
in (*prep.*), in (+*abl.*)
be inclined to think, haud scio an, nescio an (§ 205)
increase (*tr.*), augeo, -ēre, auxi, auctum; (*intr.*), augeor, cresco, -ĕre, crēvi, crētum
incur, ineo* (*tr.*)
individual (*adj.*), *use* singuli
induce, addūco* (+ *ut* clause)
infant, infans, infantis, *c.*
infantry, pedites, *m. plu.*
influence, moveo, -ēre, mōvi, mōtum; **influenced** (by), adductus
influence (*noun*), auctōritas, -tatis, *f.*

inform, (te) certiorem facio, (te) doceo
inhabitant, incola, *c.*
injure (=harm), noceo 2 (+*dat.*), laedo, -ĕre, laesi, laesum; (physically), vulnero 1; **injured** (wounded), saucius
innocent, innocens
inside (*prep.*), intrā (+*acc.*)
inspect, perspicio*
instant, punctum temporis
instead: § 503
intend, in animo habeo (+*infin.*); *use fut. part.* (§ 35)
intention, consilium, *n.*; *see* intend
intercept, excipio*
interests: *see* consider
interpreter, interprēs, -etis, *m.*
into (*prep.*), in (+*acc.*)
invade, invādo, -ĕre, invasi, invasum (in + *acc.*); irrumpo* (in + *acc.*)
invasion, incursio, -onis, *f.*
invite, invīto 1
irksome, *use* piget (*impers.*), § 402
iron, ferrum, *n.*
island, insula, *f.*
issue (*intr.*), ēgredior*; **issue -orders**, ēdico*, impero 1
Italy, Ĭtalia, *f.*

jar, cadus, *m.*
javelin, pīlum, *n.*
be jealous, invideo* (+*dat.*)
join (= attach oneself to), me adiungo, -ĕre, adiunxi, adiunctum (+*dat.*); **join battle**, proelium committo*
joke: *see note on No.* 49
journey, iter, itineris, *n.*

joy, gaudium, *n.*
joyful, laetus; **joyfully**, *use adj.*
judge, iūdico 1
judge (*noun*), iūdex, iudicis, *m.*
Jupiter, Iuppiter, Iŏvis, *m.*
juror, juryman, iūdex, iudicis, *m.*
jury, iudices, *m. plu.*
just, iustus, aequus
just as, sīcut; **just as if**, *see* § 574 (*a*)
justice, iustitia, *f.*

keen, ācer, acris, acre; **be keen on**, studeo 2 (+*dat.*)
keep, retineo*; (an oath), (con)-servo 1; **keep one's word**, fidem praesto, -āre, -stiti; **keep from** (= prevent from); **keep on a course**, cursum teneo; **keep out** (*tr.*), exclūdo 3
kill, interficio*; (in battle), occīdo*; (slaughter) trucīdo 1
kind (sort), genus, generis, *n.*
kind (*adj.*), benignus
kindness, beneficium, *n.*, benevolentia, *f.* (*not synonyms*)
king, rex, rēgis, *m.*
kingdom, regnum, *n.*
kinsfolk: *usu. omit* (*e.g.* my k., mei)
knight, equĕs, equitis, *m.*
know, scio 4; **know how to**, scio (+*infin.*); (persons, places), nōvi, (*perf. of* nosco); **do not know**, nescio 4, ignōro 1; **it is generally known**, inter omnes constat

knowledge, scientia, *f.*; **without one's —**, *use* inscius (§ 177)

Lacedaemonian, Lacedaemonius
lack, careo 2 (+*abl.*: § 543); *or use* desum (aliquid mihi deest)
lack (of supplies), inopia, *f.*
lake, lacus, -ūs, *m.*
land, terra; **by land**, terrā; (plot of land, farm-land), ager, agri, *m.*
land (*vb.*) (=disembark)
language, lingua, *f.*
large, magnus
last, ultimus, novissimus[1]; **at last**, tandem; **to the last**, ad extremum; **to the last man**, omnes ad unum
late, too late, sēro (*adv.*); **late in the day**, multus dies; **late at night**, multa nox; **later**, post, posteā (§ 156)
Latin, lingua Latīna; **in —**, Latine (*adv.*)
laugh, rīdeo, -ēre, rīsi, rīsum
be laughing-stock, lūdibrio sum (§ 294)
launch, dēduco*; (troops), ēmitto*
law, lex, lēgis, *f.*
lawyer, iūris consultus, *m.*
lay aside, dēpono*; **lay down**, depono*
lead, dūco, -ĕre, duxi, ductum; **lead out**, ēduco; **lead across**, trāduco; **the road leads**, via fert (*intr.*)

[1] These words mean 'last of all', *not* 'last up to now': last night, *proxima nocte*; in the last few days, *his paucis diebus*.

leader, dux, dŭcis, *m.*
leadership, *use* dux (§ 177)
leading (man), princeps, principis, *m.*
leaf, fŏlium, *n.*
lean, nītor, -i, nīsus sum (+*abl.*)
leap down, dēsilio, -ire, desilui, desultum; **leap on to**, insilio (in + *acc.*); **leap out**; exsilio
learn, disco, -ĕre, didici, *no supine*; **learn how to**, disco (+ *infin.*); (= find out), cognosco, -ĕre, cognovi, cognitum
learned, doctus
leave (behind), relinquo, -ĕre, relīqui, relictum; (as legacy), relinquo; (=depart), discēdo* (ab, ex), ēgredior* (+*abl.*), abeo (ab) (*all three are intr.*)
left (remaining), reliquus
left (*opp. of* right), sinister, -tra, -trum
leg, crūs, crūris, *n.*
legion, legio, -onis, *f.*
leisure, ōtium, *n.*
lend, praebeo 2
less (*adj.*), minus (+*gen.*: § 62); (*adv.*), minus; (*in value expressions*), minoris; **none the less**, nihilo minus
lest, nē
let (allow), sino, patior (*see* allow); **let down** (fail), dēstituo* (*tr.*); **let go by**, intermitto* (§ 493)
letter, epistola, *f.*, litterae, *f. plu*
levy (*mil.*), dīlectus, -ūs, *m.*
liberty, lībertas, -tatis, *f.*
lictor, lictor, lictōris, *m.*
lie, tell a lie, mentior 4

lie (= be laid), iaceo 2; **lie hidden**, lateo 2; **lie in** (= depend on), *see note on No.* 13; **lie between**, intersum
life, vīta, *f.*; **lose life** (=die) in **lifetime**, *use* vivus (§ 177)
light (natural), lux, lūcis, *f.*; (artificial), lūmen, -inis, *n.*
light (in weight), lĕvis; **think lightly of**, § 322
lightning, fulmen, -inis, *n.*
like (*vb.*), *use* mihi placet
like (*adj.*), similis (§ 424)
likely to, *use fut. part.*
line (of battle), acies, aciei, *f.*
linger behind, moror 1
lion, leo, leōnis, *m.*
listen to, audio 4 (*tr.*)
literature, litterae, *f. plu.*
little, parvus; **a little**, paullum; **a little** (*with compar.*), paullo
live (=dwell), incolo, -ĕre, incolui, incultum (+ *acc. or* in); habito 1 (+ *acc. or* in)[1]; (= be alive), vīvo, vivere, vixi, victum; **live on** (= feed on), vescor, -i (*no perf.*) (+*abl.*)
London, Londinium, *n.*
long, longus; **for a long time**, diū
long (*adv.*), diū; **no longer**, non iam; **as long as**, dum, quoad; **so long as** (= provided that), dum (§ 473)
long for, dēsīdero 1; **longed-for**, optatus
look down on, dēspicio*; **look for**, peto, -ĕre, petivi, petitum, (*tr.*); **look round**, respicio*
lose, āmitto*

---

[1] *incolo*, 'be inhabitant of' a country or region; *habito*, 'live in' a house, town, &c.

loss, *use* amitto; **with heavy losses**, multis occisis; **without loss**, *use* incolumis
lot (fate), fortūna, *f.*
loud, magnus; **so loud**, tantus
love, amo 1; **love to**, soleo
loyalty, fidēs, fidei, *f.*
luggage, impedīmenta, *n. plu.*

mad, āmens, insānus
magistracy, magistratus, -ūs, *m.*
magistrate, magistratus, -ūs, *m.*
maiden, virgo, virginis, *f.*
main body (*mil.*), ūniversi
mainland, continens, -ntis, *f.*
maintain, alo, alere, alui, altum
majesty, maiestas, -tatis, *f.*
majority of, plērique, pleraeque, pleraque
make, facio, -ĕre, fēci, factum; **be made**, fio, fieri, factus sum; **make (a speech)**, habeo; (=compel), cōgo; (money), *see* gain; **make a plan**, consilium capio; **make war on**, bellum infero* (+*dat.*); **make for**, peto
man (human being), homo, hominis, *c.*; (male person), vĭr, viri, *m.*; **men** (=soldiers), milites
man (*vb.*), compleo, -ēre, -ēvi, ētum
manage, administro 1; **manage to**, efficio* (*p.* 108, *note*)
manner, mōs, mōris, *m.*; modus, *m.*
many, multi, **so many**, tot (*indecl.*); **a good many**, nonnulli
march, contendo, -ĕre, -tendi, -tentum; iter facio

march (*noun*), iter, itineris, *n.*; **forced march**, magnum iter
market, market-place, fŏrum, *n.*
marriage, nuptiae, *f. plu.*
marry (a wife), (in matrimōnium) duco 3; (a husband), nūbo, -ĕre, nupsi, nuptum (+*dat.*)
marsh, palūs, palūdis, *f.*
Martial, Martiālis, -is, *m.*
master, dominus, *m.*; (schoolmaster), magister, -tri, *m.*; **Master of the Horse**, magister equitum
matter, rēs, rei, *f.*
matter (= be important), interest (*impers.*), § 405
may (permission), licet (*impers.*), § 403; **it may (well) be that**, § 494
meal (=food)
mean (*vb.*), significo 1; *sometimes* sum (+ *predic. dat.*)
means, modus, *m.*, ratio, -onis, *f.*
meantime, intereā
meet (assemble), convenio*; meet (*tr.*) (confer with), te convenio*; (by chance), tibi occurro*, tibi obviam fio; (go, come, march) **to meet**, obviam (+*dat.*)
meeting (public), contio, -onis, *f.*; **address a —**, contionem habeo
memory, memoria, *f.*; **in living memory**, hominum memoriā *or* post hominum memoriam
merchant, mercator, -ōris, *m.*
message, nuntius, *m.*
messenger, nuntius, *m.*
middle of, medius (*adj.*)
midnight, media nox

mile, mille passūs (*plu.:* milia passuum)
milk, lac, lactis, *n.*
mind (*vb.*), see § 84
mislead, dēcipio*
miss (chance), dīmitto, āmitto*; (= long for), dēsīdero 1
mistake, error, -ōris, *m.*; **make a mistake**, erro 1
mistrust, diffīdo, -ĕre, -fīsus sum (+*dat.*)
Mitylene, Mitylēnae, *f. plu.*
moat, fossa, *f.*
mobilize, cōgo
moderate, modicus
money, pecūnia, *f.*
month, mensis, -is, *m.* (*gen. plu.* mensum)
moon, lūna, *f.*
more (*adj.*), plūs (+*gen.:* § 62), *plu.* plūres; (*adv.*), plus, magis, potius; (*in value expressions*), pluris
moreover, praetereā
in morning, māne; **every morning**, cottidie mane; **next —**, postridie mane
most, plurimi; (= the majority), plērique
mother, māter, matris, *f.*
mountain, mons, montis, *m.*
mouth, ōs, ōris, *n.*
move (*tr.*), moveo, -ēre, mōvi, mōtum; (away), āmoveo; (*intr.*), moveor
much, multus; **so much**, tantum (+*gen.:* § 62)
much (*adv.*), multum; (= by much), multo, longe (§ 385)
mule, see note on *No.* 29

murder, neco 1; interficio*
must, *use gerundive* (*ch.* 31) *or* oportet (*impers.*), § 403

name, nōmen, nominis, *n.*; **named**, *say* 'by name'
narrow, angustus
nation, populus, *m.*; gens, gentis, *f.*
native, barbarus
natural, nātūrālis
nature, nātūra, *f.*; *see* § 172; **it is the nature of**, *use gen.* (§ 63)
near (*prep.*), prope (+*acc.*); ad (+*acc.*)
nearest (*adj.*), proximus
nearly, § 513
it is necessary, necesse est
need (*vb.*), *use* opus est (§ 182); **need to**, *use gerundive*
neglect, neglego, -ĕre, neglexi, neglectum
neighbour, fīnitimus, vīcīnus[1]
neighbouring, propinquus, fīnitimus[1]
neither... nor, neque... neque, nec... nec (*sometimes* nēve... nēve, § 214)
neither (*pron., adj.*), neuter, neutra, neutrum; **neither side**, neutri (*p.* 95, *note* 1)
never, numquam; **and never**, neque umquam
nevertheless, nihilo minus
new, novus; **newest**, recentissimus
news, *use* nuntius, *or* nŏvi (*neut. of* novus *as part. gen.*)
next, proximus; (day), posterus, *or use adv.* postrīdie.

[1] *finitimus* (from *fines*), (a state) 'on one's borders'; *vicinus*, (a person) 'whose home is near'.

night, nox, noctis, *f.*; **at night**, noctu, nocte
night (*adj.*), nocturnus
no (*adj.*), nullus
noble (*adj. and noun*), nōbilis
nobody, nēmo[1] (*sometimes* ne quis); **and nobody**, nec quisquam
noise, sonitus, -ūs, *m.*; clāmor, -ōris, *m.*
none (= nobody *or* nothing)
noon, merīdiēs, -ei, *m.*
nor, neque, nec (*sometimes* nēve)
not, nōn; **not even**, nē ... quidem
nothing, nihil, *indecl.*
notice, animadverto, -ĕre, -verti, -versum; *see* observe
now (= by now) iam; (= at this time), nunc; **now and then**, interdum; **now** (connective), autem
nowhere, nusquam; **nowhere to**, § 273
number, numerus, *m.*; **numbers** (*mil.*), multitudo, numerus (*sing.*)
numerous (= many, a good many)

oar, rēmus, *m.*
oath, iūsiūrandum, iūrisiūrandi, *n.*; **take oath** (= swear)
obey, pāreo 2 (*no supine*), (+ *dat.*)
object to (doing), recūso 1 (§ 511)
object (noun, = motive), *see* §§ 172, 176, 215
observe, conspicio*, conspicor 1; *or* video, sentio
obtain (*by chance or lot*), nanciscor, -i, nactus sum; (by asking), impetro 1; (by effort), paro 1, quaero, -ĕre, quaesivi, quaesitum
be obvious, appāret, manifestum est (+ *acc. and inf.*)
occupy (*mil.*) (= seize)
occur, fio, accĭdo* (*see* happen); **an opportunity occurs**, occasio datur, affertur*
Octavian, Octāviānus
of, *see ch.* 41, *esp.* § 415; *ch.* 42
offer to, polliceor 2
office, magistrātus, -ūs, *m.*; honōs, honōris, *m.*
officer, tribūnus mīlitum; lēgātus; praefectus: *see note on No.* 51
often, saepĕ
old, vetus, veteris; (persons), senex, senis, *c.*; **older** (in years), nātu māior; **old man**, senex, senis, *m.*; **old age**, senectūs, -tutis, *f.*; **in old age**, *say* (as) old man
omen, ōmen, ominis, *n.*, portentum, *n.*
on (*prep.*), in (+ *abl.*); *sometimes* ab (§ 195)
once (= formerly), ōlim; **at once**, statim, confestim; (= simultaneously) simul
onlooker, *use pres. part. of* specto 1
open, aperio, -ire, aperui, apertum
open (*adj.*), apertus; **it is open to**, *use* licet (*impers.*)
openly, palam
opinion, sententia, *f.*; *see* § 172; **hold opinion**, censeo, -ĕre, censui, censum

[1] for declension, see grammar.

opponent, adversārius, *m.*
opportunity, facultas, -tatis, *f.*, occāsio, -onis, *f.*, potestas, -tatis, *f.*; *see* give, occur
oppose, obsisto* (+*dat.*), resisto* (+*dat.*)
or, aut; -ve (§ 135, *note* 2); (*in alternative questions*), an; *see* whether; **or not,** § 203
oracle, ōrāculum, *n.*
orator, ōrātor, -ōris, *m.*
orchard, pōmārium, *n.*
order, iubeo, -ēre, iussi, iussum; (tibi) impero 1 (+ *rep. command*)[1]; order ... not, veto, -āre, vetui, vetitum
order (*noun,* = command), iussum, *n.*; **by order,** iussu; **without orders,** iniussu (§ 501); **issue orders,** ēdīco*, impero 1
order (=arrangement), ordo, ordinis, *m.*
ordinary, modicus
other, another, alius, alia, aliud; **the other** (of two), alter, -era, -erum; **the others** (rest), cēteri
ought, dēbeo 2; oportet (*impers.*: § 403); *or use gerundive: ch.* 31. *See* § 318; **ought to have,** § 571
out, *prefix* ex, ē; **out of,** ex (+*abl.*)
outcry, clāmor, -ōris, *m.*
on outpost duty, in statione
outside (*prep.*), extrā (+*acc.*)
over (a river), in (+*abl.*); (with numbers), amplius, § 382; **it is all over with** (him), actum est de (eo)
overpower, supero 1

overtake, consequor*
overthrow, ēverto, -ĕre, everti, eversum
Ovid, Ovidius, *m.*
owing to, propter (+*acc.*)
own (*adj.*), *use gen. of ipse* (*if needed*)
owner, dominus, *m.*
ox, bōs, bŏvis, *m.*

Palace, Palātium, *n.*
panic, terror, -ōris, *m.*; pavor, -ōris, *m.*; **panic spreads,** trepidatur (*impers.*)
paper, charta, *f.*
parade (*tr.*), convoco 1
pardon (=forgive)
parent, parens, parentis, *c.*
part, pars, partis, *f.*; **take part in,** intersum, -esse, -fui (+*dat.*)
party (banquet), convīvium, *n.*; **neither party, both parties,** &c.: *use plu. of* neuter, uterque, &c.
pass (=elapse), intercēdo*
past: for a long time past, iam diu (*see* § 152); **ride past:** *see* ride
path, via, *f.*
patrician, patricius
patrols, explōrātōres, *m. plu.*
pay, solvo, -ĕre, solvi, solutum; **pay penalty,** poenas do
peace, pax, pācis, *f.*
peasant, agricola, *m.*, rusticus, *m.*
Peloponnese, Peloponnēsus, *f.*
penalty, poena, *f.*; **pay penalty,** poenas do
penny, *use as,* assis, *m.* (*appendix* B)

[1] for difference, see § 96. Normally use *iubeo, veto.*

people (=nation), populus, *m*.; (*vague subject*), *use impers. pass.*
perceive, sentio, -ire, sensi, sensum; intellego, -ĕre, -lexi, -lectum
perform, fungor, -i, functus sum (+*abl.*); (*or* = do)
perhaps, fortassĕ
peril (=danger)
perish, pereo*; morior, -i, mortuus sum
give **permission**, (tibi) permitto* (ut)
Persian, Persa, *m*.
in **person**, ipse; cōram (*adv.*)
personally (for my part), equidem
persuade, persuādeo, -ēre, -suasi, -suasum (+ *dat. and rep. command*)
philosopher, philosophus, *m*.
pick (flowers), lego, -ĕre, lēgi, lectum; (=choose), deligo, -ĕre, -lēgi, -lectum
piece, pars, partis, *f*.
pirate, praedo, -ōnis, *m*.
pit, fossa, *f*.
pitch (camp), pōno*
pitched battle, proelium iustum; **fight a pitched battle**, iusto proelio dīmico 1
pity, miseret (*impers.*), § 402
place, locus, *m*.; in place of, loco (+*gen.*)
place (*vb.*), (things) pōno*, (persons), colloco 1; **place in, on**, impōno* (in + *acc.*)
plain, campus, *m*.
plan, consilium, *n*.; **make a plan**, c. capio
plate (= silverware), argentum, *n*.

play, lūdo, -ĕre, lūsi, lūsum
play (drama), fābula, *f*.
plead, ōro 1
pleasant, iucundus, grātus
please, placeo 2 (+*dat.*); **be pleased to**, *use* libet, placet (*both impers.*, + *dat. of person*)
pleasure, voluptas, -tatis, *f*.
plebs, plebeians, plebs, plēbis, *f*. *or* plēbeii, *m. plu*.
plight, fortūna, *f*.
Pliny, Plīnius, *m*.
plot, coniūratio, -onis, *f*., consilium, *n*.
plough (*vb.*), aro 1
plunder, praedor 1
plunder (*noun*), praeda, *f*.
poem, carmen, carminis, *n*.
poet, poēta, *m*.
poison, venēnum, *n*.
poison (*vb.*), *say* 'kill by poison'
politics, *see p.* 132, *note*
pomp, splendor, -ōris, *m*.
Pompey, Pompeius, *m*.
poor, pauper, pauperis; (=unfortunate), miser, -era, -erum
position, locus, *m*.; *and see* § 172
take **possession of** (*mil.*), potior 4 (+*abl.*)
possible, *use* possum; as . . . as possible, quam (+*superl.*), § 386
post (*vb.*) (troops), dispōno*, colloco 1
postpone, differo*
pounce on, opprimo, -ĕre, oppressi, oppressum; (from ambush), adorior (*both tr.*)
power, potestas, -tatis, *f*.; (official), imperium, *n*.; (evil), potentia; **do all in one's power**, *see p*. 171, *note* 3
powerful, potens

praetor, praetor, -ōris, *m.*
praise, laudo 1
praise (*noun*), laus, laudis, *f.*
pray to (gods), precor 1 (*tr.*)
precious, cārus
prefer, antepono* (+ *acc. and dat.*); **prefer to**, mālo, malle, mālui
prepare, paro 1; **prepare for war**, bellum paro
in presence (of), *use* praesens (§ 54)
be present, adsum, adesse, adfui (+*dat.*)
present (*noun*), (=gift)
presently, mox
preserve, conservo 1
pressed, *see under* hard
pretend to, simulo 1 (+ *acc. and inf.*)
on pretext of, per causam (+*gen.*)
prevent (from), prohibeo 2 (+*infin.*); impedio 4 (+*clause*, § 511); **to prevent**, *see* § 213
previous, superior, prior; **on previous day**, prīdie (*adv.*); **previously**, ante, anteā
price, pretium, *n.*
priest, sacerdōs, -dōtis, *c.*
prison, carcer, carceris, *m.*
prisoner, captīvus, *m.*
private, *use* suus
privilege, iūs, iūris, *n.*
prize, praemium, *n.*
profit, quaestus, -ūs, *m.*
prolong, prōduco*
promise, polliceor 2; prōmitto*; **promise to**, *see* § 143
promise (*noun*), prōmissum, *n.*; **break promise**, fidem fallo, -ĕre, fefelli, falsum

proof, documentum, *n.* (§ 294)
property, bona, *n. plu.*
propose a law, lēgem rogo 1
prosecute, reum facio; accūso 1 (*both* + *gen. of charge*)
prosperous, flōrens
protect, dēfendo, -ĕre, -ndi, -nsum; tueor 2; praesidio sum (§ 293)
protection, praesidium, *n.* (§ 293)
proud, superbus
provide, comparo 1; **provided that**, dum (+*subjunc.*), § 473
province, prōvincia, *f.*
provisions (*mil.*), commeātus, -ūs, *m. sing.*
prudence, prūdentia, *f.*
prudent, prūdens
punish, pūnio 4
punishment, poena, *f.*; (serious), supplicium, *n.*
pupil, discipulus, *m.*
on purpose, consulto; de industriā; **on purpose to**, eo consilio ut; **for the purpose of**, causā (§ 333)
pursue, sequor, prōsequor*
pursuer, *use* sequor
put, pōno*, colloco 1; **put in command** (of), praeficio (+*dat.*); **put on board**, (in navem) impōno*; **put out** (fire), exstinguo, -ĕre, -nxi, -nctum; **put to death**, interficio*; **put to flight**, fŭgo 1, in fugam verto, -ĕre, verti, versum

quality (virtue), ars, artis, *f.*
quarter (=region), pars, partis, *f.*; *see* direction
queen, rēgīna, *f.*

question (*vb.*), interrogo 1
quick, celer, celeris, celere
quite, satis; *or use compar.*

it **rains**, pluit, -ĕre
raise, tollo, -ĕre, sustuli, sublatum; (forces), cōgo, -ĕre, coēgi, coactum; (siege), *see note on No.* 9
rally, se confirmare
rampart, vallum, *n.*; munītiones, *f. plu.*
rank, ordo, ordinis, *m.*
ransom, redimo, -ĕre, -ēmi, -emptum
ransom (*noun*), pretium, *n.*
rarely, rāro
rashness, temeritas, -tatis, *f.*
at any **rate**, certe
rather, potius, magis; **would rather**, *use* mālo, malle, mālui
ravage, vasto 1
reach (= come to), venio*, pervenio, advenio (*all intr.*)
read, lego, -ĕre, lēgi, lectum
ready, paratus (§ 26); **get ready** (*intr.*), me paro 1; **readily** (=willingly)
real, vērus; **really** (= in fact), rē verā; **really** (*in question*), num
realize, intellego, -ĕre, -lexi, -lectum
rear, tergum, *n.*; **in, from the rear**, a tergo
rearguard, novissimum agmen
reason, causa, *f.*; *see* § 172
recall, revoco 1; (to mind), recordor 1 (*tr.*)
recapture, recipio*
receive, accipio*
recent, recens; **recently**, nūper

recite, recito 1
recognize, agnosco, -ĕre, agnovi, agnitum
reconnoitre, explōro 1; *or use* cognosco
recover (get back), recipio*
recovery (of health), salūs, salutis, *f.*
recruit, tīro, tironis, *m.*
refrain (from), mihi tempero 1 (§ 511)
take **refuge**, confugio*
refuse (= be unwilling), nōlo, nolle, nōlui; (in words), nego 1 (+ *acc. and inf.*)
regard as, duco*, habeo, existimo 1
region, regio, regionis, *f.*; loca, *n. plu.*; **to, in region of**, ad (*with town names*)
regret, paenitet (*impers.*) (§ 402)
in **reign of**, *see* § 54
reinforcements, novae copiae
relate, narro 1; **it is related**, *pass. of* dico, fero, trado (§ 145)
relatives, propinqui, *m. plu.*
release, lībero 1; (let go), dīmitto*
relieve, succurro*, subvenio* (*both* + *dat.*)
rely on, confīdo, -ĕre, -fīsus sum (+ *dat. of person*); **relying on**, frētus (+*abl.*)
remain, maneo, -ēre, mansi, mansum; **remain hidden**, lateo 2; **remain silent**, taceo 2
remainder (=rest)
remarkable, ēgregius
remember, memini, -isse (§ 421); memoriā teneo

remove, ămoveo, -ēre, amōvi, amōtum; tollo, -ĕre, sustuli, sublātum
renew, renŏvo 1; redintegro 1
rent, condūco*
repair, reficio*
repent, paenitet (*impers.*), § 402
replace, repono*
reply, respondeo, -ēre, respondi, responsum
reply (*noun*), responsum, *n.*
report, nuntio 1
report (*noun*), nuntius, *m.*
republic, res publica
repulse, repello, -ĕre, reppuli, repulsum
request is granted, *use* impetro (*see note on No.* 3, *line* 7)
requisition, impero (+ *acc. of thing, dat. of person*)
rescue, ēripio, -ĕre, eripui, ereptum (from: *see* § 301)
resign, me abdĭco 1 (+*abl.*: § 543)
resist (*intr.*), resisto*; (*tr.*), (*w. person as obj.*), resisto (+*dat.*); (attack, *&c.*), sustineo*
resolve, statuo, constituo*
resources, opes, opum, *f. plu.*
respite, spatium, *n.*
be responsible for, auctor sum (+*gen.*)
rest, quiesco, -ĕre, quiēvi, quiētum
rest of, reliquus (*adj.*)
restore, restituo*; (give back), reddo*
restrain, retineo*, dēterreo 2 (§ 511)
with result that, ita ut
retire (*mil.*), me recipio*

retreat, me recipio*, pedem (*always sing.*) refero*
retreat (*noun*), receptus, -ūs, *m.*; sound the retreat, § 303
return (go back), redeo*, regredior*; (come back), revenio*, regredior*; (give back), reddo*
return (*noun*), reditus, -ūs, *m.*
reveal, aperio, -ire, aperui, apertum
revolt, dēscisco, -ĕre, descivi; deficio* (*both* +ab)
reward, praemium, *n.*
Rhine, Rhēnus *m.*
Rhodian, Rhŏdius
rich, dīves, divitis
rick, acervus, *m.*
rid (=free from)
ride (on, in), vehor, vehi, vectus sum (+*abl.*); ride away, avehor; forward, provehor; into, invehor (in + *acc.*); past, praetervehor (*tr.*); up to, advehor (ad)
ridge, iugum, *n.*
rigging, armāmenta, *n. plu.*
right (*noun*), iūs, iūris, *n.*
rightly, recte; (=justly), iurĕ
ring, ānulus, *m.*
ripe, mātūrus
rise (sun or moon), orior, oriri, ortus sum; (to one's feet), surgo, -ĕre, surrexi, surrectum; consurgo
rising ground, locus superior; collis, collis, *m.*
risk, perīculum, *n.*
be rivals, inter se contendĕre
river, flūmen, -inis, *n.*
road, via, *f.*
roam, vagor 1

rob (deprive), prīvo 1 (+*abl. of thing*)
robber (=brigand), latro, -onis, *m.*
rock (reef), cautes, cautis, *f.*; (general), saxum, *n.*; (cliff), rūpes, rupis, *f.*
Roman, Rōmānus
Rome, Roma, *f.*
round (*prep.*), circum (+*acc.*)
rouse, excito 1
rout, fundo, -ĕre, fūdi, fūsum; fŭgo 1; **completely routed**, fusi fugatique
route, iter, itineris, *n.*; **by this, that route**, hāc, eā (*&c.:* § 193, *note*)
royal, rēgius
rule, rego 3
rumour, rūmor, rumōris, *m.*
run, curro, -ĕre, cucurri, cursum; **run away**, fugio*; **run forward**, procurro*
runner, cursor, -ōris, *m.*
rush out, ērumpo*, me ēicio*

sack (destroy), dīripio, -ĕre, diripui, direptum
sacred (to), sacer, sacra, sacrum (+*dat.*)
sacrifice, sacrifico 1
sad, tristis, maestus
safe, tūtus; (arrive) **safe and sound, safely**, incolumis (*adj.*)
safety, salūs, salutis, *f.*; **seek safety by flight**, fugā salutem peto
sail, nāvigo 1; (=travel by sea), vehor, vehi, vectus sum *or* nave vehor; **sail into**, invehor (in + *acc.*); (= set sail, depart),

solvo, -ĕre, solvi, solutum *or* navem solvo; proficiscor, -i, profectus sum
sail (*noun*), vēlum, *n.*
sailor, nauta, *m.*
for **sake of**, causā (+*gen.*)
Salamis, Salamis, Salamīnis, *acc.* -ina
salvation, salūs, salutis, *f.* (§ 293)
same, īdem, eadem, idem; **at the same time**, simul
satisfied, contentus (+*abl.*)
save, servo, conservo 1; **save from**, *see* § 213
say, dīco, -ĕre, dixi, dictum; *sometimes* loquor (*lit.* speak): **say that ... not**, nego 1 (§ 141)
scarcely, vix; (with difficulty), aegre; **scarcely any**, § 132, *note*
school, lūdus, *m.*
scorn (=despise)
scoundrel, homo nēquissimus
scout, speculator, -ōris, *m.*
sea, mare, maris, *n.*; **by sea**, mari
search, quaero, -ĕre, quaesivi, quaesitum
take **seat**, consīdo, -ĕre, -sēdi, -sessum
second (of two), alter
secretly, clam
secure (*vb.*) (=obtain)
see, video, -ēre, vīdi, vīsum; **see to**, cūro 1 (§ 345); **see that** (*in command*), § 84; **to see if**, § 573
seek, seek for, peto, -ĕre, petivi, petitum; quaero, -ĕre, quaesivi, quaesitum (*both tr.*)

seem, videor, -ēri, vīsus sum (§ 145)
seize (person), comprehendo*; (thing), rapio, -ĕre, rapui, raptum; (*mil.*, =occupy), occupo 1, capio; (opportunity), *use* utor
Sejanus, Seianus, *m.*
sell, vendo, -ĕre, vendidi, venditum; **be sold**, vēneo, vēnire, vēnii
senate, senātus, -ūs, *m.*
senate-house, cūria, *f.*
senator, senātor, -ōris, *m.*
send, mitto, -ĕre, mīsi, missum; **send away**, dimitto; **send back**, remitto; **send out**, ēmitto; **send forward**, praemitto; **send for** (summon), arcesso, -ĕre, arcessivi, -itum (*tr.*)
sense, prūdentia, *f.*
sentry, custōs, custōdis, *m.*, vigil, vigilis, *m.*
serious, gravis
serve well, bene mereor de (+*abl.*)
sesterce, sestertius, *m.* (*gen. plu.* sestertium)
set (go down), occĭdo*; **set out**, proficiscor, -i, profectus sum; **set before**, *see* prefer
set fire to, incendo, -ĕre, incendi, incensum (*tr.*)
set free, lībero 1
set sail, solvo, -ĕre, solvi, solutum, *or* navem solvo; proficiscor
several, complūres, -a
severe, sevērus

shade, umbra, *f.*
shadow (gloom), tenebrae, *f. plu.*
shepherd, pastor, -ōris, *m.*
shield, scūtum, *n.*
ship, nāvis, navis, *f.*
shirt, tūnica, *f.*
shoot (a missile), mitto; (a person), transfīgo, -ĕre, -fixi, fixum
shore, lītus, litoris, *n.*
short, brevis; **be short of** (=lack)
shortage, inopia, *f.*
shout, clāmo 1; clamores tollo
shout (*noun*), clāmor, clamōris, *m.*; **raise a shout**, clamorem tollo, -ĕre, sustuli, sublatum; conclāmo 1
show, ostendo, -ĕre, -ndi, -ntum; (a quality), praebeo 2; **praesto**, -are, -stiti[1]
Sicily, Sicilia, *f.*
sick, aeger, aegra, aegrum
side, lătus, lateris, *n.*; **on that side**, ab eo latere, ab ea parte; **on both sides**, ab utraque parte *or* utrimque; **sides** (=parties), *see* party
siege, obsidio, -onis, *f.*
sight, conspectus, -ūs, *m.*; **catch sight of**, conspicio*
sign (a will), obsigno 1
signal, signum, *n.*; **sound a signal**, signum do
silence, silentium, *n.*; **in silence**, silentio
be silent, taceo 2; **silently**, silentio
silver, argentum, *n.*

---

[1] Note the alternative expressions: (i) I show courage, *virtutem praesto* (*or praebeo*); (ii) I show myself brave, *me fortem praebeo* (or *praesto*).

since (*prep.*), ex (§ 154); (*conj. of time*), (= ever since), ex quo; (*causal conj.*), cum (+*subjunc.*), quoniam

sing, cano, -ĕre, cecini

sink (*tr.*) (in battle), dēprimo, -ĕre, -pressi, -pressum; (by storm, &c.), mergo, -ĕre, mersi, mersum (*both tr.*)

sir, magister

sister, soror, sorōris, *f.*

sit (be seated), sedeo, -ēre, sēdi, sessum; (sit down), consīdo, -ĕre, -sēdi, -sessum

situated, situs (*part. of* sino)

size, magnitudo, -dinis, *f.*; *see* § 172

skilful (in), perītus (+*gen.*)

skill, ars, artis, *f.*; scientia, *f.*

skilled (in), perītus (+*gen.*)

sky, caelum, *n.*

slaughter (*noun*), caedes, caedis, *f.*

slave, servus, *m.*

sleep, dormio 4

sleep (*noun*), somnus, *m.*

slow, lentus

small, parvus

smile, subrīdeo, -ēre, -rīsi, -rīsum

snake, anguis, anguis, *c.*

snatch (from), ēripio (+ *dat. of person*)

snow, nix, nivis, *f.*

so (*w. adj. or adv.*), tam; **so great**, tantus; **so many**, tot; **so completely** (*w. vb.*), adeo

soldier, mīles, militis, *m.*

Solon, Sŏlo, Solōnis, *m.*

some, § 524; **some ... others**, alii ... alii; **some time**, aliquando

sometimes, aliquando, interdum

somewhat (*w. compar.*), aliquanto

son, fīlius, *m.*

song, carmen, carminis, *n.*

soon, brevi; **as soon as**, simul atque (§ 451); **as soon as possible**, quam primum; **sooner**, mātūrius; *see* § 381

sorrow, dolor, dolōris, *m.*

be sorry, doleo 2; **be sorry for** (=regret), paenitet (*impers.*), § 402; (=pity), miseret (*impers.*), § 402; misereor 2 (+*gen.*)

sort, genus, generis, *n.*; **this, that sort of**, talis, huiusmodi, eiusmodi; **what sort of**, qualis, cuiusmodi; **the sort to**, § 283

sortie, ēruptio, -onis, *f.*; **make a sortie**, e. facio

soul, anima, *f.*

sound (a trumpet-call), cano, -ĕre, cecini (§ 303)

sound (*noun*), sonus, *m.*

sow (seed), sero, serere, sēvi, sătum

Spain, Hispānia, *f.*

spare, parco, -ĕre, peperci, *no supine* (+*dat.*); conservo 1

Spartan, Lacedaemonius

speak, loquor, -i, locūtus sum (*intr. or tr.*); *or use* dico; **speak to**, alloquor (*tr.*)

spear, hasta, *f.*

speech, ōratio, -onis, *f.*; (to the assembly), contio, -onis, *f.*; **make a speech**, o. habeo

speed, celeritas, -tatis, *f.*

spell (charm), carmen, inis, *n.*

spend, impendo, -ĕre, impendi,

impensum; (use up), consūmo, -ĕre, -sumpsi, -sumptum; (time), consumo
spirit (ghost), imāgo, -inis, *f.*
split, diffindo, -ĕre, -fīdi, -fissum (*tr.*)
spoil (*noun*), praeda, *f.*
spring (season), vēr, vēris, *n.*
spring (of water), fons, fontis, *m.*
spring up, orior, oriri, ortus sum; coörior
stab (=strike, wound)
stable, stăbulum, *n.*
stag, cervus, *m.*
stand (be standing), sto, stare, stĕti, statum; constiti (*perf. of* consisto); **stand for** (office), peto; **stand up**, surgo, -ĕre, surrexi, surrectum; **stand amazed**, *see* amazed
stand: take one's stand, consisto*
standard (*mil.*), signum, *n.*
start (=begin); (on journey), proficiscor, -i, profectus sum
starvation, fames, famis, *f.* (*abl.* -ē), inopia, *f.*
station (*vb., mil.*), colloco 1
state, cīvitas, -tatis, *f.*; (government), res publica
statue, statua, *f.*, signum, *n.*
stay, maneo, -ēre, mansi, mansum; moror 1
by stealth (=secretly)
steep, arduus
steer (straight), (rectum) cursum teneo
stick in, infīgo, -ĕre, infixi, infixum (*tr.*) (in + *acc.*)
stick (*noun*), baculum, *n.*; virga, *f.*[1]

still (*adv. of time*), adhūc
stone, lapis, lapidis, *m.*
stop (halt), moror 1 (*tr. or intr.*); (=prevent)
storm (*vb., mil.*), expugno 1
storm (*noun*), tempestas, -tatis, *f.*; **take by storm** (*mil.*), expugno 1
story, historia, *f.*; (tale), fābula, *f.*
strait, frĕtum, *n.*
strange, ignōtus; mīrus
stratagem, dolus, *m.*
strategy, consilium, *n.*
straw, strāmentum, *n.*
stream, flūmen, -inis, *n.*
street, via, *f.*
strength, vīres, virium, *f. plu.*
strike, ferio, -ire, percussi, percusum
strive, nītor, niti, nīsus sum (+*infin.*)
stroll, spatior 1
strong, validus; (forces; wind), magnus; **be strong** (in), valeo 2 (+*abl.*)
struggle (*noun*), certāmen, -inis, *n.*
stumble, prōlābor, -i, -lapsus sum
stupid, stultus
subdue, pāco 1
succeed, rem bene gero
success, res bene gesta; **without success**, frustrā (*adv.*), re infecta (§ 501)
such, talis; **such a** (+*adj.*), tam; **such** (in amount), tantus, § 113
sudden, subitus; **suddenly**, subito, repentĕ

---

[1] *baculum*, for walking; *virga* (or, heavier, *fustis*, m.), for beating.

suffer, patior, pati, passus sum; (from illness), afficior (+*abl.*); **suffer hardship**, laboro 1 (+ *abl. of cause*)
sufficient (=enough)
at suggestion of, § 177
it suits, decet (*impers.*), § 403
suitable, idōneus (+ad, +*dat.*, *or* + qui *clause*, § 286)
sum: a large sum of money, magna pecunia
summer, aestas, aestatis, *f.*
summon, arcesso, -ĕre, arcessīvi, -ītum; (call together), convoco 1
sun, sōl, sōlis, *m.*
sunrise, sōlis ortus, -ūs, *m.*
sunset, sōlis occāsus, -ūs, *m.*
supply, cōpia, *f.*; **supplies** (*mil.*), commeātus, -ūs, *m. sing.*
support, sustineo*; (a person), faveo, -ēre, fāvi, fautum (+*dat.*)
supreme (*w. abstract noun*), summus
sure, certus; **be sure** (that), pro certo habeo; **be sure to**, § 84
surprise, *see* take
surrender (*tr.*), dēdo*; (*intr.*), me dedo
surround, cingo, -ĕre, cinxi, cinctum; circumdo, -dăre, -dedi, -dătum; circumvenio*[1]
survive, supersum, -esse, -fui (+*dat.*)
suspect, suspicor 1; **suspecting**, suspicatus
suspend (interrupt), intermitto*
suspicion, suspīcio, -onis, *f.*
swamp (*noun*), palūs, palūdis, *f.*

swamp (a ship), compleo, -ēre, -ēvi, -ētum
swear, iūro 1 (§ 143)
swift, celer, celeris, -ĕ
swim, năto 1; **swim across**, trāno 1 (*tr.*)
sword, gladius, *m.*

table, mensa, *f.*
tablets (for writing), tabulae, *f. plu.*
take, sumo, -ĕre, sumpsi, sumptum; (capture), capio, -ĕre, cēpi, captum; (carry), porto, fero; (as companion), dūco; **take across**, transporto 1; **take away**, aufero, auferre, abstuli, ablātum; **take away from**, adimo, -ĕre, adēmi, ademptum (+ *dat. of person*); **take back**, refero, reduco, recipio; **take up**, sumo; **take off one's guard**, incautum capio; opprimo, -ĕre, oppressi, oppressum
take care to, § 84
take place (=happen)
take possession of (*mil.*), potior 4 (+*abl.*)
talent (of money), talentum, *n.*
talk, loquor, -i, locūtus sum
task, opus, operis, *n.*
tax, vectīgal, -ālis, *n.*
teach, doceo, -ēre, -ui, doctum (*acc. of person; also acc. of thing if needed, or infin.*)
teaching, doctrīna, *f.*
tear, lacrima, *f.*
tedious, longus (*p.* 181, *note*)

---

[1] General word, *cingo*: urbs muro cingitur; military words, *circumdo* (a place), *circumvenio* (persons).

tell (inform), (te) doceo, -ēre, -ui, doctum; (te) certiorem facio; (tibi) dico; (=order), iubeo, -ēre, iussi, iussum (*sometimes* veto); (=distinguish), discerno, -ēre, -crēvi, -crētum; *see* § 224

temple, templum, *n.*

tent, tabernāculum, *n.*

term (of agreement), condĭcio, -onis, *f.*; on . . . terms, *use abl.*

terrible, atrox

terrify, terreo, perterreo 2

territory, fīnes, finium, *m. plu.*[1]

than, quam; *or abl. of comparison*; **than if**, § 574

thank, gratias ago (+*dat.*)

thanks, grātiae, *f. plu.*; **give thanks**, gratias ago (+*dat.*)

theatre, theatrum, *n.*

theft, furtum, *n.*

then, tum; (=next), tum, deinde

there, ibi; (=thither), eo; **from there**, inde

thick, densus; (=wide), lātus; **the thick of**, medius

thief, fūr, fūris, *m.*

think, puto 1; arbitror 1; existimo 1; **thinking**, arbitratus, rătus (*from* reor); **I almost think**, haud scio an, nescio an (§ 205); **think much** (*&c.*) **of** (= value at much, *&c.*)

thither, eo

though, quamquam, etsi; cum (§ 461)

take thought for, consulo (+*dat.*)

threat, mina, *f.*

threaten, minor 1 (§ 143); **threaten you with**, tibi id minor; (*thing as subject*), immineo 2 (+*dat.*)

three days, triduum, *n.*

through (*prep.*), per (+*acc.*); (= because of), propter (+*acc.*)

throughout, per, per totum . . .; *cf.* § 192 (ii)

throw, iacio, iacĕre, iēci, iactum; (in a volley), cōnicio*; **throw aside**, reicio*; **throw down**, dēicio*

thus, ita; sīc

Tiber, Tiberis, -is (*acc.* -im), *m.*

tide, aestus, -ūs, *m.*

tie, adligo 1 (+ *acc. and dat.*)

till (=until)

timber, māteries, -ei, *f.*

time, tempus, temporis, *n.*; **in time**, ad tempus; **after a time**, mox; **time of day**, hōra (§ 158, *note*); **three** (*&c.*) **times**, *use numeral adv.*; **a long time**, diu

tired, defessus; **be tired of**, taedet (*impers.*), § 402

to-day, hŏdie

toil, labor, labōris, *m.*

to-morrow, crās

tone, *use* vōx, vōcis, *f.*

to-night, hac nocte

too, nimis; *or use compar.*; **too little**, parum; **too much**, nimis (*both* + *part. gen.*); **too . . . to**, § 354

top of, summus; **on top of**, super (+*acc.*)

toss, iacto 1

---

[1] *fines* only with the possessor stated: *e.g.* hostium fines. General words, *terra*, *ager*.

tow away, abstraho, -ĕre, abstraxi, abstractum
towards (*time prep.*), sub (+*acc.*); (*of feelings*), ergā (+*acc.*): *see p.* 155, *note*
tower, turris, -is, (*abl.* -i), *f.*
town, oppidum, *n.*
townsman, oppidānus, *m.*
train, exerceo 2
traitor, prōditor, -ōris, *m.*
Trajan, Traianus, *m.*
transfer, transporto 1
travel, iter facio
treachery, dolus, *m.*
treason, māiestas, -tatis, *f.*
treasure, treasure-house, thēsaurus, *m.*
tree, arbor, arbŏris, *f.*
tribe, gens, gentis, *f.*; (in Gaul, &c.), cīvitas, -tatis, *f.*
tribune, tribūnus, *m.*; **military —**, t. militum
trick, trickery, dolus, *m.*
triumph (victory procession), triumphus, *m.*
Trojan, Trōiānus
troops, cōpiae, *f. plu.*
trouble (woe), incommodum, *n.*; (care), *see note on No.* 29, *line* 6
Troy, Trŏia, *f.*
truce, indūtiae, *f. plu.*
true, vērus; **come true** (=happen)
trust, confīdo, -ĕre, confīsus sum (+ *dat. of person but abl. of thing*)
tell truth, vera (*n. plu.*) dico; vera loquor
try, cōnor 1 (+*infin.*)
turn back (*intr.*), revertor, -i, reverti (*act. in form*), reversum;

turn round (*intr.*), convertor, -i, conversus sum; **turn and flee**, terga vertere
two days, biduum, *n.*
type, *use* similis
tyrant, tyrannus, *m.*

unarmed, inermis
unawares, de improviso, *see note on No.* 9, *line* 9
uncertain, incertus, **feel —** (=doubt)
uncle, avunculus, *m.*[1]
under (*prep.*), sub (+*abl.*)
understand, intellego, -ĕre, -lexi, -lectum
undertake, suscipio* (§ 345)
undoing, exitium, *n.* (§ 294)
undoubtedly, sine dŭbio, haud dŭbie
unexpected, imprŏvīsus; **unexpectedly**, subito; *see* unawares
unfortunate, miser, -era, -erum
unharmed, incolumis
unite, coniungo (*tr.*)
unjust, inīquus, iniustus; **unjustly**, iniūriā
unknown, ignōtus; **unknown to him**, § 177
unless, nisi
unlike, dissimilis (§ 424)
unpleasant, molestus; **find unpleasant**, moleste fero
unscrupulous, audax, audacis
be unseemly, *use* minime decet (§ 403)
unskilled, imperītus (+*gen.*)
until (*prep.*), ad; (*with prolong or postpone*), in (+*acc.*); (*conj.*), dum, donec (*ch.* 47); (*after a neg.*), prius quam (§ 455)

---
[1] Strictly, *avunculus*, mother's brother; *patruus*, father's brother.

be **unwilling**, nōlo, nolle, nōlui; **unwillingly**, *use adj.* invitus (*p.* 151, *note*)
unwise, imprūdens
uproar, clāmor, -ōris, *m.*; strepitus, -ūs, *m.*
urge, hortor 1, cohortor; suādeo, -ēre, suāsi, suāsum
urgent, necessārius
use, ūtor, uti, ūsus sum (+*abl.*); **use up**, consūmo*
use (*noun*), ūsus, -ūs, *m.*; **of use**, usui (§ 293)
useful, utilis; usui (§ 293)
usual, solitus; ... **than usual**, solito; **usually**, *use* soleo, -ēre, solitus sum (+*infin.*)
utmost, summus

in vain, frustrā
valley, valles, vallis, *f.*
value, aestimo 1; facio (*ch.* 32)
vanguard, primum agmen
various, dīversus
Veientines, Veientes
Verres, Verres, Verris, *m.*
very (*adv.*), *use superl.*; **not very**, § 387
the very (*adj.*), ipse
be vexed at, aegre fero, graviter fero (+ *acc. or* quod *clause*); irascor, -i, iratus sum (+*dat.*)
victorious, victor, -ōris, *m.*
victory, victōria, *f.*; proelium secundum
view (=sight)
vigilant, cautus, intentus
vigorous, strēnuus, ācer
village, vicus, *m.*
violate, violo 1
violence, vīs, *f.*

Virgil, Vergilius, *m.*
visit, adeo* (*tr.*)
voice, vōx, vōcis, *f.*
volley, *see* hurl

wage war, bellum gero, -ĕre, gessi, gestum
wait, exspecto 1, moror 1; **wait for**, exspecto (*tr.*); **wait until**, exspecto dum (§ 474)
wake (*tr.*), excito 1
wall, mūrus, *m.*
war, bellum, *n.*; **declare war on**, bellum indico* (+*dat.*); **make war on**, bellum infero* (+*dat.*)
warn, moneo, admoneo 2
warship, nāvis longa
waste (time), (tempus) tero, -ĕre, trīvi, tritum
watch, specto 1
water, aqua, *f.*; **fetch water**, aquor 1
wave (gentle), unda, *f.*; (rough), fluctus, -ūs, *m.*
way (journey), iter, itineris, *n.*; **on the way**, in itinere; (=manner), modus, *m.*; (=method), ratio, -onis, *f.*
weak, infirmus
wealth, dīvitiae, *f. plu.*
weapons, arma, *n. plu.*
wear out (=exhaust)
weary (=tired)
weather (*esp.* bad), tempestas, -tatis, *f.*
weep, fleo, flēre, flēvi, flētum; plōro 1
weigh anchor, *see* anchor
weight, pondus, -eris, *n.*
welcome, accipio*

welfare, salūs, salutis, *f.*
well (*adv.*), benĕ; **it is well known**, constat
be well (in health), valeo 2
what sort of, qualis
whatever, § 522
when (*interrog.*), quando; (*conj. of time*), ubi, postquam; cum (§ 452, 463)
whenever, cum, quotiens: *see* § 464, *ch.* 53
where (*interrog.*), ubi; (*rel.*) ubi; (=where to), quo
whereas (although), cum (+*subjunc.*)
wherever, ubi, ubicumque; (= to wherever), quo, quocumque: *see ch.* 53
whether (*in rep. qu.*), num; **whether ... or**, utrum ... an (§ 204); (*in conditions*), sive ... sive
while, dum (§ 472)
white, albus
whoever, quisquis; quicumque; si quis: *see ch.* 53
whole, tōtus
why, cur, quāre, quamobrem
wicked, improbus
wickedness, improbitas, -tatis, *f.*
wide, lātus
width, lātitudo, -dinis, *f.*
wife, uxor, uxōris, *f.*
will (= be willing), volo, velle, volui
will (*noun*, =wish), voluntas, -tatis, *f.*; **against one's will**, *use* invitus (§ 177)
will (document), testāmentum, *n.*
be willing, volo, velle, volui;
not be willing, nōlo; **willingly**, libenter; *or use adj.* libens
win (*intr.*), vinco, -ĕre, vīci, victum; (*tr.*) (a victory), reporto 1; (=acquire), consequor*; quaero, -ĕre, quaesivi, quaesitum
wind, ventus, *m.*
window, fenestra, *f.*
wine, vīnum, *n.*
wing, āla, *f.*
winter, hiems, hiemis, *f.*
winter (*adj.*), hībernus; **winter camp**, **winter quarters**, hiberna, *n. plu.*
wisdom, sapientia, *f.*
wise, sapiens; (=prudent), prūdens
wish, volo, velle, volui; cupio, -ĕre, cupivi, cupitum; **not wish**, nōlo, nolle, nōlui
with (= along with), cum (+*abl.*); (in house of), apud (+*acc.*)
withdraw (*intr.*), me recipio*; pedem (*always sing.*) refero*; (*tr.*), dēduco*
within (*prep.*), intrā (+*acc.*); (time), § 151, 153
without (*prep.*), sine (+*abl.*); **without doing**, § 493, 502; **without orders**, iniussu § 501); **without knowledge**, *use* inscius (§ 177); **be without** (=lack)
withstand (=resist)
witness, testis, testis, *c.*
wolf, lupus, *m.*
woman, mulier, mulieris, *f.*; fēmina, *f.*
wonderful, mīrus

wood, silva, *f.*; (=timber), lignum, *n.*
wooden, ligneus
word, verbum, *n.*; keep word, fidem praesto, -are, -stiti
work, laboro 1
work (*noun*), (=toil), labor, laboris, *m.*; (=task, job), opus, operis, *n.*
workman, faber, fabri, *m.*
worn out (=exhausted)
be worsted, come off worst, inferior discedo*
worthy, dignus (+ *abl. or* + qui *and subjunc.*); (*complimentary*), § 388
wound, vulnero 1; **wounded**, saucius (*adj.*)
wound (*noun*), vulnus, vulneris, *n.*
wreck (a ship), frango, -ĕre, frēgi, fractum
wretched, miser, -era, -erum
write, scrībo, -ĕre, scripsi, scriptum

wrong (*noun*), iniūria, *f.*; **do wrong**, pecco 1
the **wrong** (*adj.*), *use* alius
wrongfully, iniūriā

Xenophon, Xenophōn, -ontis, *m.*

yard (of house), ārea, *f.*
year, annus, *m.*
yearly (*adv.*), quotannīs
yesterday, heri; **yesterday's**, hesternus (*adj.*)
yet (however), tamen; **not yet**, nōndum
yield, cedo* (+*dat.*)
yolk, vitellus, *m.*
young, iuvenis; **younger, -est**, nātu minor, minimus; **young man**, adulescens, -entis, *m.*; iuvenis, -is, *m.*[1]
youth (*abstract*), iuventūs, -tutis, *f.*; adulescentia, *f.*; **in youth**, *say* '(as) a youth'
youth (= young man)

---

[1] Strictly, *adulescens*, 'one not yet adult', 'in one's teens'; *iuvenis*, 'not yet senex' (say, under 46); but this distinction is not always observed.

INDEX OF LATIN WORDS

(giving the principal words of which the use is explained in the text)

causā + *gen.*, 333
cave ne, 84
coepi, 22 *note* 3
cum, 46
cum ... tum, 467
cum (*prep.*), 541
curo, 345
dico, nego, 141
dicor, 145
dignus + *abl.*, 183; + qui, 286
doleo, 556
dum, 47
fac ut, 84
fore ut, 225
gaudeo, 556
gratiā + *gen.*, 333
haud, 134; haud scio an, 205
idoneus ad, 333; qui, 286
inquam, 76 *note*
interest, 405
is = talis, 283 *and note*
is qui (+*subjunc.*), 283; (+*indic.*), 372–3
iubeo, veto, 92; *and* impero, 96
locus (*no prep.*), 192 (ii)
medius, 411
memini, 142 *note* 4; 421 *note*; (*imper.*), 86 *note*
minus (*with numbers*), 382
natus (+*acc.*), 154
-nĕ, 12
ne quidem, 131, 505
ne quis, 211–12
neu, neve, 82, 214
nescio an, 205
nonne, 14

num, 15, 161
num quis, 201
odi, 142 *note*; *pass. of*, 296
opus est + *abl.*, 182
plus (*with numbers*), 382
quae res (*clause-antecedent*), 376
quam + *compar.*, 381; + *superl.*, 386
quam ut, 355
quamvis, 564
quasi, 574 (*b*)
quidam, 524 *and note*
quin (*pron.*), 288; (*conj.*), 49; (=without), 502
quis (*indef.*), 201, 211–12, 435, 526
quisquam, 132
quisque (*with numbers or superls.*), 527
quo + *compar.* (*in final clauses*), 274
quo ... eo, 384
quominus, 51
quod (+ *noun clause*), 556
rēfert, 405 *note*
rogo, 87
similis, 424
sunt qui, 283
suscipio, 345
tamquam, 574 (*b*)
ut + *noun clause*, 225, 404, 234 *note*
utor, 182; *gerund and gerundive, p.* 111 *note*
utrum ... an, 202–4
velim, vellem, 395
videor, 145

CASE USES: SUMMARY AND INDEX

(Ordinary numerals refer to paragraphs, bold figures to chapters)

ABLATIVE

absolute, **4**; without participle, 54, 157, 177
agent, 181
cause, 414, 42 *n.*
comparison, 181, 381
description, 413
instrument, 181; with *utor, &c.,* 182
manner, 181, 541–2
measure of difference, 156, 181; (*quo . . . eo*), 384
place whence, 192
place where, 191
price, 324–7
respect, 181
road by which, 192 (iii)
separation, 543
time when, 151
time within which, 151
with adjectives, 183
with verbs (*utor, &c.*), 182

ACCUSATIVE

double object, 87, *note* 2
extent of space, 196
extent of time, 151, 154, 155
goal of motion, 192; (supine), 352, *note*
acc. and infin., **7**; of impersonal verbs, 263; as subject, 144

DATIVE

advantage, 292
agent, with gerundive, 313, 315
indirect object, with verbs of taking away, 301; parts of body, 302
predicative, **29**
purpose, 303
with adjectives (*similis, &c.*), 424
with verbs, **25**, 403; in passive, 262 (*b*); with compound verbs, 252

GENITIVE

characteristic, 63
charge, penalty, 422
description, quality, 413
objective, 333
partitive, 61, 62 (*see p.* 8, *note* 1)
possessive (= duty of, *&c.*), 63
value, 322–3
with adjectives, 333, 424
with verbs, 421–3; with impersonal verbs, 402

LOCATIVE

general, 192 *and note*
in value expressions, 322, 325

CLAUSES: SUMMARY AND INDEX

(Ordinary numerals refer to paragraphs, bold figures to chapters)

Adverbial (list of), 5
Alleged reason, 552
Causal, **55**; summary, 557
Causal relative, 554
Commands, direct, **8**; with impersonal verbs, 264; with 'any', 211
Commands, reported, **9**; summary, 95; with 'any', 211; in Or. Obl., 584
Comparison, 574
Concessive, **56**; summary, 567
Conditional (general survey), 430; summary, 445; alternative, 433; indicative, **43**; subjunctive, **44**; exceptional, **57**; in Or. Obl., 596
Consecutive, **11**; summary, 115
Consecutive relative, **28**; with *quin*, 493–4
Deliberative, 393–4
'Ever' clauses, **53**; with *cum*, 464
Exclamation, reported, 168
Fear, **23**; summary, 237
Final, **10**; summary, 106; with *ne quis*, &c., 211, 212; with *quo*, 274
Final relative, **27**
Final temporal, 454
Frequentative, **53**; with *cum*, 464
Generic relative, 287
Hindering and preventing, 511
Ideal conditions, 430 n., **44**
Ideal consecutive, 281
Indefinite relative, **53**
Indirect: *see* command, question, statement, reported speech

Inverted time clauses, 465
Noun, 3; introduced by *quod*, 556 *and n.*; introduced by *ut*, 225, 404, 234 *n.*
Preventing, &c., 511
Purpose: *see* final; *cf.* 351–2
Questions, **1**; deliberative, 393–4
Questions, reported, **16**; summary, 167; alternative, 202–4; in Or. Obl., 585; for Engl. abstract nouns, 171–2
Quoted reason, 552
Ratio (*quo . . . eo*), 384
Reason, 55
Rejected reason, 553
Relative, **37**, 4; indefinite, 522, 531–3; with superlative, 375; with sentence antecedent, 376; for Engl. abstract noun, 176
Relative (with subjunctive): final, **27**; consecutive, generic, **28**; causal, 554; concessive, 566
Reported speech (Or. Obl.), **58**, **59**; in prose, 618; *see* statement, command, question
Result, **11**
Statements, reported, **7, 14**; summary, 75; in Or. Obl., 584; with impersonal verbs, 263, 406; with *fore ut*, 225
Suboblique, 226, 591, **59**
Subordinate, general survey, 1–5; tenses in, 90
Temporal, **45**; inverted, 465; with *cum*, **46**; with *dum*, **47**; with imperatives, 437
Time, *see* temporal
Wishes, 392, 395